77 Furniture Projects
Projects
You Can Build

77 Furniture Projects
You Can Build

Editors of Family Handyman®

TAB BOOKS Inc.
BLUE RIDGE SUMMIT, PA. 17214

FIRST EDITION

SEVENTH PRINTING

Printed in the United States of America

Reproduction or publication of the content in any manner, without express permission of the publisher, is prohibited. No liability is assumed with respect to the use of the information herein.

Copyright © 1980 by TAB BOOKS Inc.

Library of Congress Cataloging in Publication Data

Main entry under title:

77 furniture projects you can build.

    Includes index.
    1. Furniture making—Amateurs' manuals.
2. Furniture, Shaker. I. Family handyman.
TT195.S45   684.1   80-21204
ISBN 0-8306-9921-X
ISBN 0-8306-1122-3 (pbk.)

Cover photo courtesy of Armstrong Cork Company.

Preface

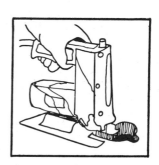

There's nothing like fine furniture to increase the beauty of your home. This book is a companion of furniture projects that do-it-yourselfers and home handymen can make without much difficulty.

All projects are clearly explained in step-by-step fashion. There are plenty of illustrations to assist you. Also included are materials lists and construction detail diagrams for many projects.

Projects include all types of desks, chests and bureaus, cabinets, tables, beds, built-in units, bars and chairs. There are guidelines for making furniture out of plywood and plastic. Learn how to assemble furniture that comes in kits. Also included is an important chapter on furniture repairs.

We hope that you'll find some useful ideas in this furniture project book. Feel free to modify projects somewhere to fit your personal needs. Above all, have fun and don't work too hard!

Editors of Family Handyman®

Contents

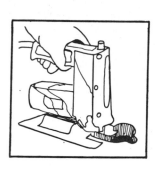

Chapter 1
Chairs

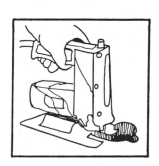

Would you like to learn how to assemble a beautiful Shaker armchair? Do you have any old chairs which you want to restore? How about a need for a Shaker bench that can seat several people? If your answers to any or all of these questions is yes, read on for step-by-step instructions for these projects.

SHAKER ARMCHAIR

Shaker furniture has become so popular with American home owners that kits have become available which make it possible for persons without any special woodworking skill to assemble an authentic piece which cannot be distinguished from the real thing. In one such kit of a ladderback arm chair all the parts are supplied with predrilled holes or slots for arms and rails. The back with its six curved slats is preassembled in this kit. Assembly is very easy (Fig. 1-1).

Assembly

The entire chair is assembled loosely without glue to see if all the parts fit. It may be necessary to sand the ends of rails slightly if too tight a fit has resulted from absorption of moisture during shipment. The chair is then disassembled and the position of each part noted.

When ready for final assembly, apply glue to the walls of the holes into which the rails fit using a small stick. Do not apply glue to

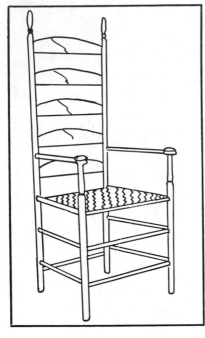

Fig. 1-1. Light and graceful, this "elder's" chair is an exact copy of the Shaker original and easy to assemble.

the ends of the rails as they may swell rapidly and make it very difficult to assemble the chair.

Glue and assemble the two front corner posts and three long rails making sure that the rail with the largest diameter goes on top (Fig. 1-2). (The rails of the seat all have a larger diameter than the others). Note that the front rails go into the holes on the front posts that are slightly lower than the side rail holes (Fig. 1-3). To insure tight joints, place assembly on its side and pound with a hammer and small block of wood (Fig. 1-4). Now lay the assembly on a flat surface and make sure the legs are parallel. If they are not parallel, twist the assembly until they are.

The side rails are then glued and assembled to the front post and the preassembled back after the arms have been placed over the front posts and secured with post caps (Figs. 1-5 through 1-7).

With front legs lying on the floor, pound the back legs with a hammer and block of wood to assure a tight fit (Fig. 1-8). Using a dry rag, remove all excess glue from the joints (Fig. 1-9).

The chair should be checked for alignment before the glue dries. All four legs should rest squarely on a level surface. If they do not, bounce the chair frame lightly on the leg that appears too long until all four legs rest on the floor.

Fig. 1-2. After loosely preassembling chair kit in order to determine exact position of each piece, glue is applied to front post holes.

Fig. 1-3. Long rails are inserted into front corner posts making sure that the largest diameter rails go at the top to receive the seat taping.

Fig. 1-4. Joints in the chair front assembly are secured by tapping the posts from the side using a hammer and wood block to prevent damaging the leg.

Fig. 1-5. Six remaining side rails are inserted into their respective holes in the front posts after alignmnet has been checked and glue is applied.

Fig. 1-6. Chair arms are mounted onto front posts after dabbing a small amount of glue inside the arm hole. Any excess glue is wiped off.

Fig. 1-7. Front and side rail assembly is joined to preassembled back by inserting the side rails into respective holes after applying glue.

Fig. 1-8. Glued joints are then tightened, again using hammer and wooden block, and front post caps are glued to the two protruding tenons.

Fig. 1-9. Wiping off excess glue around all joints is an important step. If left on the surface, glue would prevent stain from penetrating.

Fig. 1-10. After a preliminary touch-up sanding, the stain is wiped on with a rag. Brush application would be slower but would make less mess.

Measure the diagonal distance between the front and back posts. If they are not equal, put a rope around the longest diagonal and tighten by inserting a stick between the ropes and twisting until the distances are equal. Do not remove the rope until the glue dries, which should be in about 24 hours.

The chair should then be lightly sanded with the sandpaper supplied in the kit. Stain for the finish is in a can that comes with the kit (Fig. 1-10). Suggestions for finishing are on the stain can.

After staining, two coats of clear varnish may be applied, each of which should be rubbed with very fine steel wool (Fig. 1-11). An oil finish is available from the manufacturer of the kit. Liquid furniture polish or paste wax can be applied for greater luster and added protection.

For those who wish to make this armchair from scratch and have a lathe to make all the turnings, the dimensions are available in Table 1-1. Also see Fig. 1-12. Be sure to use a good grade of birch or maple. The curved slats of the back may present somewhat of a problem since these are usually shaped or bent by steaming and pressure in a special press. However, you can cut these out of a solid block of birch if you have access to a bandsaw and thus secure

Fig. 1-11. Stain is allowed to dry overnight and then clear varnish is applied in one or more coats with careful steel wool rubbing between coats.

the curved shape. Otherwise your only alternative is to make these back slats flat.

Weaving The Seat

One of the most distincitve features of Shaker chairs are seats woven of tape which the Shakers called "listing." This cloth tape, in two different colors, is supplied in the kit. Of course, rush, splint and cane seats were also used by the Shakers but the woven tape seats were the most popular.

Table 1-1. List Of Materials For The Shaker Armchair.

LIST OF MATERIALS	
A. 5 pcs, 17⅝ × 3¼ × 9/32″	H. 2 pcs, 27 × 1⅜″
B. 2 pcs, 1¼ × 47″	I. 4 pcs, 16¾ × ¾″
C. 2 pcs, 1¼ × 4½″	II. 2 pcs, 16¾ × ⅞″
D. 4 pcs, dowel ½ · × 1½″	J. 1 pcs, 17⅝ × ¾″
E. 10 pcs, dowel ¼ × 1″	JJ. 1 pc. 17⅝″ × ⅞″
F. 2pcs, 17 × 3 × ⅝″	K. 1 pc, 21⅞ × ⅞″
G. 2 pcs, ⅝ × 2″	L. 2 pcs, 21⅞ × ¾″

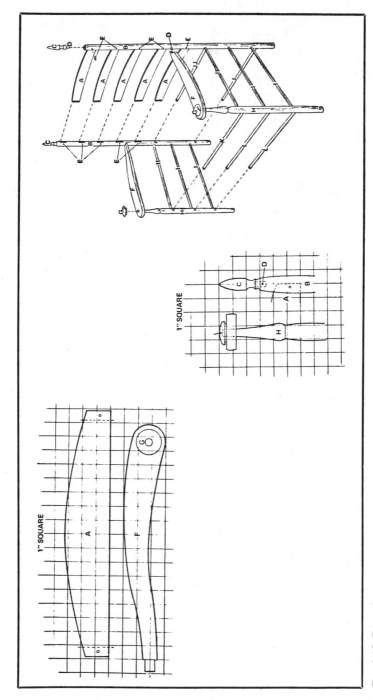

Fig. 1-12. Parts detail for the Shaker armchair.

19

Fig. 1-13. First step in weaving the chair seat is wrapping tape from front to back rungs after first tacking it inside the back rail.

The first step in seating the chair is known as warping (Fig. 1-13). This simply entails wrapping tape around the front and back rails to provide a warp both on the top and the bottom of the seat (Fig. 1-14). The procedure is as follows: the end (doubled over for strength) of one coil of tape is tacked to the inner side of the back rail as close as possible to the left back post; this doubled-over end must point toward the top of the chair. With the end firmly tacked in place, the coil of tape is brought over the back rail to the front rail at right angles to both the front and back rails. It is then brought over the front rail and returned to the back rail, which it goes under and over. It is essential that the tape not be twisted.

Fig.1-14.Wrap the tape carefully.

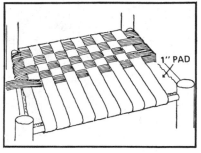

Fig. 1-15. There is a triangular-shaped area on either side of the seat which has no warps.

This procedure is continued until the back right post is reached and there is no space for another warp on the back rail (there will, however, be spaces at either side on the front rail). When this stage is reached, the tape is brought over and under the front rail to the back rail and cut off, allowing about an extra 2″. This end is doubled over and securely tacked to the bottom right side of the back rail, where it will overlap the last warp strip. Before this end is tacked in place it is important that as much slack in the warping as possible be pulled out; the tape should not be stretched but should be firm. It should be emphasized that the tape must run at right angles to the front and back rails. Because the side rails are splayed from front to back, there will be a triangular-shaped area on either side of the seat which will be without warps (Fig. 1-15). These warps will be added at a later stage.

With the warping completed, the next step is the actual weaving of the seat. This is begun by securing the end of the coil of tape which will be the weft. The end (doubled over for strength) is tacked to the inside of the left side rail as close as possible to the

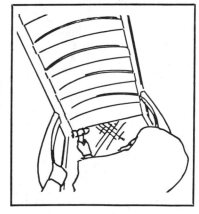

Fig. 1-16. The cross weaving or weft tape is now tacked to the bottom portion of the rear left seat rung and the wefting is begun.

Fig. 1-17. When front-to-back weaving (warp) is tightened and tacked, the cut foam pad is inserted between the rows of warping.

left back post (Fig. 1-16). The pad which has been made to fill the area of the seat is now stuffed between the top and bottom levels of the warping (Fig. 1-17). The free end of the coil of tape is then brought over the first warp strip of the top layer, under the next, over one, under one, etc., until the right back post is reached. The full length of the tape is now pulled through all the top layer of warp strips. The chair is then turned over and the process is repeated on the lower layer of warp strips (Fig. 1-18).

Next, the weft is again woven through the top layer of warp strips, this time starting under the first strip, over the second, etc., so that the result is the start of a checkerboard pattern (Fig. 1-19). The chair is again turned over and the weft is returned through the lower level of warp strips so as to form, as on the top layer, the beginning of a checkerboard pattern. It will be noted that, at the right side of the chair, the end warp of the bottom layer

Fig. 1-18. View showing underside of chair while weft is being completed. The tightened weft will be tacked to the left front rung bottom.

Fig. 1-19. A neat checkerboard pattern is produced.

(which has been tacked to the right side of the back rail) will somewhat overlap the second to the last warp on the same side. It is essential that these be treated as a single warp: i.e., the weft must be carried over or under both of them together. Only in this way can a checkerboard pattern be created on the bottom of the seat; in the finished seat, this inconsistency will not be apparent.

Keeping Weft Flat

The process described above is continued until the weft reaches the front posts of the chair. Again, it must be emphasized that the tape must not be twisted (Fig. 1-20). Also, it should be pulled firmly each time it is brought through the warp strips, and the rows should be kept as straight as possible, each touching the last. The final row on the top of the seat will abut the front posts on the side rails and should curve slightly toward the front rail to keep the warps smooth and flat.

Fig. 1-20. It is important to remember that tape should not be twisted; this would create a visible lump in the finished flat seat.

Fig. 1-21. Corner filling with shorter pieces of tape is the final step in the seat work.

As at this stage the warps will be tight, a dinner knife is useful for lifting them to permit the weft to pass under them. The weft is now cut so that it will end on the bottom of the chair and is tacked to the left side rail as close as possible to the left front post (if there is not sufficient room to weave it through to the left side of the chair as is sometimes the case, it should be tacked to the bottom of the front rail).

Splicing The Weft

If it is necessary to splice the weft, this should be done so that the splice falls on the bottom of the seat. In splicing, the ends of the tape should be firmly sewed together.

The final step in taping the chair is that of filling in the corners of the seat with added warps (Fig. 1-21). For this, two strips of tape of the color used in the warping are cut to a length which will allow them to run from the front rail to the back on both the top and the bottom of the seat (i.e., double the depth of the chair) with 2 or 3" to spare. They are then woven in parallel to the last warp on either side of the the top of the seat, are brought over the front rail, and are similarly woven on the bottom. The ends, meeting at the back rail, are then tacked in place as inconspicuously as possible on the bottom of the back rail.

One (or sometimes two or three, depending on the size and type of the chair) additional warp (or warps) will be required on either side of the seat to fill out the warping near the front posts. Because of the triangular shape of the areas to be filled in, these warps cannot be carried back to the back posts of the chair but should be woven through the wefts until they meet the side rails. Their ends should be tucked under the wefts and secured either by tacking to the side rails (tacking them under a weft, which may be lifted with a dinner knife) or by carefully gluing them to the bottom of the weft with cloth glue.

Putting in these added warps demands care. The quality of the finished seat depends to a great extent on the workmanship of this finishing stage. If done with care, the seat will fill out smoothly at the front.

RESTORING OLD CHAIRS TO RENEWED BEAUTY

The more hopeless that first piece looks before you begin to restore it, the more you may become a fanatic on restoring old chairs.

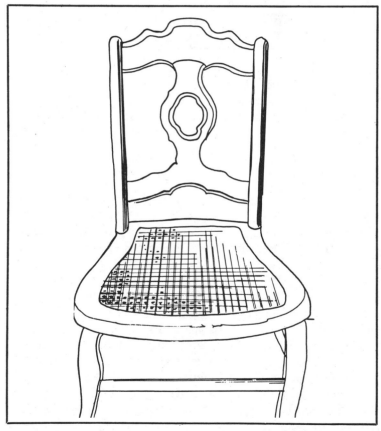

Fig. 1-22. This old chair's finish was stripped off without marring the wood.

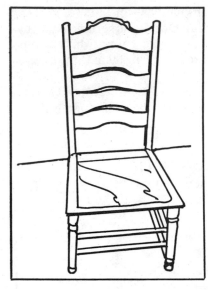

Fig. 1-23. Despite a blistered finish, this old chair was well worth restoration.

It seems that everyone already has the basic raw material—a dilapidated chair forgotten in the basement or attic for years.

It isn't really such a hopeless case, despite the six layers of paint and varnish, a rail or two missing, and a plywood seat tacked on a generation or two ago to replace the original cane seat (Fig. 1-22).

Stripping The Finish

The first step is to wash down the old chair with a mixture of vinegar and water. Try a strong solution of a heavy-duty cleaner like "beatsall" if the dirt does not yield easily. Brush on a thick, sudsy coating and let stand for 10-15 minutes. Then rinse, rinse, rinse!

Next, strip down a piece of the wood to determine if you really think you should go any further with it. The entire process of bringing new life to an old chair takes a good deal of time. Be patient, however, for chances are that you will find an amazing wealth of detail once you have completely stripped it. In one instance we uncovered a very intricate and attractive dark veneered insert design on the centerwork of a solid old maple chair.

An originally caned seat is recognized by a perimeter of holes approximately ¼″ in diameter and spaced at approximately ½″ intervals. If there are any portions of the original seat remaining, remove them. Clean out the holes with an awl or an icepick.

Do not try to sand, scrape or otherwise mar the wood when removing the old finish. The antique patina which will remain after the finishes are removed contributes to the appeal of the eventually restored chair. Remember, the objective is not to make a new item from the derelict with which you begin, but to restore the piece, perhaps a century or more old, to its highest state—an old chair which looks as if it had been used, yet preserved, down through the years (Fig. 1-23).

We found "Zip-Strip" non-flammable remover, a semi-liquid, nowash stripper easiest to work with on this type of project (Fig. 1-24). It can be laid on liberally with a 1" or 1½" brush. A discarded toothbrush is great for working the remover into scroll work and turned rails. Just be sure to give it 15 or 20 minutes to do its work before removing.

The bulk of the old finish can then be stripped with a dull putty knife. A sharpened wood dowel will do the job of cleaning out any grooves. A second pass with a wad of fine (#00 grade) steel wool dipped into the remover should complete this step. After stripping an area, wipe it down with a soft cloth dampened with alcohol.

Next, inspect the chair for loose rails or missing pieces and make the necessary repairs. White glue is the solution here. If any parts have to be replaced, you may have to stain the new wood to match the old.

Fig. 1-24. With the plywood seat removed, the finish will be stripped with non-flammable paint remover.

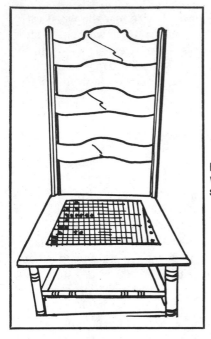

Fig. 1-25. With the finish restored, weaving of the new cane bottom is shown in progress.

After a complete stripping, cleaning with alcohol, and making the necessary repairs, the chair should be refinished before beginning to cane the seat. Use two coats of a satin finish, clear varnish which gives a soft but durable result. Rub with extra fine steel wool between coats. Remove dust with vacuum cleaner and tack rag.

Caning The Seat

Caning entails weaving the seat from lengths of natural cane. Some firms also offer a plastic version of cane which is claimed to be easier to work with (it doesn't have to be soaked before using) and is slightly less expensive. If the chair you are working on, however, is a worthy antique or has other redeeming qualities, use the natural cane (Fig. 1-25).

There is nothing difficult about the caning process, although it is a time-consuming one. Detailed information regarding caning is readily available from the firms providing the materials. Your county cooperative extension offices are another valuable source of information (Fig. 1-26).

The only "equipment" you will need for caning is an awl or icepick, scissors, a basin for soaking natural cane, and a dozen or so tapered wood pegs to hold the ends of the cane in place until they can be tied or drawn taut. Ideal pegs can be made from ⅜″ dowels cut into 2½″ lengths and tapered in a pencil sharpener.

SHAKER BENCH

Here's a delightful bench that has all the charm, grace and simplicity of Shaker craftsmanship (Fig. 1-27). It's very easy to build because it consists of only seven parts. You can make this bench from the parts described in Table 1-2. All of the parts supplied in the kit are made of clear pine. See Figs 1-28 and 1-29.

Positioning The Seat Support

The first step in the assembly of the parts is to place the seat top (C) face down on the floor. Then place the seat support (D) in the center of the underside of the seat which is now facing upward (Fig. 1-30). The slots and predrilled screw holes of the seat support (D) should face upward and should be directly over the dado or groove in the underside of the seat that crosses its width.

To make sure that the seat support (D) is properly in position, place the slot in one of the legs (E) over the slot in the seat support so that both slots interlock (Fig. 1-31). Then press the leg down firmly into its own dado. Using a hammer and block of wood, tape the edge of the leg so that it lines up flush with the edge of the seat

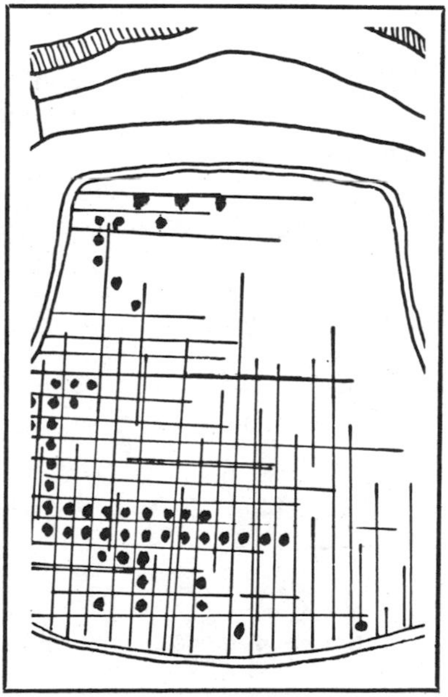

Fig. 1-26. Different chair showing a finished cane seat.

Fig. 1-27. This Shaker bench is easy to make.

as shown in Fig. 1-32. For good measure, also tap the leg down into its groove with the block and hammer. Repeat this operation with the remaining leg at the other end of the seat support. All this should be done without glue or screws.

You now have the seat support in precisely the right position. Mark this position accurately with a pencil and remove both the seat support (D) and the legs (E). Apply glue to the top of the seat support, place it in the marked position and drive screws through the predrilled holes into the underside of the seat (Fig. 1-33).

Back Rest Supports

Glue should then be applied to the slot and upper edges of the legs. With a hammer and block of wood drive the legs down firmly

Table 1-2. Materials Required For the Shaker Bench.

LIST OF MATERIALS	
A. 1 pc. 60 × 3 × ¾″ B. 2 pcs. 29⅞ × 3 × 1¼″ C. 1 pc. 60 × 9¾ × 1¼″	D. 1 pc. 54 × 4 × ¾″ E. 2 pcs. 16 × 9¾ × 1¼″

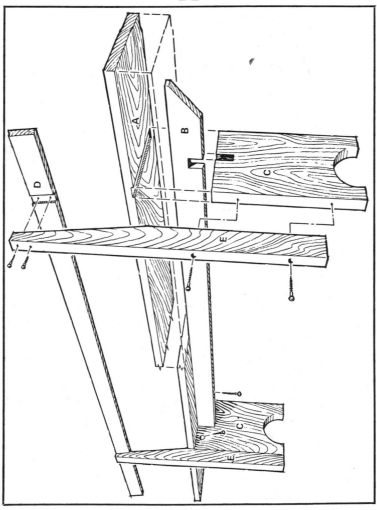

Fig. 1-28. Diagram of the Shaker bench.

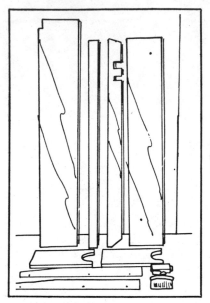

Fig. 1-29. Seven basic structural parts of the Shaker bench are shown here.

so that their slots interlock with those of the seat support and their upper edges are seated in the dadoes that cross the width of the seat. The legs should also be fastened with the 2" screws (Fig. 1-34).

Place the assembly with its front edges face down on the floor. Now attach the supports (B) for the back rest with glue and 2½" screws, driving the screws through the predrilled holes into the back edges of the legs (E) (Fig. 1-35). Make sure that the bottoms of the back rest supports are flush with those of the legs (Figs. 1-36 and 1-37).

Fig. 1-30. Assembly begins by properly lining up the seat support and seat top.

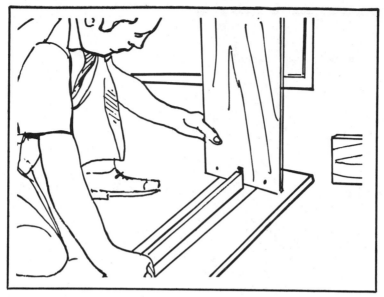

Fig. 1-31. Seat legs are now set into place. Note that slots in leg and support interlock and also that the top leg fits into a dado which has been precut on the underside of the seat top.

Now put the assembly on its legs. Using glue and 1″ screws, attach the back rest (A) to its supports. These supports (B) should be inserted into the grooves at the back of the back rest. The tops of the supports should be flush with the top of the back rest. Glue and tap the hole buttons into the holes in the back supports (B), tapered ends first.

Fig. 1-32. A hammer and block of wood are used to assure a flush line along the back of the leg and seat top.

Fig. 1-33. Support and legs are finally fastened using proper length round head screws.

Fig. 1-34. Shown is the final fastening of leg support pieces to the bench top.

Fig. 1-35. With the bench placed on its front edge, the back rest supports are positioned.

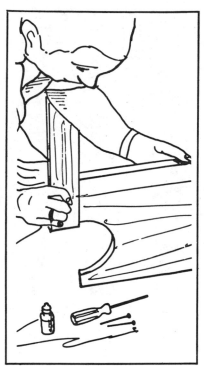

Fig. 1-36. Flush lineup with leg bottoms is important. A wooden block is used as a straightedge.

Fig. 1-37. The 2½" screws are driven home through the back supports and into the bench legs.

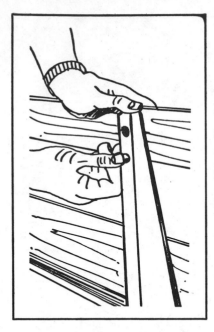

Fig. 1-38. The back rest has been joined to the supports, and hole buttons are being inserted to finish the assembly. After wiping glued joints and allowing glue to dry overnight, the bench can be sanded, stained and finished using shellac, varnish and paste wax.

Remove excess glue from all joints with a dry rag and allow glue to dry overnight. Lightly sand bench with sandpaper provided in the kit or use 100 grit. Finish with stain in kit or use your own medium walnut stain (Fig. 1-38). After stain has dried overnight, apply white shellac thinned half and half with alcohol and rub with fine steel wool when it is dry. Follow with two coats of light varnish, sanding each coat when dry and finish with paste wax buffed to a satin glow.

Chapter 2
Desks

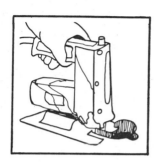

Every person in a household should have his or her own desk. In this chapter are guidelines for making many types of desks, including an antique merchant's desk, a Queen Anne secretary desk and a captain's style desk.

SHAKER DESK

Simple and sturdy is one way to describe this Shaker desk. And with the addition of the cove or bead moldings, the desk becomes almost elegant (Fig. 2-1).

The dimensions of this piece are small, so the use of solid, ¾" stock is practicable (Table 2-1). The bottom part of the desk is essentially a table with sides enclosing it. The top part is simply two shelves. The suggested method of construction is to make the table, including the four legs, first, before attempting the top portion. As can be seen both in Figs. 2-1 and 2-2, the legs are fluted on all four sides. The tops of the legs are cut diagonally and extend into the enclosed portion of the desk as is shown in Detail B (Fig. 2-2). This method of construction does away with having to use some means of attaching them to the desk other than with nails and glue, although both may also be used for additional stability.

The ¾" cove or bead molding (K,L) goes completely around the upper portion of the desk. Additionally, ½" cove or bead molding goes around the top opening of the desk (M,N) as is shown in Detail A (Fig. 2-2).

Fig. 2-1. This handsome Shaker desk is also sturdy.

Attaching the extreme upper part of the desk (G,H,I) to the top part can be done with nails and glue. And although the sides, back, and front of the desk (D,E,F) are attached using butt joints, they of course could also be attached using either dovetail or lock joints.

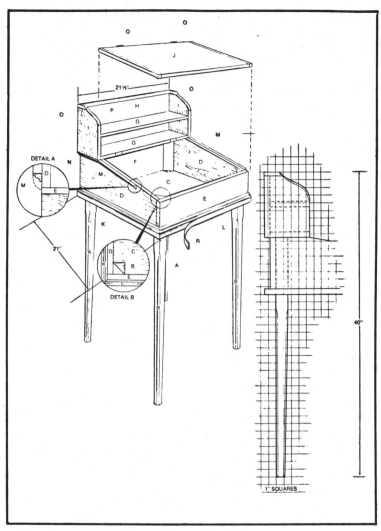

Fig. 2-2. Construction details for the Shaker desk.

Table 2-1. Required Materials For the Shaker Desk.

Two legs, fluted, each 31½″
 Each leg 1¾″ square at top, 1¼″ at the bottom
 Two legs, fluted, each 28¾″
 Each leg 1¾″ square at top, 1¼″ at the bottom
 One piece, 21½ × 21 × ¾″
 Two sides, each: 18¾″, 6¾″ at rear, 4″ at front,
    5¼″ at top
 One piece, 20 × 4 × ¾″
 One piece, 18½ × 6¾ × ¾″
 Two pieces, each: 19 × 5¼ × ¾″
 One piece, 20 × 8 × ¾″
	I. Two pieces, each: 8 × 6 × ¾″
	 J. One piece, 21½ × 15½ × ¾″
	 K. Two pieces cove or bead molding, each: 21 × ¾″
	 L. Three pieces cove or bead ' molding,
	    each: 21½ × ¾″ (two not shown)
	 M. Two pieces cove or bead molding, each: 14¾ × ¾″
	 N. Two pieces cove or bead molding,
	    each: 6 × ¾″ (one not shown)
	 O. Two pieces cove or bead molding, each:2½ × ½″
	 P. One piece cove or bead molding, 21½ × ½″
	 Q. Two hinges
	 R. One piece 1/16″ veneer strip, 85″

39

Fig. 2-3. The original of this desk is in the Philadelphia Museum of Art.

It's not indicated, but some of you may want to include a paper stop on the front edge of the lid (J) with brads and glue. Actually, rather than go through the trouble of making this piece (J) yourself, you could simply buy a drawing board and cut it to size. One of the final steps is attaching the hinges (Q) to the lid. If you feel the need, you could attach a 1/16" strip of veneer (R) edges of the plywood bottom (C). Finishing depends on your own taste but the original Shaker piece was stained a dark, reddish color.

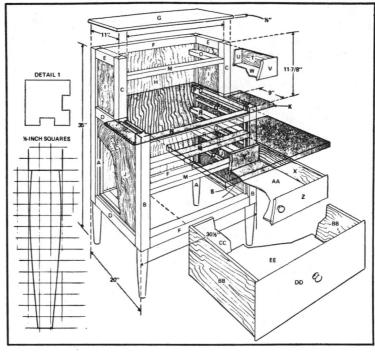

Fig. 2-4. Construction details for the sewing desk.

SHAKER SEWING DESKS

The original of this interesting sewing desk is in the Philadel-phia Museum of Art (Fig. 2-3). Like most Shaker furniture it combines graceful simplicity of style with practical utility.

Table 2-2. Materials Required For the Sewing Desk.

LIST OF MATERIALS	
A. 2 pcs, 1½·× 1½·× 35″ B. 2 pcs, 1½·× 1½·× × 23⅛″ C. 2 pcs, 1½ × 1½ × 12⅛″ D. 4 pcs, 1½·× 1½·× 17½″ E. 2 pcs, 1½·× 1½·× 8½″ F. 3 pcs, 1½·× 1½·× 27½″ G. 1 pc, ½·× 11¼ × 30½″ H. 1 pc, ½·× 27½·× 25½″ I. 2 pcs, ½·× 8½·× 10⅞″ J. 2 pcs, ½ × 17½ × 13⅝″ K. 1 pc, ¾ × 34 × 20″ L. 1 pc, ¾ × 26⅞ × 17″ M. 3 pcs, ¾ × 1½·× 27½″ N. 1 pc, ⅜ × 1½·× 27½″ O. 2 pcs, ¾ × 1½·× 8½″	P. 2 pcs, ½·× 1½·× 17½″ Q. 6 pcs, ½·× ½·× 17″ R. 4 pcs, ¾ × 1½·× 17½″ S. 2 pcs, ¾ × 1 × 17″ T. 2 pcs, ½·× 2 7/16 × 9½″ U. 1 pc, ½·× 2 7/16 × 25⅞″ V. 1 pc, ¾ × 2¾ × 27½″ W. 1 pc, 3/16 × 26⅜ × 9″ X. 4 pcs, ½·× 2 15/16 × 19″ Y. 2 pcs, ½·× 2 15/16 × 25⅞″ Z. 2 pcs, ¾ × 3½·× 27½″ AA. 2 pcs, 3/16 × 26⅜ × 18½″ BB. 2 pc, ½·× 515/16 × 19″ CC. 1 pc, ½·× 515/16 × 25⅞″ DD. 1 pc, ¾ × 6½·× 27½″ EE. 1 pc, 3/16 × 26⅜ × 18½″

The framework consists of 1½" × 1½" pieces (A-B-C-D-E-F) each of which has a ½" groove down one side. See Table 2-2 for materials. The corner pieces or leg posts (A-A-B-B) have an additional groove as shown in Detail 1 (Fig. 2-4). The ½" grooves are used to receive the sides and back (I-J-H) which are slid into place from above.

Note that all members of the framework join each other with short tongues that fit into corresponding grooves. All joints are glued, of course.

Fastening Parts

The top (G) and main surface (K) are fastened with pegs in each corner and glue. Both of these parts are made in one piece. You may have difficulty finding a single board wide enough for K, in which case it is suggested that it be made of two pieces glued and doweled edge to edge. A similar problem may arise in regard to the pull out shelf (L), the actual work surface. Again a similar solution is suggested—two pieces edge glued and doweled. The guides (P) on which the pull-out shelf rests have stops at their ends to prevent the shelf from going in too far.

All four drawers have grooves in the fronts, back and sides to receive the bottoms. The drawer fronts are rabbeted so that they overlap the openings into which they fit and have rounded edges.

The legs are turnings which are part of the corner posts (A-B). If you have difficulty fashioning the posts and legs as one piece, the turning may be done separately and joined to the posts with a ¾" dowel or a steel pin that is threaded on both ends.

The original wood used in this piece was cherry and pine but it may be made entirely of pine. The finish is a brownish tan stain followed by a clear, hard wax buffed to a satin sheen.

Building Twin Desks

Made by Elder Henry Green in the Shaker community at Alfred, Maine, around 1890, back-to-back twin sewing desks combine the advantages of a chest of drawers and a sewing desk or table (Fig. 2-5). They have the storage facilities of a chest of drawers and the convenience of a desk or table in the form of a sturdy pullout leaf (N) (Fig. 2-6). The two sewing desks in Fig. 2-5 are separate, independent pieces placed back to back, each being an exact duplicate of the other. The plan shown here can therefore be used for both, if you feel like making two of them. See Table 2-3.

Fig. 2-5. A chest of drawers is the key feature of these twin sewing desks.

Despite the complexity of its appearance, this sewing desk is relatively simple to build. Mainly, it consists of a framework of 1 × 2s (F, E, K) joined to the 2 × 2s (A, B, C) used here as corner posts. Of course, the 1 × 2s and 2 × 2s are really ¾ × 1½ and 1½ × 1½, respectively.

Large sheets of ¼″ plywood (LL, MM, NN) are used to cover the framework of the sides and back from the inside. The corner posts (A, B) and the side rails (D) are rabbeted to receive the plywood, as shown in Detail 2 at Fig. 2-6. The same detail also

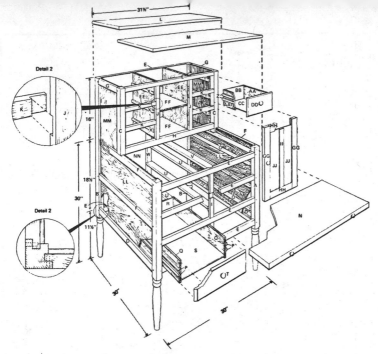

Fig. 2-6. Diagram of the twin desks.

Table 2-3. Necessary Materials For the Twin Sewing Desks.

LIST OF MATERIALS	

A. 2 pcs, 1½ × 1½ × 29¼"
B. 2 pcs, 1½ × 1½ × 45¼"
C. 2 pcs, 1½ × 1½ × 17½"
D. 2 pcs, 1½ × 1½ × 27⅜"
   (⅜" tenons each end)
E. 9 pcs, ¾ × 1½ × 27¾"
   ⅜" tenons each end;
   2 pcs not shown)
F. 4 pcs, ¾ × 1½ × 27¾"
   (1 pc not shown)
G. 2 pcs, ¾ × 1½ × 9¾"
   (⅜" tenons each end)
H. 1 pc, ¾ × 2¼ × 27¾"
   ⅜" tenons each end)
I. 1 pc, ¾ × 1½ × 17⅜"
   (both ends half lap)
J. 2 pcs, ¾ × 1½ × 16¾"
   (both ends half lap)
K. 4 pcs, ¾ × 1½ × 9⅞"
   (1 end half lap, 1 mortise)
L. 1 pc, ¾ × 12¾ × 31½"
M. 1 pc, ¾ × 18¾ × 31 ½"
N. 1 pc, ¾ × 18 × 26¾"
O. 6 pcs, 1 × ¾ × 27"
   (3 pcs not shown)
	P. 24 pcs, ½ × ¾ × 26¾"
	Q. 12 pcs, 26¾ × 3¾ × ½" plywood
	R. 6 pcs, 10¾ × 3¾ × ½" plywood
	S. 6 pcs, 11¼ × 27 × ¼" plywood
	T. 6 pcs, 4¼ × 12¼ × ¾"
	U. 3 pcs, 2½ × ¾ × 27¾"
	V. 1 pc, 2½ × ¾ × 28½"
	W. 1 pc, 1½ × ¾ × 16⅛"
	X. 6 pcs, ½ × ¾ × 10¼"
	Y. 6 pcs, 1 × ¾ × 10¼"
	Z. 24 pcs, ½ × ½ × 10¼"
	AA. 12 pcs, 3 5/16 × 10¾ × ½" plywood
	BB. 6 pcs, 3 5/16 × 6 × ½" plywood
	CC. 6 pcs, 11 × 6½ × ¼" plywood
	DD. 6 pcs, ¾ × 313/16 × 8½"
	EE. 2 pcs, 10¼ × 13½ × ½" plywood
	FF. 2 pcs, 8 × 10¼ × ½" plywood
	GG. 2 pcs, 1¼ × ¾ × 12⅞"
	HH. 2 pcs, 1½ × ¾ × 6"
	   (¼" mortise each end)
	II. 1 pc, 1¼ × ¾ × 10⅜"
	JJ. 2 pcs, 2⅝ × 10⅜ × ¼" plywood
	LL. 2 pcs, 27½ × 16½ × ¼" plywood
	MM. 2 pcs, 9½ × 16¾ × ¼" plywood
	NN. 1 pc, 27½ × 33¼ × ¼" plywood

shows how the blind mortise and tenon joints (where side rails meet the corner posts) are pinned with ¼" pegs. All the joints are glued.

Interior joints where K meets J and where I intersects or meets the three front rails (E) are of the half lap type. The drawer runners (P, Z) are wood strips that ride on guide X, Y and O. Note that both sides of the brace (U) that unite front and back are used as drawer guides.

The pull-out desk leaf (N) should be made from a single piece of plywood preferably 1" thick. If the 1" thickness is not available, ¾" thickness will do.

SHAKER DESK AND WORKING TABLE

We've billed this handsomely designed piece of Shaker furniture as a desk and work table (Fig. 2-7). It is that and more, too.

Fig. 2-7. This Shaker desk and working table has 13 drawers.

With its 13 drawers and the top section's middle area (with door), it is also a bureau piece that provides abundant space for storage. In addition, the top of the six small drawer section (G) offers a mantle-like area for placing objects, while the good-sized counter (J) and the large pull-out section (K) are available for use as a desk, work table, or drawing board (Fig. 2-8). This Shaker item will fit handily into a corner so that both front and side sets of drawers are easily accessible.

The basic frame of the piece is constructed of varying lengths of 1½ × 1½s (A,B,D,E,F,H) attached with mortise and tenon joints glued together (Table 2-4). The front, bottom crossbar of the top section (I) is 1½ × 2¼, however, to allow ¾" as a backstop for the counter (J). The verticals (C) for the panels were originally attached to the horizontals (D,F) with mortise and tenon joints and pegged. If, however, you find this too difficult, you can half lap the verticals to the horizontals and show externally the same results. If you don't want to bother with pegs, you can use countersunk screws with a plug in the top cavity to conceal the screw. In addition, the verticals (C) are recessed in the back 1⅛" to allow insertion of ¼" panels, leaving a ⅜" recess in front.

The members of each of the rectangular drawer guides (M,O,Q) are rabbeted together, with the front members flush with the rest of the basic frame to form the exterior areas between the drawers. The six small drawers (N) of the top section, when pushed all the way in, reach the back panel of the section and have bottoms which are simply glued directly to the sides, backs and fronts of the drawers. The seven drawers of the bottom section have bottoms which are attached under the sides, backs, and fronts of the drawers with nails and glue. The four equal-size drawers of the bottom section, when pushed all the way in, reach approximately two-thirds of the full depth of the bottom section; otherwise, the drawers would be much too unwieldy.

The counter (J) can be made from one sheet of plywood, but it is best not to use plywood, because the edges will clearly show its layers. It would be best to use two pieces of hardwood (the original was made of maple) edge glued together and rounded off at the outer edges. The top piece (G) is simply glued to the frame (F,H).

The floor (U) of the middle area between the two sets of drawers in the top section also provides a stop for the flush door (L). The door is joined together with mortise and tenons and has a recessed panel. Finally, the legs of the desk are turnings shaped as shown in Fig. 2-7.

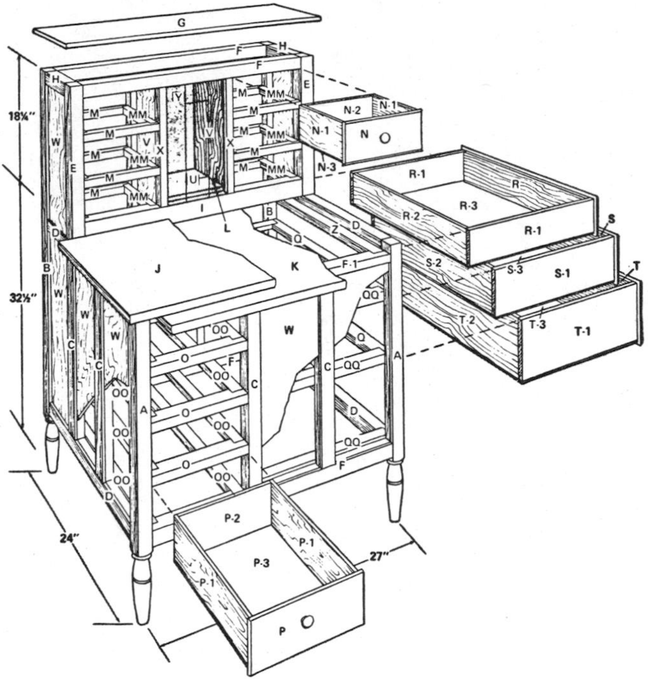

Fig. 2-8. Construction details for the Shaker desk and working table.

Table 2-4. Materials For the Shaker Desk and Working Table.

LIST OF MATERIALS	
A. 2 pcs, 1½ × 1½ × 32½"	P-1. 8 pcs, ½ × 4½ × 15"
B. 2 pcs, 1½ × 1½ × 50¾"	P-2. 4 pcs, ½ × 4½ × 7⅞"
C. 6 pcs, 1½ × 1½ × 21½"	P-3. 4 pcs, 3/16 × 8¼ × 15"
D. 4 pcs, 1½ × 1½ × 21"	Q. 4 pcs, 1 × 1½ × 21"
E. 2 pcs, 1½ × 1½ × 18¼"	QQ. 6 pcs, 1 × 1½ × 16½"
F. 4 pcs, 1½ × 1½ × 24"	R. 1 pc, ¾ × 4 × 21½"
F-1. 1 pc, 1½ × ¾ × 24"	R-1. 2 pcs, ½ × 3⅜ × 15"
G. 1 pc, ⅜ × 28 × 8½"	R-2. 1 pc, ½ × 3⅜ × 19⅞"
H. 2 pcs, 1½ × 1½ × 5"	R-3. 1 pc, 3/16 × 20¼ × 15"
I. 1 pc, 2¼ × 1½ × 24	S. 1 pc, ¾ × 6½ × 21½"
J. 1 pc, ¾ × 30 × 18"	S-1. 2 pcs, ½ × 5⅞ × 15"
K. 1 pc, ¾ × 24 × 23"	S-2. 1 pc, ½ × 5⅞ × 19⅞"
L. door, 6 × 15⅝"	S-3. 1 pc, 3/16 × 20¼ × 15"
M. 10 pcs, 1 × 1 × 8	T. 1 pc, ¾ × 9½ × 21½"
MM. 12pcs, 1 × 1 × 5½"	T-1. 2 pcs, ½ × 8⅞ × 15"
N. 6 pcs, ¾ × 4-13/16 × 8½"	T-2. 1 pc, ½ × 8⅞ × 19⅞"
N-1. 12 pcs, ½ × 4 × 7½"	T-3. 1 pc, 3/16 × 20¼ × 15"
N-2. 6 pcs, ½ × 4 × 6⅞"	U. 1 pc, ⅜ × 6 × 5¾"
N-3. 6 pcs, 3/16 × 7½ × 6⅞"	V. 2 pcs, ⅜ × 15⅝ × 5¾"
O. 6 pcs, 1 × 1½ × 9"	W. ¼" plywood panels to fit
OO. 8 pcs, 1 × 1½ × 22½"	X. 2 pcs, 1 × 1 × 15⅛"
P. 4 pcs, ¾ × 5⅛ × 9½"	Y. 1 pc, 8 × 15⅛ × ¼"
	Z. slide guide, 1 × 1 × 21"

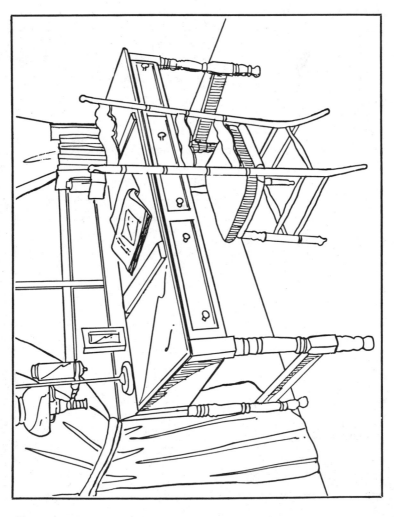

Fig. 2-9: This merchant's desk can be easily reduced.

ANTIQUE MERCHANT'S DESK

Once a sturdy work desk in a mercantile establishment, this large handsome piece bears the scars of its long years of service (Fig. 2-9). Some surfaces are distressed, and the front edge of the top shows nail holes where there once must have been fastened a small lip that prevented ledgers from sliding to the floor.

Because of the desk's generous dimensions, a large room would be its best setting. To fit your scale of living, however, a smaller version may be desirable. The piece is easily reduced, losing none of its authentic look in the transition. Elimination of one drawer and minor reduction of the front-to-back dimension and leg thickness is recommended.

The original, with its liberal use of dadoes and mortise-and-tenon joints, shows the builder's careful attention to detail. Those who wish to duplicate its original condition will want to know there is evidence that another 2 × 4 once stretched from one side 2 × 4 to the other; this is not shown on the plans.

With all parts cut, construction is quite simple. See Fig. 2-10 and Table 2-5. Assemble one front and one rear leg with its side and 2 × 4 brace; glue and clamp. When dry, fit the front 1 × 4 horizontal members and back panel in their dadoes, glue and clamp. With the main framework now constructed, the drawer separators and drawer slides can be screwed and glued in. It is suggested that the drawers be cut and fitted next, as access to the interior is, of course, much easier before the top is attached.

The sloping top is made from two pieces of clear 1 × 12 pine doweled and edge glued, cut to 20″ deep. The forward edge of the

Table 2-5. Materials For the Merchant's Desk.

MATERIALS LIST
All stock clear pine. 2 front legs, 3 × 3 × 30 2 rear legs, 3 × 3 × 32¼ 2 leg spacers, 2 × 4 × 23¾ 2 slides, ¾ × 9 × 22¼ 2 separators, ¾ × 9 × 22¼ 2 front horizontals, 1 × 4 × 68½· 1 back, ¾ × 9 × 65¼ 1 sloping top, ¾ × 20 × 70½· 1 horizontal shelf, ¾ × 9 × 70½· 3 drawer fronts, ¾ × 3⅞ × 19⅞ 3 drawer backs, ¾ × 3⅞ × 18⅜ 6 drawer sides, ¾ × 3⅞ × 24⅜ 3 drawer bottoms, ¼ × 19⅛ × 24 6 drawer slides

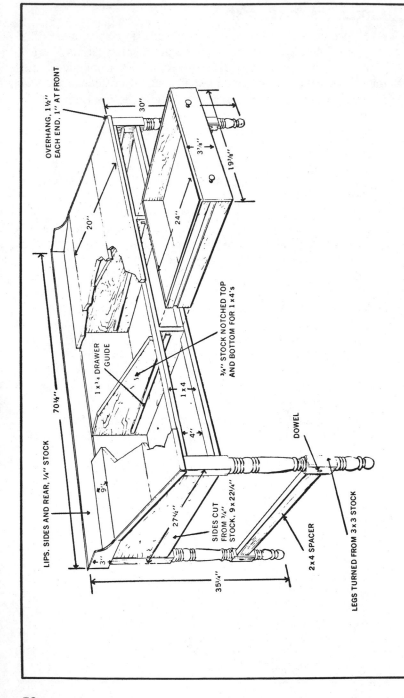

OVERHANG, 1½"
EACH END, 1" AT FRONT

30"

3⅛"

19⅞"

24"

20"

¾" STOCK NOTCHED TOP
AND BOTTOM FOR 1 x 4's

1 x 3 ½ DRAWER
GUIDE

70½"

1 x 4

4"

DOWEL

LIPS, SIDES AND REAR, ¼" STOCK

9"

27½"

SIDES CUT
FROM ¾"
STOCK, 9 x 22¼"

2 x 4 SPACER

3"

35¼"

LEGS TURNED FROM 3 x 3 STOCK

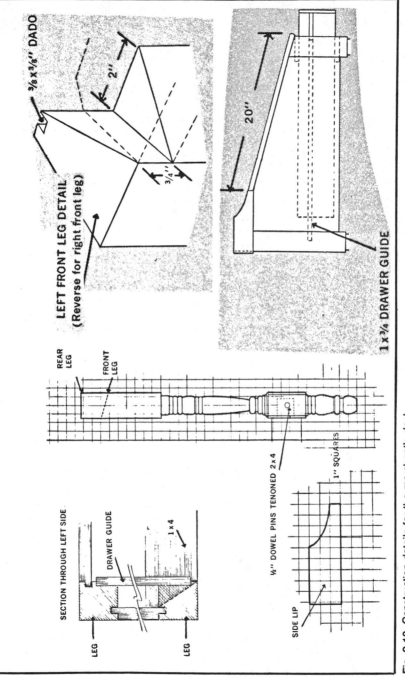

³⁄₈ x ³⁄₈" DADO

2"

3⁄4"

LEFT FRONT LEG DETAIL
(Reverse for right front leg)

1 x ¾ DRAWER GUIDE

20"

REAR LEG

FRONT LEG

½" DOWEL PINS TENONED 2 x 4

1" SQUARES

SECTION THROUGH LEFT SIDE

DRAWER GUIDE

1 x 4

LEG

LEG

SIDE LIP

1" SQUARES

Fig. 2-10. Construction details for the merchant's desk.

51

horizontal shelf across the back of the top is mitered to the angle which is formed by the back edge of the 20" piece with the vertical. Seal the undersides and edges of the top before attaching to prevent warping. Several coats of thinned shellac will suffice.

The final construction step is attaching the side and rear lips. Use glue and fasten with small finishing nails to hold until the glue dries.

Special care must be taken with the front legs, the top of which have a complex shape. The special leg detail drawing shows the slope of the top surface; the triangular section which is sawed from the inside corner to provide a bearing surface for the top front 1 × 4; and the dado for the side (Fig. 2-10). For the sake of clarity, the dado for the bottom front 1 × 4 is not indicated in this drawing.

The type of finish is something the builder will want to decide. In the original, the finish is a rich, deep mahogany with a high gloss surface that gleams in the light.

QUEEN ANNE SECRETARY DESK

We have assembled and finished successfully both the large and small kit models of the Emperor Clock Company's Grandfather clocks. The quality of the wood, both cherry and walnut, was excellent, and the parts were nicely cut. With some care in assembly and finishing, the final result was a very attractive grandfather clock for less than half the cost of a factory finished clock. So, when the announcement of the company's new Queen Anne secretary arrived in the mail, it was too good a deal to pass up.

At first, we had a doubt or two about whether the finished secretary would be as handsome as the clocks (Fig. 2-11). Obviously, many more parts were involved and it seemed to me that assembly and finishing would be considerably more difficult for an amateur. But we decided to try it anyway.

When the kit arrives you will find that the parts in each of the three boxes are packed in shredded paper from old business forms plus millions of little paper dots or circles. We suggest that you open each box on a large sheet of wrapping paper and take the shredded paper out very carefully; otherwise the little paper dots will be all over the house.

Instruction Booklet

Look for the instruction booklet as soon as you remove the master carton. It should be lying on top of the three boxes, each of which is identified by number (Fig. 2-12). Do not open any box until

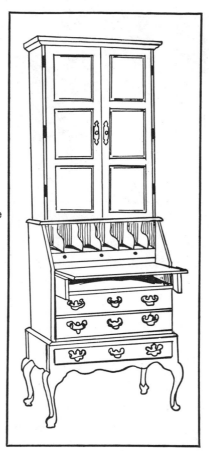

Fig. 2-11. A completed Queen Anne secretary desk.

you have found the instruction booklet. In our case the book was buried in the third box and we opened all the boxes to find it with the result that 135 wood parts were all mixed up. Actually, it wasn't hard to separate them into the three boxes in which they belonged after consulting the instruction booklet and identifying all the parts. However, it is unlikely that you will run into this problem since the company now packs the instruction book so that it is immediately visible when the main carton is removed.

All the wooden parts are packed in separate boxes or compartments according to the different assemblies to which they belong. These assemblies or sections include the base, waist (drawers, letter compartments, sides, back, etc.), and hutch.

The exposed surface of each part is presanded at the factory, and the job is done well. Before assembly of each section, how-

Fig. 2-12. The entire secretary desk is contained in three large boxes in a carton.

ever, we carefully sanded the exposed surface of each part, using the recommended garnet paper. Grade 100 was used first, followed by a light sanding with grade 180. The precision of the factory sanding was excellent. Having had some experience with several brands of clock kits, we had expected to find deep sanding marks across the grain of the wood on some pieces. That was not the case with this kit, though, and very little work was needed to bring each part up to a smooth, satiny feel, with no sign of sanding scratches.

Desk Base

The first assembly is the desk base (Fig. 2-13). With the preformed legs and leg posts, this is a relatively easy operation. Dowel pegs are used to fasten the base sides to the leg posts, and the instructions say to hammer these parts together using a padded surface. But it might be better not to try it. Once before, we had hammered two parts together on one of the clock kits and never did get all the marks out. Use a bar clamp with small scraps of wood between the clamp surfaces and the parts. The screws of the clamps. The base sides will slide easily and snugly onto the leg posts.

It is important at this point to make sure that the four legs, base sides, and front and rear rails are truly square. Again, the bar clamps were used crosswise to square the assembly while the glue dried. White glue was used, as recommended in the instructions. Considerable care was used in wiping off excess glue with a damp cloth. Any glue left on an exposed surface will reject stain and cause an unsightly spot during the finishing operations. In spite of the care used in wiping away excess glue, we found two small

Fig. 2-13. Base of the desk assembled from its precut but unfinished parts.

places later on where the stain didn't take. We rubbed these out with steel wool, and succeeded in completely erasing them.

Brads As Drill Bits

Part of the base assembly calls for the use of ¾″ brads on the drawer runners, for example. The instructions suggested using a brad as a drill bit, and cautioned against nailing without first drilling a pilot hole. At first, we balked at using a brad as the drill bit, and hunted up a bit with a smaller diameter than the brad. Later, we decided to try out the brad-drill idea, and were surprised to find that it works beautifully, at least on the cherry wood in this secretary.

Following assembly of the base, the next step is to assemble the waist (Fig. 2-14). Essentially this is done with two precut sides and a series of four front and rear rails, and an equal number of side rails. The cross rails have a square tenon on each end, and the sides have matching mortises. This was another case where the job could

Fig. 2-14. Waist assembly includes top, sides, back and spaces for three drawers.

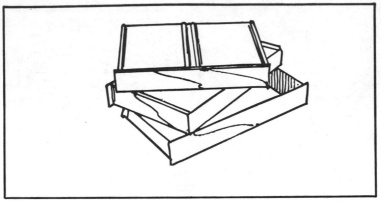

Fig. 2-15. The three drawers after being assembled. Note the centered guides.

probably not have been done nicely by hammering the rails into the sides. We used the trusty bar clamps, and the whole assembly went together smoothly.

In some places, glued joints are reinforced with counterset 1¼″ flat head screws. At first, we used three different bits for each screw hole: first, a shank bit; second, a slightly larger bit for the unthreaded part of the screw; and finally, a counterset bit. That's a lot of drill bit changing. We soon acquired one of the wood screw bits which drill two-sized holes and a countersink all in one operation. They are available in any hardware store for each screw size.

Checking Squareness

Again, squareness must be checked carefully, and our check showed an out of square condition. We nailed four wood blocks, one for each corner of the waist, on the workbench, and set the waist

Fig. 2-16. Assembled letter compartment is now ready for installation in desk.

assembly inside the blocks. Then, using wedges between the sides and the wood blocks we pushed the assembly into square and left it there until the glue dried. It was right on.

From the length of detailed instructions for the waist assembly, we judged that the manufacturer considers this section to be the most difficult to assemble. We did not find that to be the case. The only disconcerting thing was the practice of naming each part, in addition to identifying it in the instructions. For example, one step said "trial fit the top drawer front lower side rails (SW6 c&d) to the top drawer front lower cross rail (SW 2 a)". We soon ignored the name of the part and simply read the instruction as "trial fit SW 6-c&d to SW-2-a", and referred to the exploded drawings.

Drawer Assembly

Assembly of the waist drawers was very easy, and there were no problems (Figs. 2-15 through 2-18). The same was true of the

Fig. 2-17. Waist section fastened to the base. A fourth drawer has been assembled and placed in the opening.

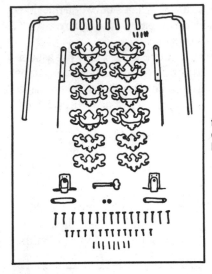

fig. 2-18. Waist section hardware includes drawer handles and desk locks.

hutch (Figs. 2-19 and 2-20). Installation of the drop lid hinges and the arms that pull out the supporting side rails when the lid is opened looked difficult but turned out to be fairly simple. The lid worked perfectly, and the support rails slid in and out beautifully with no problems (Figs. 2-21).

With a final overall light sanding and a careful wiping with a tack rag, as instructed, we were ready for staining (Fig. 2-23). In finishing our Emperor clocks, we had used an alcohol stain and a nationally-known lacquer. This time, we used Emperor's stain and varnish package. They sent two 1-pint cans each of oil stain and varnish (Fig. 2-24).

Staining and Varnishing

The stain is excellent—easy to brush or rub on, and the color is beautiful, a medium light fruitwood with little or no red. The overall result is outstanding. After staining, although the instructions did not call for it, we rubbed the whole piece with fine steel wool. This cut off all tiny raised wood grains and made a very smooth surface for the finish.

The varnish in Emperor's package is very slow drying. Twenty-four hours after the first coat, the finish was still tacky, and it finally took three days to dry thoroughly. After another light rubbing with steel wool, a second coat of varnish was brushed. Three days later, the nearly finished secretary was ready for the final fine steel wool light rub and a coat of paste wax.

Hardware installation was quite easy and presented no problems.

When finished, this secretary is a fine piece of furniture. Beautifully designed with pleasing proportions, the desk and hutch will grace any home. And not the least of its charm is the great measure of personal satisfaction its builders will attach to it. Every one of them built with reasonable care will be a treasured heirloom a generation from now.

CAPTAIN'S DESK

The traditional captain's desk originally was created to make the best use of a small space, like the confines of a shipboard cabin. Its rail-edged top held quill and ink, and inside its hinged lid was a convenient storage space for such things as stationery, logbooks

Fig. 2-19. Bookcase section or hutch shown here after completion has three hinges on doors and three shelves.

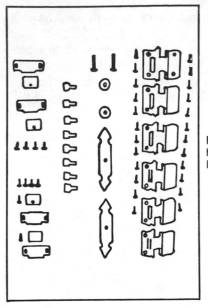

Fig. 2-20. Hardware parts for the hutch include two sets of magentic latches.

and packets of important papers. With the lid closed, it provided an adequate writing surface.

Today, captain's cabins are larger, and you'd be hard pressed to find this functional piece of furniture aboard ship anywhere. Now authentic captain's desks are considered antiques, and bring thousands of dollars at auctions.

You can, however, have one of these beautiful relics with a seagoing history for your living room or den by building it yourself. And if yours is a small den, the desk you build can serve the dual purpose of being—of all things—a desk!

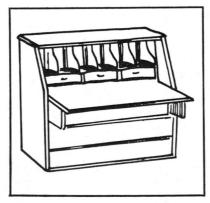

Fig. 2-21. Completed waist section. Note supports that extend under cover.

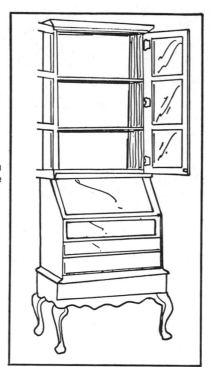

Fig. 2-22. Fully assembled desk with hutch doors open showing all the hinges.

Fig. 2-23. Cherry wood Queen Anne desk shown fully assembled but still unfinished.

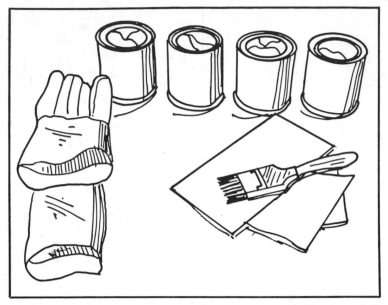

Fig. 2-24. Shown is the finishing material which is part of the kit. Two cans of oil stain and two cans of varnish are provided.

All you'll need is an electric drill, a power saw and other tools normally found in any ordinary home workshop. The wood will run $50 to $75, depending on the grade you use; and the whole project can be done in about a week, if you devote several hours after supper each night. You can plan out the desk pattern yourself, if you are a reasonably skild craftsman.

Get Your Lumber

The first step is to purchase select pine boards that are straight-edged and flat (Table 2-6). It's best to choose boards that are similar in color, avoiding dark wood or wood with pronounced grain textures. If you use boards with knots, make sure the knots are small and sound.

Lay out your cutting patterns and transfer their outlines to the wood. It's best to leave extra wood in the flat areas to allow for planning or squaring up the piece. To do this, move the pattern in from the normal flat edge of the board about 1/8". To make sure the finished desk will stand upright, check all transferred patterns with a carpenter's square.

Next step is to cut out the pieces. Use a saber saw, if you can, when cutting the planks. A coping saw can be used but will take much more time. If you have access to a table or radial arm saw, either will make it easier to cut the large rabbets needed to join feet, legs and box support pieces. You cut out all the pieces except cutouts in the legs; these are made with a hole saw after the legs are assembled.

After cutting, the next step is to smooth the edges of all parts, particularly the curved cuts, with a sanding drum attached to your drill. The assembly dowels, to be used to reinforce glue joints, should be beveled on both ends with sandpaper or drill sanding attachment. A flat area, about ⅛" deep, on each end of the dowel will provide a vent for excess glue.

Dowel locations are transferred onto the boards after they are cut out, and a doweling jig is used to bore the holes (Fig. 2-25). Next the dowels are inserted dry to make sure everything fits. It should be possible to bring the parts together without excessive pressure. If not, the dowels which are causing trouble can be shaved down. Then white liquid resin glue is applied to all joining surfaces and the pieces are set in bar or pipe clamps.

Joining Pieces

All pieces except the legs and braces are glued where they fasten to the desk box. See Figs. 2-26 and 2-27. Screws will be sufficient to hold the box, and you'll be able to easily disassemble the desk if you have to move it.

Fig. 2-25. After cutting out the desk legs, a doweling jig provides location when boring dowel holes.

Table 2-6. Materials Needed For the Captain's Desk.

Pieces	MATERIAL LIST (Sizes listed below are lumber common sizes)	
Pieces	**Dimensions**	**Parts**
1	1 × 4 × 10'	Box bottom
1	1 × 10 × 10'	Box sides, lid
1	1 × 10 × 30"	Box ledge
1	5/4 × 10 × 48"	Feet, box Supports & bottom, bracing
1	5/4 × 8 × 8'	Legs
1	⅛" Hardboard or ¼" Plywood x 24" × 30"	Bottom of desk box
1	5/16" Dowel × 36"	Rail uprights
2	⅜" Dowel × 36"	Fastening dowels
1	½" × ¾" Parting stop × 48"	Railings
3	2" Cabinet butt hinges	Lid
2	Lid and fall supports	Lid

¾" brads, 4-penny finishing nails, (12)1" No.10 flat-head wood screws, (28) 1-¼" No. 10 flat-head wood screws, (26) 1½" No. 10 flat-head wood screws, (4) 1-¾" No. 10 flat-head wood screws, plastic wood or wood putty, liquid white resin glue.

To end up with a beautiful final finish, make sure the un-finished wood stays smooth and unstained as you work. All excess glue should be removed with a warm, damp cloth immediately after joining pieces to avoid stain penetration. Soft wood blocks should be used under clamp jaws to prevent marring of exposed surfaces.

To make screw holes, you can use a wood screw pilot bit. The bit's depth stop is set so the screw head is recessed ¼" below the surface. Cut ⅜" dowel plugs ¼" long, and glue them to each hole after the screw is in. Let the plugs protrude slightly, and you can sand them flush after the glue has set.

The box and its base frame are assembled with glue and screws (Fig. 2-28). Next the two pieces of the lid and its braces, plus the legs, feet and braces are assembled. Then the leg cutouts are finished with 2" hole saw and saber saw (Figs. 2-29 and 2-30). The box and legs are joined and the desk bottom is fastened in with

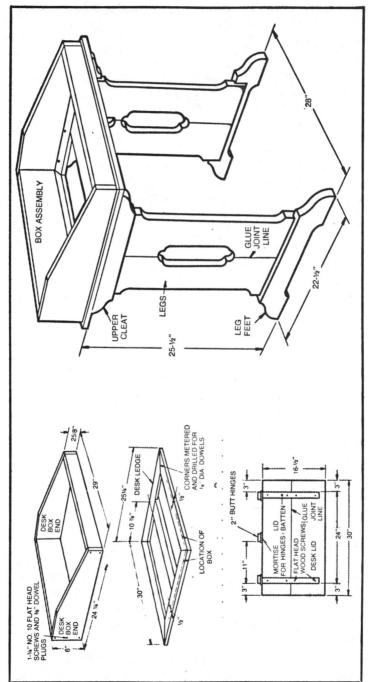

Fig. 2-26. Assembly details for the captain's desk.

65

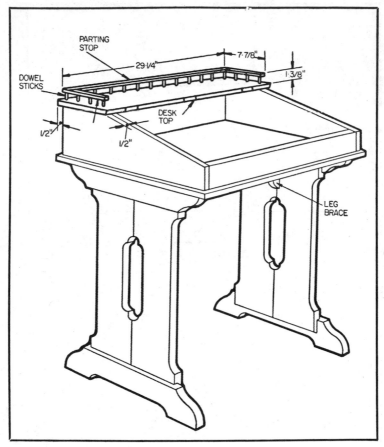

Fig. 2-27. Diagram of the captain's desk.

A drop of glue is used on each dowel hole in the ledge, before driving the railing dowels up through it. A scrap of wood can be used to keep the dowels protruding evenly 1⅛″ above the ledge. Next a drop of glue is applied to each dowel hole in the railing and the rail pushed onto the dowels with firm even pressure (Fig. 2-32). After the rail has been started, a wood block and hammer can be used to tap the rail into its final position.

How to Finish

The desk is sanded with a very fine paper. A silky smooth final surface is obtained by "raising the grain" with a damp cloth or sponge after the first sanding, and then sanding again after the

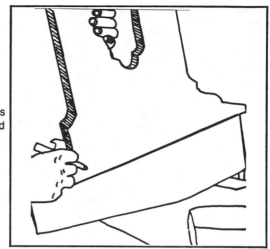

Fig. 2-28. Desk box is assembled with wood screws.

surface has dried. The dampening causes loose wood fibers to rise, and the second sanding removes them.

It's best to try out stains and seals on a scrap of wood first. Then brush on stain liberally, let it stand and then wipe it off with a cloth. The longer the stain stands, the darker the finish will be. You can use a satin varnish, rubbed down with extra fine steel wool after it has dried, followed by an application of a hard furniture wax.

STUDY DESK

This duplex study area offers abundant desk space, shelves, and drawers (Fig. 2-33). Construction on the shelves begins with

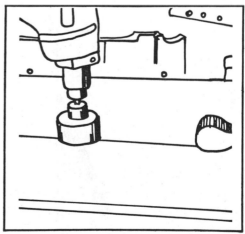

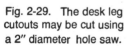

Fig. 2-29. The desk leg cutouts may be cut using a 2" diameter hole saw.

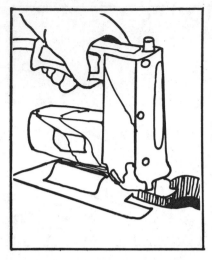

Fig. 2-30. After using the hole saw, the leg cutouts can be completed using a saber saw.

brads or small screws (Fig. 2-31). Next rabbets are cut for the desk hinges in the ledge front and the lid is positioned.

cutting grooves in (A) for the sliding door panels. See Fig. 2-34 and Table 2-7. Make two 40" long, 3/16" wide grooves ½" from the edge. Make a similar groove 3/16" from the first cut. The depth of the cuts on the lower (A) are ⅛". The upper (A) cuts are 5/16", to allow for the insertion and removal of the door panels by lifting them out of the bottom cut. Waxing the grooves lets the panels slide easier. If a power saw or router is not available, plastic guide tracks that are nailed to the surface can be obtained at the hardware store. Back cleats (B) and two end cleats (D) are fastened to the wall studs by screws.

Fig. 2-31. Leg sections are glued. Then upper cleats and leg feet are attached.

Fig. 2-32. The gallery rail is assembled before gluing onto desk box.

Fig. 2-33. The good looking desk and wall cabinets offer plenty of storage and working space for your young scholars.

Table 2-7. Materials Needed For the Study Desk.

LIST OF MATERIALS	
A. 2pcs, ¾" × 9½." × 8'	N. 8 pcs, ½· × ¾ × 35¼"
B. 2 pcs, 1½· × 2½· × 30"	O. 1 pc, ¾ × 2½· × 15½."
C. 4 pcs, ⅛ × 10¼" 20"	P. 2 pcs, 1½· × 2½· × 12½."
D. 2 pcs, 1½· × 2½· × 10"	Q. 1 pc, ½· × 8¾ × 10¼"
E. 4 pcs, ¾ × 10 × 9½."	R. 1 pc, ¾" × 36" × 8'
F. 1 pc, 1/16" × 36" 8' Formica	S. 4 pcs, ¼ × 11¼ × 34¾"
G. 1 pc, ¾" × 2½." 8'	T. 1 pc, ½· × 8¾ × 11¼"
H. 1 pc, 1/16" × 3 5/16" × 8' Formica	U. 2 pcs, ½· × 8¾ × 34¼"
I. 2 pcs, ¾ × 29¼" × 35¼"	V. 3 pcs, ½· × 4¾ × 11¼"
J. 2 pcs, ¾ × 2½· × 36"	W. 6 pcs, ½· × 4¾ × 34¼"
K. 3 pcs, ¾ × 5 × 14"	X. 2 pcs, 1½· × 2½· × 35¼"
L. 1 pc, ¾ × 9'× 14"	Y. 2 pcs, 1½· × 2½· × 35"
M. 16 pcs, ½· × ¾ × 30"	Z. 3 pcs, ½· × 4¾ × 10¼"

The drawer unit is a box frame of ½" pine (T), (U) and (Q), with a bottom of ¼" plywood (S) glued and nailed to it. The front end of the box (Q is glued and screwed to the back of the birch face (K) or (L). Fastened by screws to I, birch veneered plywood, is a runner (N) that fits between guides (M), nailed 1" apart on the faces of (U). Cleats (P) are fastened by screws to the floor and wall, and the sides (I) are nailed to these. Two more cleats (X) are placed to lie beneath the ends of the table top (R). Be sure the end of the cleat is in line so as to furnish support for the 3" wide strip (G), which is screwed to R, X and P before R is covered with contact glue and Formica (F). Formica H covers (G), and a router or a file creates the proper bevel between the two Formica edges. Finish with two coats of clear varnish. Hide the counterset nail holes with birch colored wax stick.

DESK FOR BOY'S ROOM

You can make an extremely practical desk for a boy's room that is easy to make, provides plenty of storage and ample work space on the top surface (Fig. 2-35).

The top (A) is a sheet of ¾" plywood with a 1¾" skirt of ½" thick lumber fastened with finishing nails and glue (Fig. 2-36 and Table 2-8). The left end of the desk top is supported by a cleat attached with screws driven through the plasterboard and into the studs.

The right end of the desk top is supported by a cabinet which is really a three-sided box made up of the back and two sides (D) nailed to a top and bottom (J). The top of this box (J) is attached to the underside of the desk top (A) with glue and 1¼" No. 8 screws.

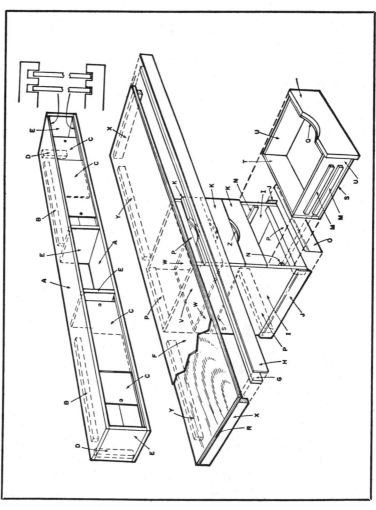

Fig. 2-34. Diagram of the study desk.

71

Fig. 2-35. This practical desk is easy to make.

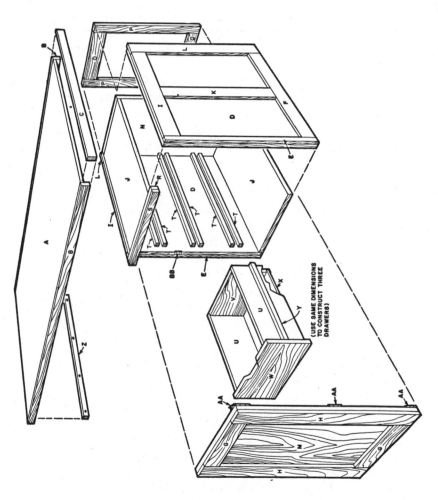

Fig. 2-36. Diagram of the desk shown in Fig. 2-35.

73

Table 2-8. Materials Required For the Desk Shown in Fig. 2-35.

LIST OF MATERIALS	
A. 1 pc, ¾ × 22½· × 59¼″	O. 1 pc, ½·× 3¼ × 10½″
B. 2 pcs, ¾ × 1¾ × 59¼″	P. 2 pcs, ½·× 1½·× 28¼″
C. 1 pc, ¾ × 1¾ × 24″	Q. 1 pc, ½·× 2 × 10½″
D. 2 pcs, ¾ × 20¾ × 28¼″	R. 1 pc, ¾ × 1¼ × 14½″
E. 2 pcs, ½·× ¾ × 28¼″	S. 1 pc, ½·× 1¼ × 14½″
F. 2 pcs, ½·× 2 × 18½″	T. 12 pcs, ¾ × ¾ × 18¾″
G. 2 pcs, ½·× 2 × 10½″	U. 6 pcs, ½·× 6⅝ × 16″
H. 2 pcs, ½·× 2 × 28″	V. 3 pcs, ½·× 6⅝ × 9¼″
I. 2 pcs, ½·× 3¼ × × 18½″	W. 3 pcs, ¾ × 6⅝ × 11¾″
J. 2 pcs, ¾ × 12 × 20″	X. 3 pcs, ¼ × 9¾ × 15¾″
K. 2 pcs, ½·× 2 × 23″	Y. pcs, ¾ × ¾ × 16″
L. 2 pcs, ½·× 2 × 28¼″	Z. 1 pc, ¾ × 1 × 22½·″
M. 1pc, ¾ × 14½·× 28″	AA. 3 pcs, Hinges
N. 1 pc, ¾ × 12 × 28¼″	BB. 1 pc, Magnetic Latch

The door of the cabinet is equipped with a touch latch and therefore needs no exterior handle.

The decorative frames (E, F, I, L, K) and (H, G, H, G), on the surfaces of the door, sides, and back of the cabinet are made of ½″ lumber with routed edges. If you are not equipped to do this kind of routing, just round of the corners and smooth them with sandpaper. The frames are fastened with countersunk finishing nails and glue and the nail holes filled with wood putty.

Note that the cabinet door has ⅛″ clearance at the bottom so that it can swing freely over the Armstrong vinyl floor.

The plywood for the desk top should be good one side and sanded when purchased. It should then be sanded again with 100-grit and then with 150-grit aluminum oxide open coat sandpaper. Follow this with two or even three coats of fresh shellac diluted half and half with alcohol. Each coat of shellac should be rubbed smooth with fine steel wool. Spray with a wood primer followed by two coats of the enamel color of your choice. Rub both coats of enamel lightly with very fine steel wool and then apply a good grade of paste wax.

SHAKER CHILD'S DESK

This handsome student's desk reflects the beauty, practicality, simplicity, and sturdiness characteristic of Shaker furniture (Fig. 2-37). The original dates back to the last half of the nineteenth century and was made of black walnut, cherry, and poplar. It is now on display in the Philadelphia Museum of Art.

Note that the desk is intended for a child to stand at and work or play. It features two side drawers, the smaller one near the top for such items as pens, pencils and crayons and the larger one for other supplies such as paper. Both drawers are made of ½″ material. See Table 2-9.

The desk top is hinged in the back, preferably with two small antique-styled hinges if obtainable. There is an interior partition (B) which separates a main compartment at the left from the two drawers at the right. See Fig. 2-38.

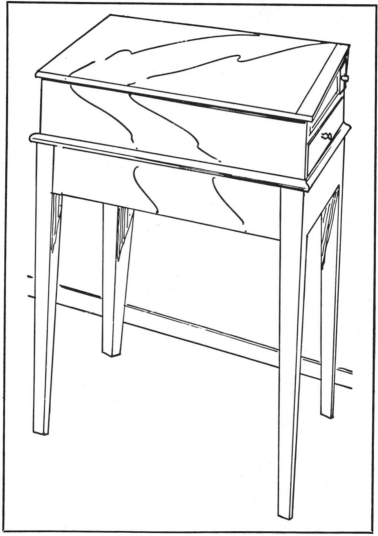

Fig. 2-37. This Shaker child's desk is both beautiful and simple.

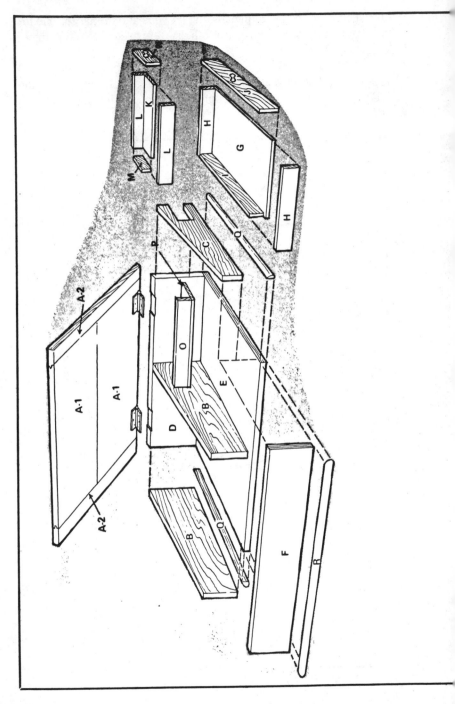

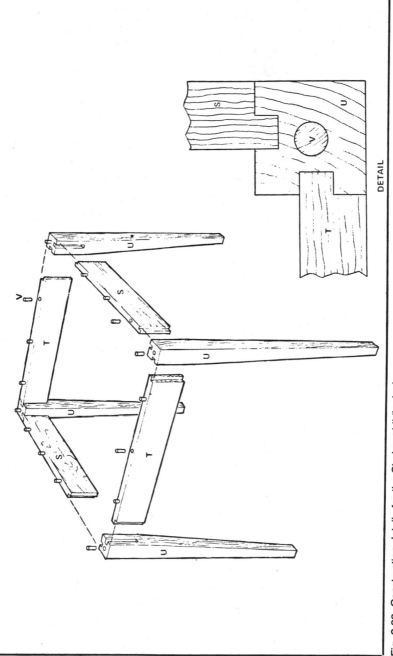

DETAIL

Fig. 2-38. Construction details for the Shaker child's desk.

Table 2-9. Materials Needed For the Shaker Child's Desk.

LIST OF MATERIALS	
A-1. 2 pcs, 15½ × 13¾ × ¾"	K. 1 pc, 8⅛ × 3 × ½·"
A-2. 2 pcs, 13¾ × 2 × ¾"	L. 2 pcs, 8⅛ × 2½· × ½"
B. 2 pcs, 11½· × 7½· × ¾"	M. 1 pc, 3 × 2 × ½"
C. 1 pc, 11½· × 4½· × ¾"	N. 1 pc, 4 × 2½· × ½"
D. 1 pc, 18 × 7½ × ¾"	O. 1 pc, 7⅞ × 3 × ½"
E. 1 pc, 18 × 13 × ¾"	P. 1 pc, 7⅞ × 4 × ½"
F. 1 pc, 18 × 6 × ¾"	Q. 2 pcs, ¾ × ¾ × 13¾"
G. 1 pc, 11½· × 8⅛ × ½"	R 1 pc, ¾ × ¾ × 19½"
H. 2 pcs, 8⅛ × 2½· × ½"	S. 2 pcs, 11½· × 5 × ¾"
I. 1 pc, 10½· × 2½· × ½"	T. 2 pcs, 16½· × 5 × ¾"
J. 1 pc, 11½· × 3 × ½·"	U. 4 pcs, 1¼ × 1¼ × 21"
	V. 16 pcs, ⅜" Dowels × 1½"

In addition, the top is made of four pieces (A-1, A-2). The two larger ones (A-1) are simply edge glued to each other and the two end pieces (B, C) are fastened to the ends of the larger boards (A-1) with glued tongue-and-groove joints.

The front (F) is 1½" lower than the back panel (D). The moldings are three separate pieces (Q-Q, R) which are butted at the front and nailed and glued to the edges of the bottom (E) of the interior compartment.

The skirts (S, T) are attached to square tapered legs (U) with mortise and tenon joints shown in Fig. 2-38. The tops of the skirt pieces should be fastened to the bottom (E) of the inner compartment with glue and dowels (V).

Chapter 3
Chests

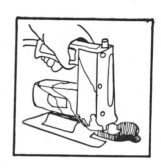

Most homeowners have need for more storage space. This chapter explains how to make chests for storing things like toys, clothes and bed linens. You can even build a couch whose interior has room to hold plenty of toys and other items.

SHAKER CHEST OF DRAWERS

This tall Shaker chest of drawers is frankly utilitarian but it has a homespun charm about it which is characteristic of these early American craftsmen (Fig. 3-1). The original is made of pine and is now in the Philadelphia Museum of Art.

Getting the material should pose no problem since ¾" pine with a minimum of knots is readily available in any lumber yard. See Fig. 3-2 and Table 3-1. The two verticals (A) are nailed and glued to the drawer supports (R). Note that the front drawer spacers (Q) are notched at the front corners to accommodate the two front pieces (B). Also note that the two verticals (A) and the top (E) are rabbeted at their back edges to accept the back (D) which is a ¼" thick sheet of plywood. In addition, E is notched in front to fit the two pieces (C) on either side of the little door.

The panel of the door (L) is ½" thick and is set in a notch or rabbet set back ¼" from the front of the frame (J-J-K-K). The two rails of the door (K) have ⅜" tongues or tenons at each end that fit into corresponding grooves or mortises. The tenons are pinned with ¼" pegs or dowels. The latch on the cabinet door is of a type

Fig. 3-1. The Shaker chest of drawers has a homespun quality about it.

that is no longer made and you will have to shop around to get something similar.

Another construction point to take note of is the bottom frame and drawer support which has double sides (U-T) to strengthen the bottom area of the drawer section.

The drawer openings are all 6⅝" by 25½". The drawers have a 5/16" groove on the inside of the sides, back and front, ½" up

Fig. 3-2. Diagram of the Shaker chest of drawers.

Table 3-1. Materials Needed For the Shaker Chest of Drawers.

LIST OF MATERIALS	
A-2 pcs. ¾ × 15¼ × 84"	L-1 pc. ½ · × 9½ · × 20¼"
B-2 pcs. ¾ × 1¼ × 55½"	M-7 pcs. ¾ × 7 × 25⅞"
C-2 pcs. ¾ × 6½ · × 28½."	N-7. pcs. ½ · × 6½ · × 24⅜"
D-1 pc. ¼ × 27¼ × 83¼"	O-14 pcs. ½ · × 6½ · × 15½."
E-1 pc. ¾ × 26½ · × 16"	P-7 pcs. ¼ × 15½ · × 24⅞"
F-1 pc. ¾ × 26½ · × 15"	Q-14 pcs. 1 × 2 × 26½."
G-1 pc. ½ · × 26½ · × 15"	R-14 pcs. 1 × 2 × 12¾"
H-4 pcs. ¾ × 1½ · × 15"	S-1 pc. ¾ × 2¼ × 26¾"
I-2 pcs. ¾ × 1½ · × 5¾"	T-2 pcs. ¾ × 2¼ × 15"
J-2 pcs. ¾ × 3 × 27¾"	U-2 pcs. ¾ × 2¼ × 14¼"
K-2 pcs. ¾ × 4 × 9¾"	V-1 pc. ¾ × 2¼ × 25"

from the bottom to receive the bottom (P) which is made of ¼" plywood. The drawer fronts are rabbeted on all four sides to permit a ¼" overlap all around the drawer opening. The drawer sides are nailed and glued to the front and back.

SHAKER CLOTHES BUREAU

Here is a handsome Shaker chest of drawers for you to build that duplicates the original 19th century piece owned by Eldress Josephine Wilson of Canterbury, New Hampshire (Fig. 3-3). This pine bureau, now exhibited in the Philadelphia Museum of Art, is a fine example of Shaker craftsmanship, combining plenty of functional storage space with the beauty of simple, clean lines. Table 3-2 lists materials.

Constructing the piece is very easy: the unit simply consists of a series of interior frames (G-H-I) nailed and glued to the sides (B) and back (D) (Fig. 3-4). The interior frames (G-H-I), on which the drawers slide, have half lapped joints at the front and rabbeted joints at the rear. The front separator portions (G) of the interior frames (G-H-I) are notched into the sides (B), a divider panel (C) is inserted with additional drawer glides (K) for the four smaller drawers to ride on, and middle braces (K) are installed for the bottom two larger drawers to ride on.

Note that the back piece (D) is rabbeted to the side pieces (B) and that the top (A), a solid piece, is attached to the top of the framing (G-H-I-K) by drilling holes through these members for screws which are driven from below into the underside of the top (A). The upper surfaces of G,H,I, and K are covered with glue before the screws are driven.

The base (E-F-E) has beveled top edges with mitered joints. The front section of the base (F) is nailed and glued to the front piece (G) of the bottom interior frame (G-H-I), as well as two small blocks (L) which provide additional gluing and nailing surface.

All of the drawers are of standard construction, having the backs (N) (R) flush with the sides (M) (Q) rabbeted to the fronts (O) (S), and the bottoms (P) (T) recessed into the sides (M) (Q), backs (N) (R), and fronts (O) (S). In addition, the edges of the drawer fronts (O) (S) are rounded off. Finally, if you wish, the pine can be attractively finished with a light brown stain.

SHAKER STORAGE CHEST

The handsome Shaker pine chest shown in Fig. 3-5 features a large bottom drawer, a hinged top, and a deep storage section.

Fig. 3-3. This beautiful Shaker clothes bureau has plenty of storage space.

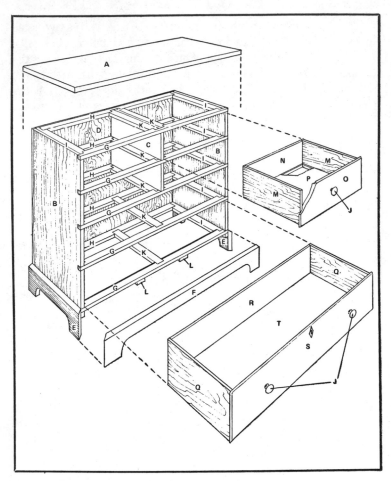

Fig. 3-4. Diagram of the clothes bureau.

Table 3-2. Materials Required For the Clothes Bureau.

LIST OF MATERIALS	
A. 1 pc, 1¼ × 44¼ × 21"	K. 8 pcs, ¾ × 1½ × 17¼"
B. 2 pcs, ¾ × 36¾ × 19"	L. 2 pcs, ¾ × 1½· × 2"
C. 1 pc, ¾ × 16¼ × 18¾"	M 8 pcs, ⅜ × 6⅞ × 18½"
D. 1 pc, ¼ × 36¾ × 37¾"	N. 4 pcs, ⅜ × 6⅞ × 17⅛"
E. 2 pcs, 1¼ × 6 × 20¼"	O. 4 pcs, ¾ × 7½· × 18½"
F. 1 pc, 1¼ × 6 × 40¾"	P 4 pcs, ¼ × 17½· × 18¼"
G. 5 pcs, ¾ × 1½· × 38¼"	Q. 4 pcs, ⅜ × 7⅞ × 18½"
H. 5 pcs, ¾ × 1½· × 35¼"	R. 2 pcs, ⅜ × 7⅞ × 36"
I. 10 pcs, ¾ × 1½· × 18"	S. 2 pcs, ¾ × 8½· × 37¼"
J. 8 wooden knobs	T. 2 pcs, ¼ × 36⅜ × 18¾"

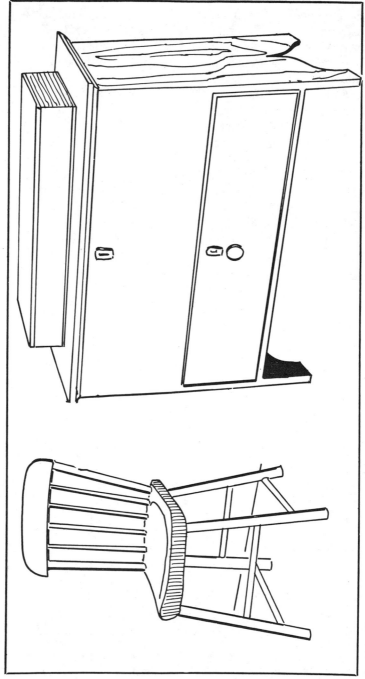

Fig. 3-5. The spacious top area and large bottom drawer in the easy-to-build Shaker chest provide plenty of storage space.

(The pine seed box shown on top of the chest is not included in our construction plans.) The original Shaker chest belonged to Eldress Rosetta Cummings, was made at Enfield, New Hampshire, and can now be seen at the Philadelphia Museum of Art. Table 3-3 lists materials.

First note that the cover (F) is a solid piece of wood and is hinged to lift up for access to the top storage area. The hinges (N) are mortised as shown in Detail 1 of Fig. 3-6. Molding (M), which is mitered at the corners, is attached around the edges of the cover (F).

The drawer is very solidly built with ¾" material. It has an overlapping front (J) rabbeted all around. The thick sides (H) and bottom (G) are held together by simple butt joints, glued and nailed together. Detail 3 of Fig. 3-6 shows the side view of the drawer, with the drawer front (J), with ¼ × 1" rabbet, overlapping the front horizontal cross piece (K). The drawer is supported by a three-

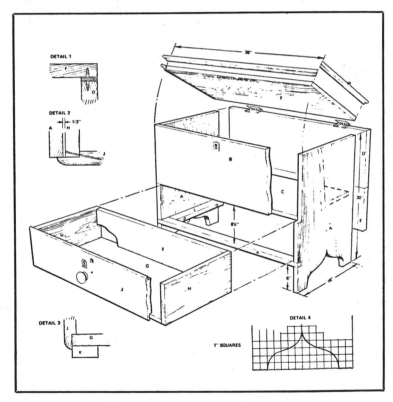

Fig. 3-6. Construction details for the storage chest.

Table 3-3. Materials Needed For the Storage Chest.

LIST OF MATERIALS	
A. 2 pcs, ¾ × 14 × 30″	H. 2 pcs, ¾ × 8 × 13¼″
B 1 pc, ¾ × 15 × 36″	I. 1 pc, ¾ × 7¼ × 32⅞″
C. 1 pc, ¾ × 13¼ × 34½″	J. 1 pc, ¾ × 8¾ × 35″
D. 1 pc, ¾ × 15 × 36″	K. 1 pc, ¾ × 2 × 36″
E. 1 pc, ¾ × 9 × 36″	L. 2 pcs, ¾ × 2 × 12″
F. 1 pc, ¾ × 14¾ × 36″	M. ¾″ lid moulding, 6′
G. 1 pc, ¾ × 14 × 32⅞″	N. 2 pcs, 3″ butt hinges

sided frame (K-L-L); two of the rails (L) are screwed to the sides of the chest (A). Detail 2 of Fig. 3-6 shows the top view of the drawer in relation to the side of the chest (A). Note that the side of the drawer (H) is toenailed to the front of the drawer (J) as shown and that the front of the drawer (J), with ¼ × 1⅛″ rabbet, overlaps the side of the chest (A). Top edge of the drawer front (J) is rabbeted ¼ × ½″.

The sides of the chest (A) are notched with ¾″ square notches to accept the front horizontal crosspiece (K). In addition, they (A) are notched to receive the front panel (B), which is held with finishing nails and glue. The profile of the cutout in each of the sides (A), which forms the legs of the chest, is done with a jigsaw. (See Detail 4 of Fig. 3-6).

The back consists of two pieces (D,E) which are simply nailed to the back edges of the sides (A). The shelf (C) at the bottom of the upper section is nailed through the sides (A) with finishing nails which are countersunk and filled with wood putty. Finish the chest by using a medium brown stain.

SHAKER LINEN CHEST

This simple pine chest is one of the easiest to build of the Shaker furniture pieces (Fig 3-7). The Shakers had used it as a practical storage unit for their bedding and linen, and you can make one to serve the same or some other functional purpose as, for example, a graceful hope chest. Table 3-4 lists materials.

The front (A), back (B) and side panels (C) which serve also as the frame for the chest, are butted, nailed and glued (Fig. 3-8). Solid pine had been used by the Shakers for these panel pieces because it was readily available to them, but you will probably have to substitute a good grade of interior plywood, unless you are willing to glue two boards edge to edge.

Follow the cross-hatched detail as a guide for marking and cutting the scrolled legs on the panel bottoms, including the lower

Fig. 3-7. A functional and attractive linen chest.

molding panel (D). The inside shelf (E), lower drawer supports (F) and side guides (O) are fastened inside the chest frame by nails driven from the outside. Glue is also used here and on the butted drawer joints which are nailed as well. All nails, of course, should be counterset, and the holes puttied.

The front drawer panel (M) is rabbeted and rounded to create the overlapped closure, and the drawer bottom (N), cut from either hardboard or plywood, fits into grooves around the sides, front and back. Molding strips (I-J-I) conceal any unevenness in the flush joint made when the hinged chest lid (H) is closed; the molding pieces also hide the end grain of the lid panel.

After properly sanding the piece, a light stain can be rubbed on, and two coats of urethane varnish will complete your Shaker chest. A hint when finishing is to shellac and sand end grain surfaces to prevent them from absorbing too much stain.

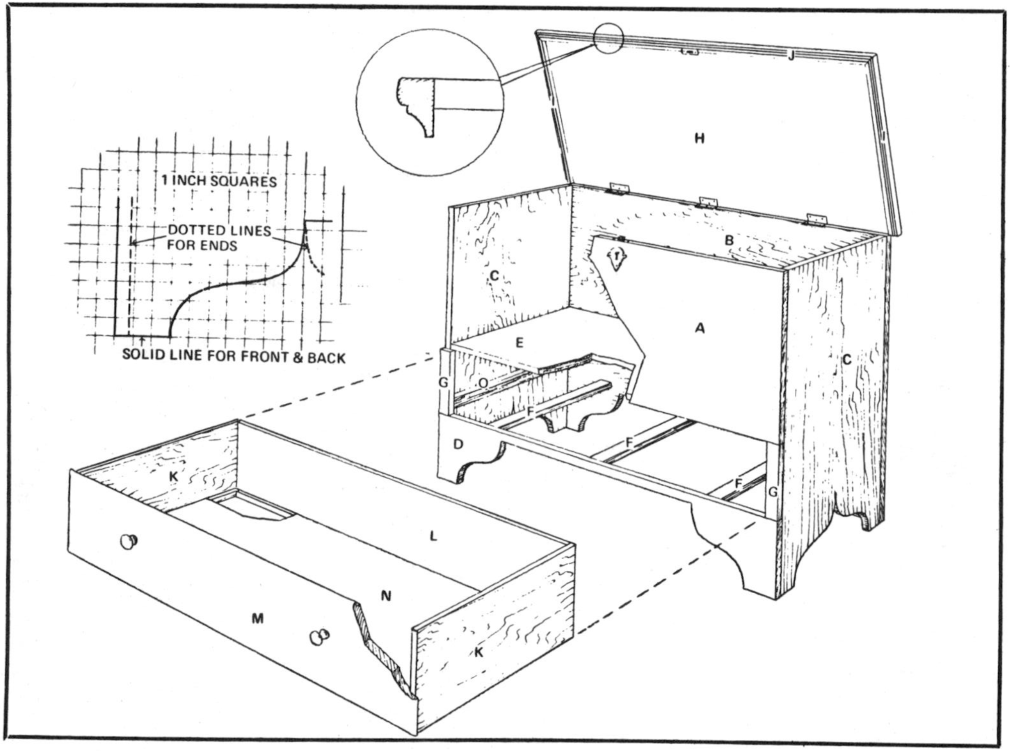
1 INCH SQUARES
DOTTED LINES FOR ENDS
SOLID LINE FOR FRONT & BACK
H
J
B
A
C
C
E
G
O
F
D
F
F
G
K
L
N
M
K

Fig. 3-8. Construction details for the linen chest.

Table 1-1. List Of Materials For The Shaker Armchair.

LIST OF MATERIALS	
A. 1 pc, ¾ × 42 × 17¼"	H. 1 pc, ¾ × 42 1/16 × 20 1/16"
B. 1 pc, ¾ × 42 × 32¼"	I. 2 pcs, 1 × 1½ × 21 1/16"
C. 2 pcs, ¾ × 18½ × 32¼"	J. 1 pc. 1 × 1½ × 44 1/16"
D. 1 pc, ¾ × 42 × 7½"	K. 2 pcs, ½ × 7 3/3 × 19"
E. 1 pc, ¾ × 40½ × 18½"	L. 1 pc, ½ × 7⅜ × 37⅞"
F. 3 pcs, ¾ × 1½ × 18½"	M 1 pc, ¾ × 7⅞ × 39⅜"
G. 2 pcs, ¾ × 1½ × 7½"	N. 1 pc, ¼ × 38⅜ × 19"
	O. 2 pcs, ¾ × 1½ × 18½"

SHAKER TOY CHESTS

Those who like Shaker furniture will find these two toy chests typical of Shaker craftsmanship and simplicity. The chest on the right in Fig. 3-9 was made about 1800 in the Shaker community at Alfred, Maine; and the one on the left with a drawer was made in the same place about 1848.

The upper part of the chest with the drawer is a close copy of the simpler chest on the right. both are made of solid pine but you may find it more convenient to use ¾" plywood. See Table 3-5 for materials.

The bottom, sides, and ends of the upper part are made with butt joints fastened with glue and finishing nails. Note that the cover (O) has moldings (P) on both ends that overlap the sides of

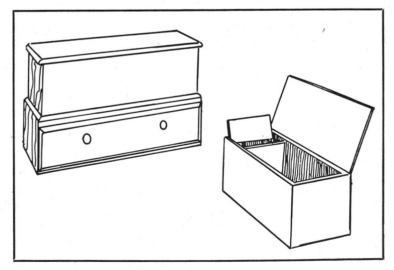

Fig. 3-9. These chests will hold plenty of toys.

the upper part (J) (Fig. 3-10). A strip of molding of different shape is nailed to the front edge of the cover.

The swinging cover (L) of the little compartment in the top section pivots on two dowels (N) and must be fitted to the little cover when the front and back (I) are assembled. The outer wall of the compartment (M) is nailed through the front and back (I).

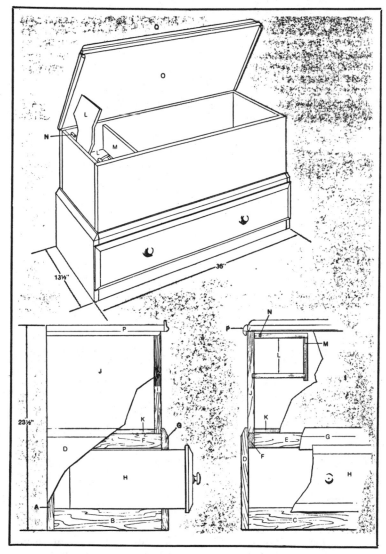

Fig. 3-10. Diagram and dimensions for the toy chests.

Table 3-5. Required Materials For the Shaker Toy Chests.

A. One piece. 34 × 11-½ × 1"
B. Two pieces. each: 11-½ × 3 × 1"
C. One piece. 34 × 3 × 1"
D. Two pieces. each: 13-½ × 12 × 1"
E. Two pieces. each 32 × 2 × 1"
F. Two pieces. each: 13-½ × 2 × 1"
G. One piece. 34 × 3 × 1"
H. One drawer: one front. 36 × 8 × 1";
two sides. 12-¾ × 7 × ½"; one back, 32-⅞
× 7 × ½"; one bottom, 33-⅞ × 12 .¾ × ¼"

I. Two pieces. each: 34 × 12 × 1"
J. Two pieces. each: 12-½ × 12 × 1"
K. One piece. 34-½ × 12 × ½"
L Two pieces. each: 11 × 7 × ½"
M. One piece. 10-½ × 5-¾ × ½"
N. Two dowels. each: ¾" long × ¼" diameter
O. One piece. 34-⅛ × 12-9/16 × ¾"
P. Two mouldings. each: 12-½ × 1-¾ × ¾"
Q. One moulding. 34 × 1-¼ × ¾"

The sides of the drawer section (D) are beveled at the top and this bevel is continued along the front by the strip above the drawer (G). The drawer itself is assembled with nails and glue and the beveled drawer front is nailed through its front to the sides. The drawer has no guides and rides on two cleats (B) nailed to the sides (D) on the inside.

When the upper part is ready to be assembled to the drawer section, spread glue on the upper edges of the cleats above the drawer (E, F). Insert the top part and nail through its bottom (K) into the cleats below.

You may find it difficult to get exact replicas of the cotter pin hinges made by Shaker craftsmen for the cover but other types of small antique hinges can be substituted.

The finish of the original piece is a medium brown stain. A modern oil stain of this color will not only preserve the wood but will give the chest the authentic appearance of a Shaker piece.

STORAGE COUCH

There are many handsome ways to convert wasted wall/floor space in the family room or den, and this practical storage couch is one of them (Fig. 3-11). It's a simple piece to make, requiring no more than an afternoon's work. There's ample room in the 3 × 6' interior to hold lots of toys, seasonal items or the family luggage. And Papa may find it an ideal spot to recline for his Sunday afternoon snooze. Materials are given in Table 3-6.

For structural rigidity, two of the vertical rear supports (G) are firmly anchored to the wall (Fig. 3-12). Since our bench was built against a brick surface, we used lead anchors and lag screws. On wooden-framed walls fasten one vertical leg to a wall stud using countersunk 3½" lag screws and screw the opposite leg to the wallboard with countersunk wall board anchors.

Now nail the second pair of vertical legs (G) to the already anchored pair and also nail the 2 × 4 rear support (D) in place across the top. After this, mount the seat/lid (A) to the rear support

Fig. 3-11. This couch also serves as a storage area.

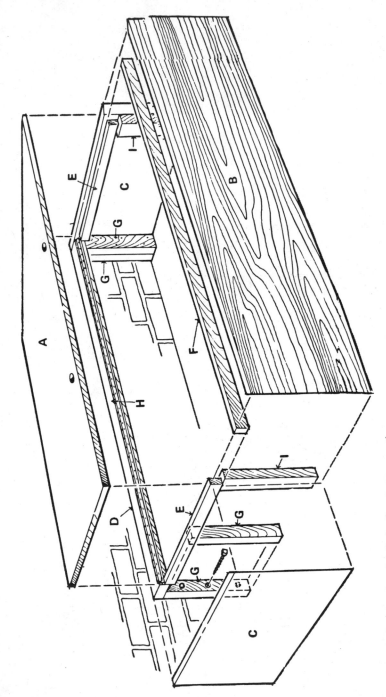

Fig. 3-12. Construction details for the storage couch.

Table 3-6. Materials Needed For the Storage Couch.

LIST OF MATERIALS
A. 1 pc, ¾ × 34⅝ × 73½"
B. 1 pc, ¾ × 16 × 75"
C. 2 pcs, ¾ × 16 × 39"
D. 1 pc, 1⅝ × 3⅝ × 73½"
E. 2 pcs, ¾ × 1½ × 33⅞"
F. 1 pc, ¾ × 1½ × 73½"
G. 4 pcs, 1⅝ × 2⅝ × 14⅜"
H. 73½" piano hinge
I. 2 pcs, 1⅝ × 2⅝ × 13¾"

using the long piano hinge. If you cannot find this hinge in a 6' length, then use two hinges 3' long. Don't forget the two finger holes for lifting the front of (A). Make these 1" in diameter.

The most difficult part is mitering the corners of side panels (C-C) and front panel (B) to avoid overlapped joints on the front of the couch. These miters can be accurately cut using a portable jig or circular saw equipped with an angle adjustment. Clamp a straightedge next to the cutting line to guide your saw for a clean, even stroke.

Screw the three support pieces (E-E-F) ¾" from the top edges of the side and front panels so that the seat/lid (A) will close flush with these top surfaces. The vertical front supports (I) are screwed to side panels (C) also from the inside. Finishing nails driven into (I) at both ends hold the front panel (B) in place. These nail heads should be counterset and the holes puttied.

Sand all surfaces and finish the couch using a quality enamel or apply a suitable stain followed by two or more coats of standard or urethane varnish. The cushion is made of 6" foam rubber covered with sail cloth. A zipper in the cushion back permits easy cleaning.

Chapter 4
Cabinets

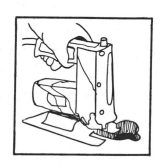

There's nothing like fine cabinetry to improve the appearance of your living quarters. Here's how to build and assemble sewing cabinets, kitchen cabinets, stereo cabinets and more.

SHAKER SEWING CABINET

This sewing stand, shown in the Visiting Elder Sisters' Room of the Sabbathday Lake Shaker Community in New Glouster, Maine, can be easily put to uses other than sewing. Of course, the sewing stand, built around 1815, is ideal for sewing supplies since it contains more than adequate storage space for pins, needles, thread, patterns, and materials (Fig. 4-1). And, because of its simple, sturdy lines, it could also blend in with many different decors and be used equally as well as a chest of drawers. Table 4-1 lists materials.

While there's no set way to build this project, it is recommended that you save the drawers for last. A combination of different types of joints are used to secure the various pieces of pine wood together. Many of the smaller structural members are secured using dadoes and rabbets. Refer to Fig. 4-2. Some of the larger items, such as piece E and F, are joined with simple butt joints. The four fillers (II) can be cut to size from the scraps left after piece "I" has been cut from its original stock. These fillers are optional and do not appear in the original. Nails and glue are used throughout to make joints secure.

Fig. 4-1. The cabinet can store many sewing supplies.

A peculiarlity of this sewing stand is the several different sizes of drawers used—the original had not less than five different drawer sizes. For fewer headaches, we've reduced the number of drawer sizes to four. As noted in Fig. 4-2 the top two drawers (Q) go into the space indicated by the dashed lines. The same is true of

Table 4-1. Materials needed for the sewing cabinet.

A. Six pieces, each: 25-½ × 2-½ × ¾″ (one not shown)
B. Four pieces, each: 14-½ × 2-½ × ¾″
C. Four pieces, each: 38 × 3-½ × ¾″
D. Eight pieces, each: 17-⅛ × ¾ × ⅜″ (two not shown)
E. One piece, 43 × 26-¼ × ⅜″
F. Two pieces, each: 33 × 18 × ⅜″
G. One piece, 25½ × 17⅝ × ¾″
H. Eight dowels, each: 2-½″ × ⅜″ diameter), (seven not shown)
I. Two pieces, each: 17⅝ × 9¼ × ¾″
II. Four pieces, each cut to fit from "I" (one not shown)
J. Two pieces, each: 24-¾ × 5-½ × ¾″
K. One piece, 5-½ × 4-1/16 × ¾″
L. Two pieces, 1″ molding, each: 18″ (one not shown)
M. Two drawers, each: one front, 24-11/16 × 7-¼ × ¾″; two sides, 16-⅝ × 7-¼ × ¾″; one back, 23-3/16 × 7-¼ × ½″; one bottom, 23-3/16 × 16.⅜ × ¼″ (not shown)
N. One drawer: one front, 24-11/16 × 7 × ¾″; two sides, 16-⅝ × 7 × ¾″;one back, 23-3/16 × 7 × ½″; one bottom, 23-3/16 × 16-⅜ × ¼″ (not shown)
O. One drawer: one front, 24-11/16 × 5-½ × ¾″; two sides, 16-⅝ × 5-½ × ¾″; one back, 23-3/16 × 5-½ × ½″; one bottom, 23/3/16 × 16-⅜ × ¼″
P. Sixteen drawer slides, each: 16-⅝ × ¾ × ⅜″ (fourteen not shown)
Q. Two drawers, each: one front, 11-15/16 × 3-½ ×¾″; two sides, 5-⅛ × 3-½ × ½″; one back, 11-7/16 × 3-½ × ½″.; one bottom, 11-7/16 × 5-⅛ × ¼″ (one not shown)
R. Six drawer pulls (not shown)

All dimensions shown in the drawing and list of materials are actual measurements in keeping with the recent National Standard for softwood lumber. Thus 2 × 4's are shown as 1-½″ × 3-½″, the actual size you get at the lumber yard when you ask for 2 × 4's.

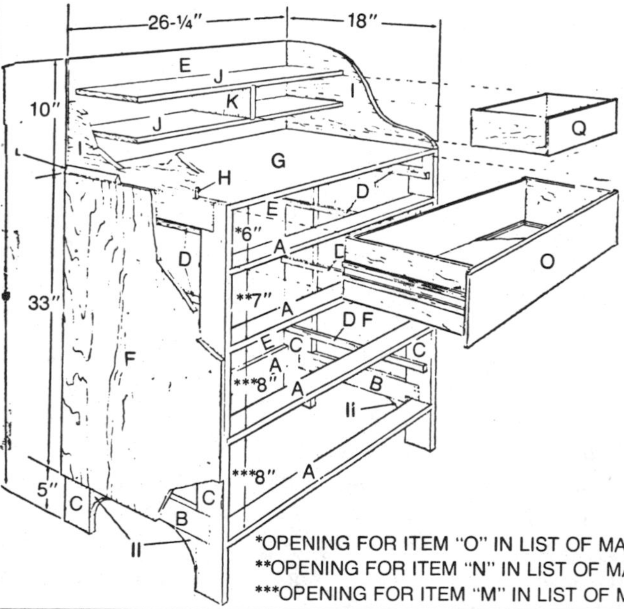

*OPENING FOR ITEM "O" IN LIST OF MATERIALS
**OPENING FOR ITEM "N" IN LIST OF MATERIALS
***OPENING FOR ITEM "M" IN LIST OF MATERIALS

Fig. 4-2. Diagram of the sewing cabinet.

the drawer designated "O" in Fig. 4-2 and noted at the lower part of Fig. 4-2 by a single asterisk. Also in the lower part of Fig. 4-2, the item "N," designated with two asterisks, goes into the area immediately below drawer "O." The two spaces immediately below "N" receive drawer "M", noted with the three asterisks.

Instead of the wooden drawer pulls (R), you could easily lend a distinctive note to the sewing stand by substituting procelain. As far as finishing the unit is concerned, the original pine had a reddish orange stain.

KITCHEN CABINETS

If you spend $1,000 remodeling your kitchen you'll likely add $2,000 to the value of your home. That's when you pay someone else to do the work. But if you remodel a kitchen and install new cabinets yourself, the rule of thumb is that you'll add four times the cost of the materials to your home (Figs. 4-3 and 4-4).

That means that if you spend $1,000 for materials, you'll add $4,000 to your home's value. In the interim your family enjoys a kitchen that is updated for both efficiency and convenience.

Laura Hawkins, decorating consultant for 57 Plywood Minnesota stores, says that you can often redesign an outdated kitchen to cut out three-fourths of the steps needed to handle meals. "That may not sound like much," she says, "but multiplied by three meals a day, seven days a week, you have miles and miles of needless walking."

By planning carefully you can make a new kitchen work for you rather than against you. There are three basic steps to making a new kitchen a reality: planning, shopping for cabinets, and installation. Here's a breakdown.

Planning

Before heading out to buy cabinets, plan carefully. In addition to meal preparation, kitchens are often the center of family activities. "It can be the most used room in the house," says Hawkins, "one with the highest amount of foot traffic. A well-designed kitchen can accommodate these activities as well as storing, preparing, serving and cleaning up after daily meals."

Be realistic and evaluate what you use the kitchen for— whether it's a message center, storage area, a place for hobby projects, a herb garden, a kid's play area, or even a place to clean your car's carburetor.

Because both personal tastes and space available varies from home to home, it's impossible to set hard and fast rules. Hawkins suggests you pay particular attention to storage, including space for dishes, cleaning supplies, appliances and pots and pans.

Consider the size of your family and meal schedules—a snack bar may be an energy saver for families on the go. If a lot of canning is done, you may want to consider a center island with a chopping block. You may want to use the kitchen to display items such as a collection of copper pots. How do you entertain? A peninsula island can bring entertaining into your kitchen and take the strain off of other living areas.

Also consider the location of doors, walls, windows, plumbing, gas/electrical outlets, appliances and venting ducts. Hawkins points out that a kitchen is made up of cabinets, countertops and appliances which together make up work centers: mixing and preparations, cooking and serving, and cleanup. Here are tips she offers to make these work centers more efficient:

- Have the refrigerator located nearest to the door where the groceries are brought int. Plan for at least 15" of counter space on the handle side so you have a place to set food instead of on the stove, for example.
- Store food near where it will be used. Try not to locate range and refrigerator side by side. Provide for about 36" of counter space for mixing.
- Pay particular attention to sink location, since it's used for most kitchen activities. Locate it centrally is possible. Consider putting it under a window. You can't use a 30" cabinet over a skin anyway, so why not use a window to make sink work more pleasant.

Kitchen cabinet manufacturers and suppliers offer special planning aids which can be invaluable in kitchen planning. Hawkins says to keep the "working triangle" in mind, which indicates footsteps required: "Draw a line from your stove to your sink to your refrigerator, and measure the lineal footage. The rule of thumb is that if you have more than 22 lineal feet you will be doing too much running."

A straight wall kitchen won't have a working triangle. In this case, length of the kitchen determines footsteps. The L-shaped kitchen is generally the most efficient, she says, while the U-shaped kitchen offers the most amount of space unbroken by traffic patterns. You can use an island peninsula to turn a straight

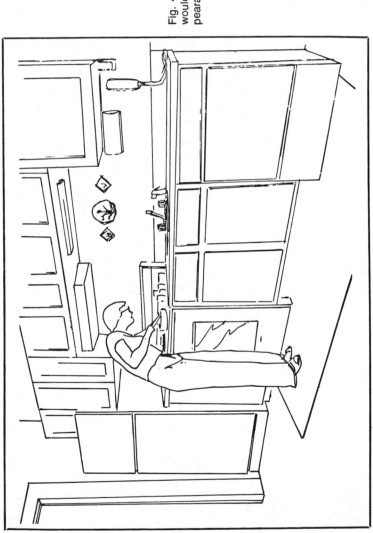

Fig. 4-3. These beautiful cabinets would enhance any kitchen's appearance.

Fig. 4-4. Kitchen remodeling is a feasible do-it-yourself project.

wall kitchen into an L-shaped kitchen, or an L-shaped kitchen into a U-shaped kitchen.

The next step is to determine the style of cabinets you want to use, as well as appliances, single or double sinks, faucet styles, wallpaper and flooring.

Shopping For Cabinets

The largest part of your kitchen, and probably the most expensive, is the kitchen cabinets. Just a few years ago most retailers believed kitchen cabinets could not be merchandised as a do-it-yourself project. Now, according to Bob Erikson, Minneapolis-based rep for Kitchen Kompact, more and more home centers are demonstrating it's not only a feasible do-it-yourself project, but one that adds up big savings for the homeowner.

"Selling kitchen cabinets on a custom basis," Erikson says, "meant about a $50 investment by the store for estimating. Then if only one out of four customers bought cabinets that meant the store had to tack on an additional $150 to the price of those cabinets. Retailers buying cabinets by the carload and selling to do-it-yourselfers avoid that extra mark-up."

Wall cabinets attach to the wall; base cabinets sit on the floor. You'll find several choices in width and height, even in standard cabinets and you'll have to decide the best combinations to use. (For example, an 84″ space will allow room for two 42″ cabinets, or a 30″-24″-30″ combination.) Besides wall and base cabinets, most manufacturers offer cabinets designed to handle corners, appliance installations, peninsulas, and special needs such as broom storage, what-nots, or simply to fill space where standard cabinets won't fit.

In past years many installations left dead space in the corner, wasting an average of 12 cubic feet per corner. Angle wall cabinets, ("blind corner" cabinets), base corner cabinets, lazy susan cabinets, butted base corner cabinets and peninsula cabinets can be used to keep this wasted space at a minimum.

You also can get sink fronts (front with one or two doors, dummy drawer section and toe space), plus oven cabinets with adjustable opening sizes for various makes of ovens. Wall peninsula units are available to use over bars or base peninsula cabinets when access from both sides is desired. Your cabinet supplier can help you match up all of these options to the design of yoru kitchen.

There are three basic areas to look at in kitchen cabinets: the box, the drawer assembly and the door. Here, according to Erikson, are things to look for:

The box. The frame is the most expensive part of the box. Frames of hardwood are preferred because screws hold much better in hardwood than, say, particleboard. Check for good end panels and look to see if the interior of the cabinet is finished, and if the shelves are adjustable.

The drawer assembly. Drawer quality varies widely, but good drawers will have dove-tailed construction. They may have hardwood fronts, fronts of laminate, or be made completely of materials such as polystyrene.

The doors. The door is the most expensive part of the cabinet, often accounting for 35%—even 45%—of the cabinet's cost. The most popular today is the "picture frame" style in oak. Check the wood and finish. Most good cabinet companies use a synthetic finish. Kitchen Kompact, for example, uses a finish with a ureaformaldehyde base rated vastly superior to regular hot spray lacquers. Expensive cabinets have many coats of finish, but the average is two or three.

What about ceilings? Most cabinets sold today are 30" high, says Erikson and are installed 7' high. This means if you have an 8' ceiling, you'll have an extra foot of space above the cabinets; if you have a 9' you'll have an extra 2' of space. The most common use of this space is to build a soffit. A standard soffit is built 14" deep over wall cabinets which are 12" deep. This gives you 2" extra to put in molding. Soffits are generally built of 2 × 2s and covered with drywall.

Other options, says Erikson, include putting in a plate rail over the top of the cabinet. Or, you can build a soffit 20" deep and use the overhang for track lighting. Another alternative, if you have a 7½ or 8' ceiling, is to cut a window above the cabinets to bathe your entire kitchen in soft light. Still another treatment is to install sliding doors at the front of the soffit so you can make use of the space for storage.

Measuring for Cabinets

Measure your kitchen accurately before you buy. Use a steel measuring tape if you have a helper; if not, use a folding rule. Measure the room from wall to wall each way. After getting the room outline on paper, place the rule against the wall at a height of about 36″. Begin at one corner and measure to the nearest door or window. Measure to the edge of the trim. Also measure the width of the trim and check the possibility, if needed, of cutting down the trim.

Next measure the width of doors or windows including casing or trim. Label doors according to where they lead. (When finished, add the detailed dimensions for each wall to see that they tally with the overall dimensions you took earlier.) Also measure from floor to the bottom of the window stool. This is a check to see if cabinets can go beneath the windows, and also determines the height of the backsplash. If there isn't sufficient clearance under the sill, check and note the possibility of cutting it down. If necessary use a windows notch in the backsplash. Also measure from the bottom of sill to top of window trim.

Finally, measure the height of the room from floor to ceiling. It is a good idea to measure this at two diagonally opposite points to see if an allowance may have to be made for the floor being out of level. This method will not show up an unlevel floor if the ceiling also slopes at the same angle. As an added precaution, check floor with level.

Check for wall features which must be considered in building the sink top and counter and in planning proper use of fillers. One way to do this is to measure from wall to wall at a point 2′ from the wall and 2′ from the floor. You will need help to do this. If this dimension differs from the dimension against the wall, you know that you'll have to make allowance for the discrepancy. Even if dimensions are the same, the corners may not be square. Check these with a square. This is not that critical for installation of cabinets, but is for installing a custom sink top.

If an existing range, refrigerator, or any other appliance is to be used, whether old or new, note the width, height and depth. If the appliances are on order, get dimension data from manufacturer's brochures. When measuring depth of range, include handles and hardware. Show the door swing of the refrigerator and whether hinged on inside or outside.

Show size and location of radiators, registers, a water heater, and any other appliance or fixture. Indicate whether location can be changed. Measure and show all pipes, obstructions, ventilating grills, and other such construction features. If combination range is used, show exact location of center of chimney opening. If pipe columns of window cutouts are needed, measure size and location accurately.

Installing Cabinets

The tools you'll need for a typical installation include a tape measure, a level, hammer, electric drill, screwdrivers, two C-clamps, straightedge, crosscut saw, crowbar and belt sander (if you have one). According to Erikson, there are a couple of different ways you can install kitchen cabinets. The first is to put all your wall cabinets up, then the base cabinets. The second is to put the base cabinets in first, then the wall cabinets. "If you only have the kids or wife to help you, the first way is the easiest," he says.

Before attaching the cabinets, Erikson advises to first mark on the wall and floor where each cabinet will go to avoid hanging the wrong cabinet in the wrong place. The basic procedure is to start in a corner first, find the location of the wall studs and drill holes in the cabinet—all before lifting the cabinet up on the wall. (If you find one stud, you can generally assume the rest will fall 16" apart center to center.)

When attaching wall cabinets, a helpful tool is what is known as a "kicker," simply a 2 × 4 stud cut to length so you can "kick" it under the cabinet positioned on the wall to hold it in place. Figures 4-5 through 4-19 show how cabinets are typically installed. For troublefree installations, read and follow the manufacturer's installation instructions carefully. For best results, Erikson suggests keeping these points in mind:

- Always use screws in fastening cabinets together. Never use nails for anything other than for attaching molding. Fasten bases, fillers, and wall cabinets together through front frame with screws.
- Install all wall units before installing base cabinets.
- Do not use countertops as work benches.
- Attach cabinets to wall and to one another so that they can be removed if necessary. Check plumb and level of each unit before securing. Cut off shims at floor even with toe space.
- Use molding wherever possible for a neater, more attractive installation. Be sure to putty and touch up nail holes in the molding.

- Align all doors, if possible.
- Do not unpack units from the cartons until ready for installation.

Fig. 4-5. Removing old ceiling-high cabinets begins after plans for a new efficient kitchen layout are firmed up.

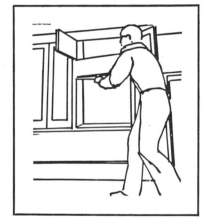

Fig. 4-6. Work carefully when removing the old cabinets.

Fig. 4-7. The old cabinets and backsplash yield easily to pry bar.

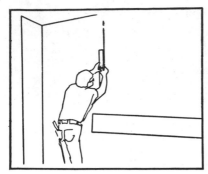

Fig. 4-8. Installation of new cabinets begins with accurate measuring and marking of their position.

Fig. 4-9. Cabinets are installed perfectly level with screws and a power drill.

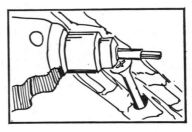

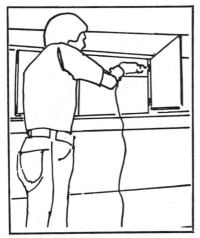

Fig. 4-10. Take pains when installing the wall cabinets.

Fig. 4-11. Secure the laminated countertop from below using screws with a variable-speed screwdriver.

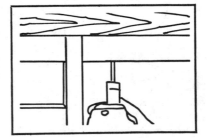

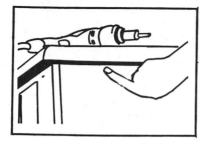

Fig. 4-12. Edges fit over and extend past cabinets for clean installation.

Fig. 4-13. The countertop looks nice when it's finished.

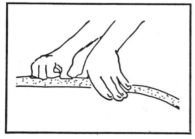

Fig. 4-14. Linoleum makes a good floor covering. Install the linoleum, edge it with plastic molding, and then you can glue down rubberback level-loop kitchen carpeting.

Fig. 4-15. Carpeting was trimmed to size around moldings with a utility knife.

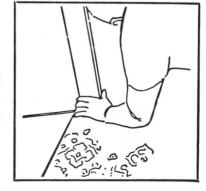

Fig. 4-16. The completed floor covering.

Fig. 4-17. View of a kitchen before remodeling.

Fig. 4-18. A view of the kitchen in Fig. 4-17 after remodeling.

Fig. 4-19. A compact "work triangle" between stove, sink and refrigerator also eliminates wasted steps.

ISLAND KITCHEN CABINET

If you are fortunate enough to have a large kitchen, you will find an island cabinet very useful. Not only does it provide convenient storage space and a large work surface, but it also saves the lady of the house a great deal of walking back and forth because of its central location.

Although the cabinet in Fig. 4-20 is made of random width boards to match the style of the original cabinets in the room, it can easily be made out of plywood with a few modifications to match your own kitchen cabinets. See Table 4-2 for materials.

The iron pipework frame is easier to make than it looks. You can cut the pipe with a hacksaw, and the mitered joints can be put together for you by a professional welder. The hooks are made of ¼" soft steel rod bent into shape and welded or brazed into holes previously drilled. The little spice shelf under the pots has a

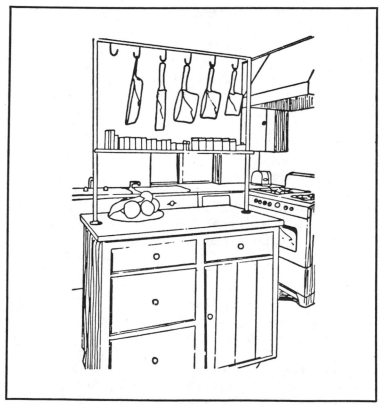

Fig. 4-20. This island kitchen cabinet could be made out of plywood.

Table 4-2. Materials Needed For the Island Kitchen Cabinet.

A. 1 pc., 24 × 48 × ¾"
B. 3 pcs., 20½ × 44½ × × ¾"
C. 2 pcs, 1½ × 1½ × 44½" (1 pc. not shown)
D. 2 pcs., 1½ × 1½ × 17½" (1 pc. not shown)
E. random width boards, 31¾ × ¾"
EE. random width boards, 35¼ × ¾"
F. 2 pcs, 11 × 20½ × ¾"
G. 1 pc., 7½ × 20½ × ¾"
H. 2 pcs., 2½ × ¾ × 44½" (a pc. not shown)
I. 3 pcs., 3½ × ¾ × 19" (1 pc. not shown)
J. 2 pcs., 2 × ¾ × 31¾"
K. 1 pc., 2 × ¾ × 29¾"
L. 1 pc., 2 × ¾ × 42"
M. 4 pcs., 1 × 1½ × 20½"
N. 4 pcs., 1 × ⅞ × 20½"
NN. 8 pcs., ½ × ¾ × 19½" (7 pcs, not shown)

O. 5 pcs., ¾ × ¾ × 20" (1 pc. not shown)
P. formica top, 24 × 48"
Q. 12 ft. of metal edging
R. 1 pc., 6 × 48 × ¾"
S. 10 ft. of 1" galvanized iron pipe
T. 9 ft. of 1" edge molding
U. 4 pcs., 5½ × 20⅛ × ⅜" (2 pcs. not shown)
V. 2 pcs., 5½ × 19 × ⅜" (1 pc. not shown)
W. 2 pcs., 6 × ¾ × 20" (1 pc. not shown)
X. random width boards, 22¾ × 20 × ¾"
Y. 2 pcs., 20 × 10⅞ × ¼"
Z. 36 in. of 5/32" wire bent to hooks
ZZ. 4 pcs., 20½ × 18⅝ × ¼"
Not shown : 2 Large Drawers
UU. 4 sides, 11 × 20⅛ × ⅜"
VV. 2 backs, 11 × 20 × ⅜"
WW. 2 fronts, 11½ × ¾ × 20"

molding around it that sticks up just high enough to prevent the spice cans from falling off. The ends of the shelf are secured by a screw that goes through holes drilled in the pipe into the shelf ends.

Note that the door on the right side has random width boards (X) fastened together with glue and screws to two sheets of ¼" plywood or hardboard (Y) (Fig. 4-21). The guides on the drawers (NN) should be located so that they ride on guides in the cabinet (M and N). When cutting the sides of the drawers remember to cut the front edges at an angle so that the drawer fronts slant as shown in Fig. 4-20. Also note that while the random width boards (E) around the back and ends are 33¾" long, those that extend to the floor on both ends (EE) are 35¼".

The edging around the laminated plastic top is stainless steel and is available in larger hardware stores. It is best to bend this edging around the corners rather than cut it into four separate strips. The bending is very easy once you have notched the edging for mitered corners.

HEIRLOOM SEWING CABINET

The original sewing machine was invented by Elias Howe in the 1800s, and even today is in great demand—but not for sewing. Almost everything is being done with the wrought iron legs—desks, marble-top tables, you name it—but the machines themselves are being dumped by the thousands. More is the pity, for the great majority of the machines are in perfect working order and can, and do, tackle jobs that nothing else short of an industrial electric can handle.

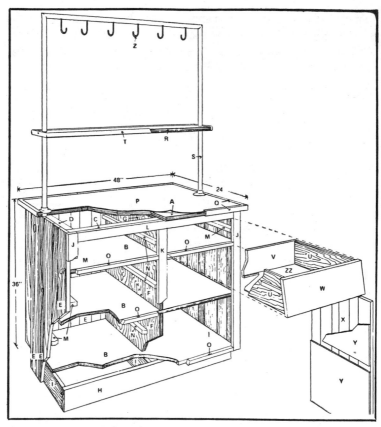

Fig. 4-21. Construction details for the island kitchen cabinet.

Face Lifting the Machine

You may decide that your beloved machine deserves a face-lift. Make it to resemble an old-time captain's cabinet, with catch rim around the top, shutter doors, and pegged sides (Fig. 4-22). A ready-made drawer case (Sears or Montgomery Ward), trimmed to a height of 28⅞" and attached to the existing unit, gives plenty of extra storage space for patterns and threads. The new drawer fronts were shaped with a router to give the illusion of apothecary-type drawers, to which is added the white china knobs. The pin dish that is recessed flush with the top is ever so handy. The inside of the lid is perfect as a pin-board for the patterns, or it can be opened 180° to form a convenient cutting table.

If you follow Fig. 4-23, you will soon have a beautiful—and functional—heirloom of your own for about $40 worth of materials.

Just pick up a measuring tape and the saw. When it is all done, it's such a delight to hand your husband the stain and varnish and the wallpaper for inside the lid. After all, joint projects do enrich family life, don't they? See Table 4-3 for materials.

Construction Steps

To start with, the original small drawers should be removed and the hinged top discarded. (Save the hinges for the new lid.) Cut off beveled edges across front, right side and back. Cut off left side to leave final top measurement 17¼" × 28½". Screw shim (D) to front edge. Place drawer assembly against left side of machine top

Fig. 4-22. The heirloom sewing cabinet has shutter doors.

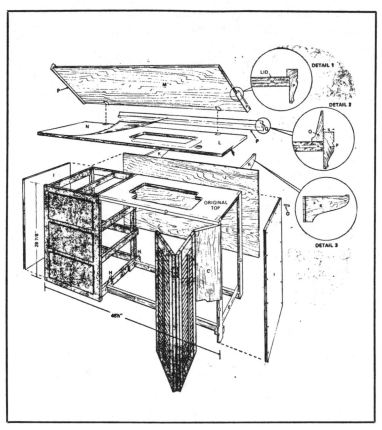

Fig. 4-23. Construction details for the heirloom sewing cabinet.

with face of drawer case in front of the left front iron leg. Since you will want the weight borne by the iron legs, shim all pieces about ¼" from the floor during construction. Cut case front to same height as machine top. Screw through top brace of drawer case horizontally into machine top with 2" screws. Install frame (E-F-G). Attach sides (I) with doweling and the back with ½" screws. Cover all new raw plywood edges with wood trim or fir veneer strips.

Remove machine head from top, also raised portions of wood which held it, and use these as pattern for opening in new top. Make all necessary adjustments to accommodate machine head. Cut opening for pin dish. Cover entire top with good grade of heavy adhesive-backed vinyl (we used a white marble pattern). Screw top (L) in place from underside (Fig. 4-24).

Stack original small drawer units and reattach to machine top. Hinge and install shutters (B) and panel (C) (Fig. 4-25). Miter panel to conceal all hinges.

Cut fancy molding as in Detail 1 of Fig. 4-23 attaching to hinged lid, front and sides, mitering front corners but extending sides 1¼" beyond back edge (Fig. 4-26). Hinge lid to top. Measure and notch remainder of same molding at ends to fit back edge. Attach plain molding (Q) between notches as in Detail 2 of Fig. 4-23. This remains a removable piece. With coping saw, cut sides to conform to shape a back piece.

For lid supports (K), cut the ½" plywood as in Detail 3 of Fig. 4-23. Attach with piano hinges to back of cabinet ¾" from sides and at correct height to support top when swung completely open. Pad top of supports with felt.

TV HI-FI CONSOLE

Why spend hundreds of dollars for a TV hi-fi console when you can take the television and hi-fi that you have now and build your

Table 4-3. Required Materials For Hierloom Sewing Cabinet.

LIST OF MATERIALS	
A. one 18 × 18 × 32" three drawer case	K. 2 pcs, ½" plywood, 14 × 8"
B. two 12 × 28½" shutters	L. 1 pc, ¾" plywood, 21 × 49"
	M. 1 pc, ½" plywood, 21 × 49"
C. 1 pc, 5 × ¾ × 28⅞"	
D. 1 pc, ¾ × ¾ × 24"	N. vinyl, 21 × 49"
E. 1 pc, ¾ × ¾ × 18"	O. 14 pcs, ⅜" doweling × 2"
F. 2 pcs, 1½ × ¾ × 28½"	P. 13' molding, 2¼ × ¾"
G. 2 pcs, 1½ × ¾ × 28⅞"	Q. 49" molding, 2¼ × ¾" 2 pr. chest hinges, ¾ × 1½" 1 pr. flat hinges, ¾ × 1½" 2 piano hinges 8" long 13' fancy molding, 2¼ × ¾" 49" plain molding, 2 × ¾" 1 roll flexible wood-trim 6 china knobs 1 (antique) door ctach
H. 4 pcs, 1½ × ¾ × 1½"	
I. 2 pcs, ½" plywood, 28⅞ × 17¾"	
J. 1 pc, ½" plywood, 46½ × 28⅞"	

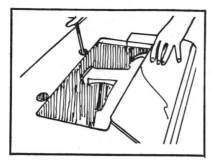

Fig. 4-24. Round hinges were saved from the original machine top. Marble pattern sheet vinyl was used to cover the new top.

Fig. 4-25. Ready-made shutter can be opened to allow access to treadle.

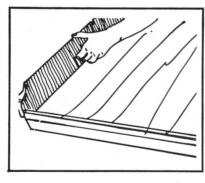

Fig. 4-26. Back molding of the lid is removable.

own cabinet with separate compartments to house them? Although the console shown looks as if it were made of fine hardwood, it is actually made from plywood which was painted and then artifically antiqued with an antiquing kit commercially available at many hardware, paint, and department stores (Fig. 4-27). See Table 4-4 for materials.

The construction is very easy as the cabinet is simply an open box structure with divider panels and doors. Start by securing

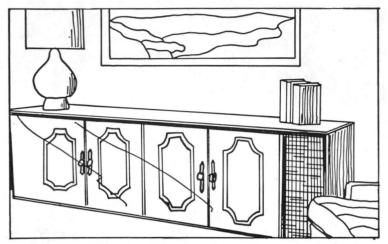

Fig. 4-27. This TV hi-fi console is made of plywood.

cleats (F) to which the divider panels (B, C) will be attached, to the bottom and top panels (A) with glue and screws (Fig. 4-28). Only one cleat at the top and one at the bottom is needed for each panel.

Frame

Five of the six divider panels (B) are glued and screwed into place flush with the rear edge of the bottom panel (A) and ¾" in from the front edge. The sixth partition (C) is also set flush with the rear edge but is more narrow than the other divider panels (B) to allow room for the front stringers (J).

The two center panels (B, C) are notched so that the top and bottom rear stringers D) will be flush with the backs of these panels. These stringers (D) are secured with cleats (K) to the bottom (A). The four front stringers (J) are set in ¾" from the front edges of the divider panels (B) to permit the doors (E) to close against them.

At this point, you may wish to modify the basic frame as it is given by adding a back panel to the three main compartments in order to have a fully dustproof construction. Note that the design as shown does already allow for panels (H) at the rear of the two speaker compartments. Only screws are used for the installation of these two rear panels (H) to permit quick and easy accessibility to the speakers.

The four vertical cleats (G) inside each of the speaker compartments are attached ¾" in from the panels' (B) front or back edges so that the rear panels (H) and the frames (I) with grille cloth stapled to them fit flush with the edges of the panels (B). Screen molding, ¼ × ¾", (T) is used on the front and side edges of the top and bottom panels (A) as well as on the front edges of the partition panels (B). Glue and brads are used to secure the molding. The trim (T) is mitered at the corners of the top and bottom panels (A).

Base Frame and Doors

The base (L,M) is nailed together with butt joints centered on the bottom of the base panel (A), and attached to the base panel with glue and screws through cleats (G). Also, 1½" casters (N) are screwed to the bottom panel inside the base frame and spread out as much as possible to distribute weight of the cabinet.

The folidng doors (E) are hinged at the outer corners (R) with TV type invisible hinges and in the center with piano hinges (Q) on each set of doors. Then each pair of doors is hung carefully. Some clearance should be left in fitting the doors to allow for later paint buildup. Use some method of indexing the doors as to their positions on the console (scribing the hinges is one way) so that when you begin painting you can identify which doors go where. When the doors are satisfactorily hung, molding (O) for the doors is cut to

Table 4-4. Necessary Materials For the Console.

LIST OF MATERIALS
A. 2 pcs, ¾ × 20¼ × 96"
B. 5 pcs, ¾ × 19½· × 23¾"
C. 1 pc, ¾ × 16 × 23¾"
D. 2 pcs, ¾ × 4 × 74"
E. 8 pcs, ¾ × 9⅛ × 23⅝"
F. 12 pcs, ¾ × 1½· × 15"
G. 14 pcs, ¾ × ¾ × 18"
H. 2 pcs, ¾ × 8¾ × 23¾'"
I. 2 pcs, ½· × 8⅝ × 23⅝" (centers cut out)
J. 4 pcs, ¾ × 1½· × 36⅝"
K. 3 pcs cut to fit from ¾ × ¾ × 72½"
L. 2 pcs, ¾ × 1¾ × 60"
M. 4 pcs, ¾ × 1¾ × 13"
N. Casters
O. Door Panel Molding, 2 kits
P. 4 Door Pulls
Q. 4 Piano Hinges
R. 8 Concealed Hinges
S. 2 Magnetic Catches
T. Screen Molding, ¼ × ¾ × 96"
U. Grille Cloth

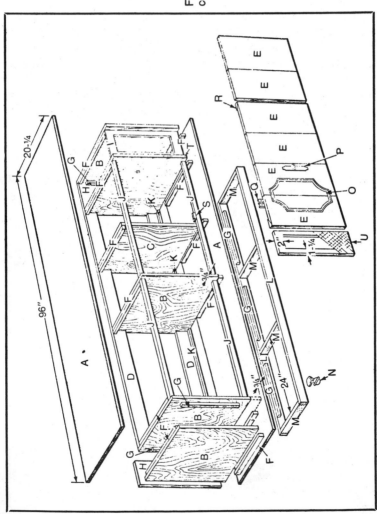

Fig. 4-28. Diagram of the TV hi-fi console.

120

size, positioned, pinned with brads and glued. Decorative trimming is available in wood or plastic in many hardware or building supply stores.

The final step is to very lightly sand all surfaces and apply two coats of semi-gloss enamel. Then the base coat of antiquing kit should be applied, perferably two coats. Some plywood grain will show through even after the painting, but this enhances the antiquing effect. Then apply the antique glaze and wipe to the grain desired, following the directions on the antiquing effect. The application of two coats of varnish, supplied in most antiquing kits, completes the project.

SHAKER WORK CABINET

This handsome work cabinet of white pine and maple is the latest of our continuing Shaker series projects (Fig. 4-29). The three drawers and enclosed shelves make it an ample storage unit. And the top work surface extends to nearly 7' when the hinge side leaf is in use. It would make an ideal piece for sewing or other household work. See Table 4-5 for materials.

Cutting and Rabbeting Pieces

Before any assembling is begun all pieces should be cut to proper dimensions, notched and rabbeted according to Fig. 4-30. Although joints on the original piece are anchored with dowels, you can do a satisfactory job by substituting wood screws which are counterbored and plugged. However, the spline joints holding the cabinet door frame (CC-DD) are not intended for screw fastening; these must be doweled and glued or at least glued.

The vertical center panel (E) and left side panel (D) are notched to receive four of the eight side braces (L) which serve as drawer supports. Both side panels (D) are rabbeted on the bottom edge to join the long base frame members (O) and (N). The bottom rabbet on the left panel extends higher because (L) is also a part of that lower joint. The center panel (E) is notched at the lower front and rear corners also in order to fit around (O) and (N).

A vertical rabbet along the inside front of the right panel (D) permits a sturdy joint with upper frame member (G) and right and vertical piece (H). The vertical pieces (H) are rabbeted on top to join (G), and the center vertical is also notched to accept front drawer supports (K). (G) joins the left panel at a notch in the upper corner.

Fig. 4-29. This work cabinet is made of white pine and maple.

Assembly

The two upper side pieces (L) fit flush against the side and center panels (D) and (E). They are joined to the panels with the ¾″ dimension upward while the lower pieces labeled (L) are joined with their 2″ surface upward. Note that the side pieces (R) and (S), which support the three shelves between the center and right side panels, are attached also with the narrow or ¾″ side up.

The rear panel (F) butts flush with the rear edges of the side and center panels. These panels may be either cut from cabinet grade plywood or built by dowel-joining and edge-gluing narrower pieces of solid stock. Use ½″ stock for the rear panel and ¾″ for the center, side and top panels (D-E-D-C), as well as for the extension leaves (B) and (A).

The drawer faces (V) and (Z) are rabbeted all around to conceal the closing edges. Front edges of the drawer faces are beveled for effect. The sides, rear and front of each drawer are grooved to accept the bottom panels (Y) which may be cut either from hardboard or plywood of ¼" thickness. The door panel (EE), which may be cut from solid ¼" stock, or plywood if the stock is not available, is supported within the door frame (CC-DD) by ¼-round molding strips glued outside and inside.

The finished cabinet can be sanded and treated with standard furniture or urethane varnish. Hinges for mounting the side and rear leaves, 2" plate-mounted casters and drawer pulls, wood or porcelain, are available from hardware dealers.

PLANTER-CABINET

A planter which also serves as a cabinet and room separator can be both highly decorative and practical. This design which was created by the editors of *Family Handyman* easily and handsomely fulfills all three functions (Fig. 4-31).

The design was submitted to Bernard Gladstone, a well known writer on home improvement subjects, who built the planter in his well equipped workshop. All of the exterior parts are made of teak-veneered ¾" plywood (Table 4-6). Of course, your own copy

Table 4-5. Required Materials For the Shaker Work Cabinet.

A. 1 pc, ¾ × 6 × 60"
B. 1 pc, ¾ × 24 × 25"
C 1 pc, ¾ × 24 × 60"
D. 2 pcs, ¾ × 23½ × 40¼"
E. 1 pc, ¾ × 22¼ × 40¼"
F. 1 pc, ½ × 58¾ × 40¼"
G. 1 pc, ¾ × 2 × 58¾"
H. 2 pcs, ¾ × 3½ × 40¼"
I. 1 pc, ¾ × 3 × 37⅝"

S. 2 pcs, ¾ × 1½ × 17¼"
T. 3 pcs, ¾ × 21½ × 22¼"
U. 21 pcs, 2" dowel × 44⅛"
  (based on 2" casters)
V. 1 pc, ¾ × 36⅝ × 9⅝"
W. 2 pcs, ⅜ × 9⅛ × 22⅞"
X. 1 pc, ⅜ × 9⅛ × 35⅜"
Y. 3 pcs, ¼ × 35¾ × 22⅞"
Z. 2 pcs, ¾ × 12½ × 36⅝"

J. 1 pc, ¾ × 2½ × 19⅝"
K. 2 pcs, 1 × 3 × 37"
L. 8 pcs, 1 × 2 × 22¼"
M. 2 pcs, 1½ × 5½ × 22¼"
N. 1 pc, 1½ × 3½ × 58¾"
O. 1 pc, 1½ × 1½ × 58¾"
P. 2 pcs, ¾ × 5½ × 3½"
Q. 2 pcs, ¾ × 1½ × 5½"
R. 4 pcs, ¾ × 1½ × 22¼"

AA. 4 pcs, ⅜ × 11⅞ × 22⅞"
BB. 2 pcs, ⅜ × 11⅞ × 35⅜"
CC. 2 pcs, ¾ × 4 × 35⅝"
DD. 2 pcs, ¾ × 5½ × 15"
EE. 1 pc, ¼ × 7 × 24⅝"
FF. ¼ rd. mldg, ¼ × 126½"

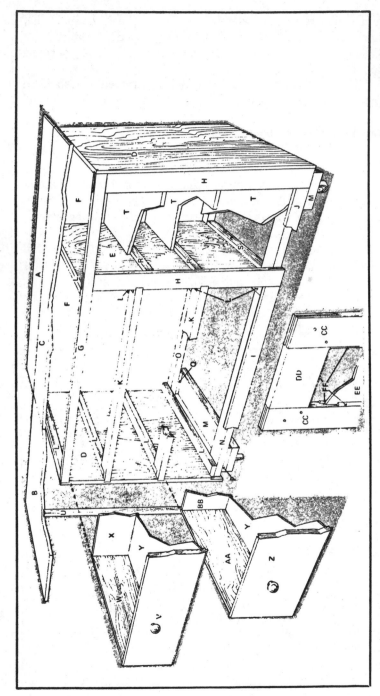

Fig. 4-30. Construction details for the Shaker work cabinet.

Fig. 4-31. This planter serves as a cabinet and room separator.

of this piece need not be teak-veneered. Teak, birch, walnut or any other, suitable furniture veneer or even painted plywood can be used, depending on the decor of your rooms.

Cutting Parts

Refer to Fig. 4-32. Some parts, such as the mitered joints where the sides (D) and ends (E) meet can be cut on a bench or radial arm saw. If you don't have either of these tools, have these parts cut by a professional carpenter or cabinet maker. However, a portable electric circular saw turned to 45° or a powerful portable saber saw can easily make the bevels required for miter joints.

Both sides of the planter are identical, since in this case it was used to separate a living room from a dining room. Therefore both sides have exactly the same kind of doors so that access to the contents of the cabinet is possible from the dining or living room.

Table 4-6. Materials Needed For the Planter-Cabinet.

LIST OF MATERIALS	
A. 2 pcs, ¾ × 5¾ × 72″ B. 2pcs, ¾ × 5⅜ × 21″ C. 2 pcs, ¾ × 21 × 36″ D. 2 pcs, ¾ × 21 × 72″ E. 4 pcs, ¾ × 26 ×21″ F. 3 pcs, ½· × 19½· × 70½″ G. 6 pcs, 1 × 1 × 17⅜″ H. 4 pcs, 1¾ × 1¾ × 4″	I. 4 pcs, 1 × 1 × 61″ J. 4 pcs, 4 × 4″ × thickness to suit K. 4 engages for rollers L. 4 nylon roller catches M. 2 pcs, 1 × 1 × 68⅜″ N. 4 pcs, 1 × 1 × 8″ O. 2 pcs, 1 × 1 × 62⅜″ P. 16 feet of ¾″ veneer tape Q. 1 pc, ¾ × 19½ × 70½″

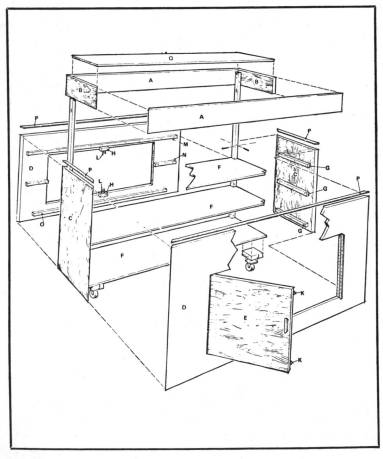

Fig. 4-32. Diagram of the planter-cabinet.

The sides (D) are cut from one piece of plywood and the doors (E) are also cut in one piece to preserve the continuity of the veneer grain (Fig. 4-33). The method of cutting the doors is very interesting. After marking the width and the combined length of both doors on the face of the side (D), a wooden straightedge was clamped to the side and a portable circular power saw with a fine-tooth blade was placed against the edge in a plunge cut and run along the marked line almost to its end (Fig. 4-34). This was repeated on the remaining marked lines of the door. The corner ends were completed with a portable saber saw and filed to make the width of the cuts by two different kinds of blades identical (Fig. 4-35).

The door panel was then lifted out of the larger sheet (D) and cut in halves to form the two doors (E-E). You don't have to have a portable circular or table saw to perform this operation since it can also be done with a good portable jig or saber saw.

Gluing and Fastening Pieces

The sides have three cleats (O-N-M) fastened with glue and screws to support the front and back edges of the three shelves inside. The shelves are smoothly sanded ½″ plywood. The ends of the shelves are supported by cleats (G) screwed and glued to the inner sides of the ends (C) (Fig. 4-36). All four doors swing on continuous hinges because they are so wide (Fig. 4-37).

The corner joints where the sides (D) and ends (C) meet are mitered. These joints were fastened with glue and held in clamps overnight. If you use plain plywood which will be covered with a paint finish, you can join the sides and ends with simple butt joints fastened with glue and finishing nails and then fill the nail holes with water putty.

The middle and upper shelves (F) are both notched at the corners to permit the four chrome 1″ square tubing supports which hold up the "roof" of the planter to pass through (Figs. 4-38 and 4-39). The lower ends of these tubes rest on the bottom shelf.

Each piece of square tubing has eight pairs of holes drilled through it for round head screws. There are two pairs above each shelf (in every corner on the inside) and two pairs in each corner where the tubing supports the roof. The pairs of holes are slightly offset so that you can drive screws through the tubing into the end pieces (C) and also into the sides (D). This, of course, also applies to the roof where the screws are driven into the ends (B) and sides (A) in each corner. This not only anchors the tubing but braces all the corners firmly.

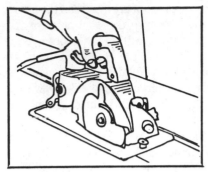

Fig. 4-33. To preserve continuity of veneer grain, two doors and one side are cut from one piece of plywood.

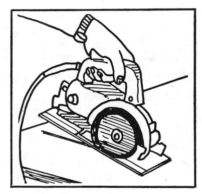

Fig. 4-34. Carefully cut the door panels.

Fig. 4-35. A cleanly cut panel from which two doors will be made is lifted from the larger side piece. A saber saw was used to square the corner cuts. Unevenness was smoothed by filing.

Fig. 4-36. End pieces are being fitted to the partially assembled frame, with shelves clamped temporarily for gluing.

Fig. 4-37. Flush-fit doors are mounted to the side pieces with piano-type hinges.

Fig. 4-38. Corner notching of the middle and upper shelves is easily done with a saber saw. Notches accommodate tubing supports.

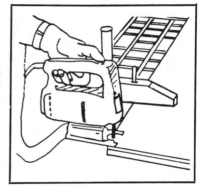

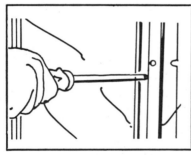

Fig. 4-39. With the main planter box assembled, the chrome 1"-square tubing supports which hold up the roof of the planter are passed through the notched shelf corners and screwed to the sides.

Fig. 4-40. The view of the planter shows 5¾" recess that will hold the soldered sheet metal pan. Actually the upper shelf forms the bottom of this recess. Note the offset holes in the square tubing. Each tubing section has eight pairs of these holes.

The top of the planter has a recess in it that is 5¾" deep (Fig. 4-40). The upper shelf (F) forms the bottom of this recess. The recess is designed to contain a pan made of sheet metal with well soldered joints so that it will not leak. It should be filled with small gravel on which flower pots for house plants can be placed.

Light Box

The roof or light box supported by the four square tubes is assembled with the same kind of glued mitered joints as the cabinet. The upper edges of the roof sides (A) and ends (B) enclose and are flush with a sheet of plain well sanded plywood (Q) which is glued into place (Fig. 4-41).

The underside of the light box or roof has three rows of fluorescent lights, each row being made up of a 40- and a 20-watt lamp (Figs. 4-42 and 4-43). One of the corner square tubes has a large enough hole in it at the top so that the electric cable for the fluorescent lamps can be passed down through the tube to a hole in the bottom of the cabinet and out to an electric outlet.

Strips of matching veneer tape go all around the top of the recess to provide this top edge and exposed low edges of A and B with a finished look. The underside of the bottom shelf (L) has four swiveling casters mounted on wood blocks deep enough to allow ⅜" clearance between the bottom of the cabinet and the floor (Fig. 4-44).

The finish depends on the material you have used. If it is plywood with a hardwood veneer, use an appropriate stain and finish with clear lacquer, urethane or standard varnish. In this particular case, the plain plywood top and shelves were stained to match the teak and the entire assembly was treated with a penetrating finish, rubbed with very fine steel wool and waxed.

STEREO HI-FI CABINET

If you have the components of a record player hi-fi , you'll find this project an interesting and unusual cabinet in which to house them (Fig. 4-45). In fact, when the whole thing is closed you won't know that it's a hi-fi. It's cleverly made inexpensive.

The back and the bottom can be cut from a single piece of standard size of ½" plywood panel. There are four hinged covers over each of the four compartments. See Fig. 4-46 and Table 4-7.

Notice the detail of how the covers work. These are ingeniously hinged behind the rear wall of the cabinet so that by pressing downward on the rear of any of the covers it will rise enough to be lifted from the front. The advantage of this construction is that no

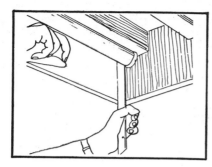

Fig. 4-41. Planter roof or light box is placed on the four tubing supports and fastened by driving a pair of round wood screws into the side pieces at each of the corners.

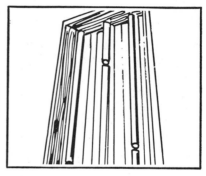

Fig. 4-42. Planter roof is also a light box that supports three rows of 40 and 20-watt fluorescent lamp fixtures.

Fig. 4-44. Four swiveling casters are mounted on wood blocks which in turn are fastened to the underside of the bottom cabinet shelf.

Fig. 4-43. View from underside of the finished planter roof shows fluorescent fixtures wired in place. Note access hole filed in the upper end of the support tubing. Fixtures are wired in parallel.

Fig. 4-45. When this cabinet is closed, you won't know it's a hi-fi.

knobs or pulls are necessary and the top can retain its smooth clean lines.

The two compartments at the left contain the electronic works, the turntable for records being in the compartment second from the left. The front is one long solid piece scored in three places to give the impression of four separate panels. While the bottom, back, and compartment dividers can be of ordinary construction plywood, the long front piece should be of smoothly sanded plywood to assure a better finish and to avoid a lot of hard sanding. This, of course, applies also to the cover tops and exterior faces of the end panels.

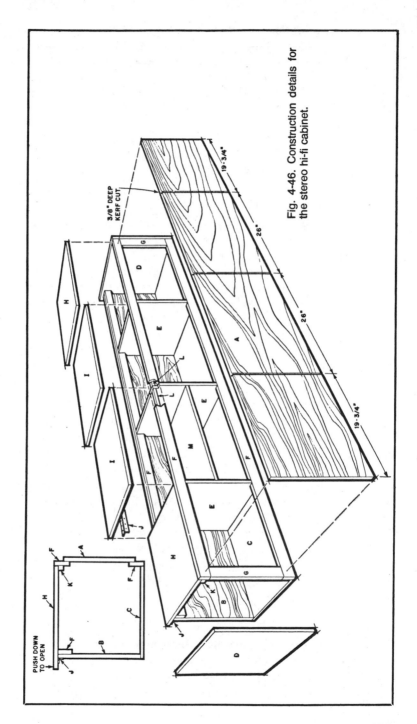

Fig. 4-46. Construction details for the stereo hi-fi cabinet.

PUSH DOWN TO OPEN

3/8" DEEP KERF CUT

19-3/4"
26"
26"
19-3/4"

133

Table 4-7. Materials Needed For the Stereo Hi-Fi Cabinet.

LIST OF MATERIALS
A. 1 pc, ¾ × 13 × 91½"
B. 1 pc, ¾ × 14¾ × 94½"
C. 1 pc, ½ × 15½ × 94½"
D. 2 pcs, ¾ × 15¼ × 16¼"
E. 3 pcs, ¾ × 14¾ × 15½"
F. 3 pcs, ¾ × 2½ × 94½"
G. 2 pcs, ¾ × 2½ × 11"
H. 2 pcs, ¾ × 18 × 21¼"
I. 2 pcs, ¾ × 18 × 26"
J. Piano Hinge
K. 2 pcs, ¾ × ¾ × 20⅞"
L. 2 pcs, ¾ × ¾ × 25¼"
M. 1 pc, ¾ × 15½ × 25¼"

The two compartments at the far right can be used for storage of records or anything else you like. The exterior of the cabinet is finished in white enamel over a white prime coat. The front and the insides of the compartments including the undersides of the covers are stained a very dark, rich brown. Of course, you can follow your own color scheme.

GRANDFATHER CLOCK

Grandfather clocks have become enormously popular with homeowners (Fig. 4-47). In the past these marvelous combinations of cabinetmaker's and clockmaker's arts were expensive luxuries for the wealthy. Today, you can buy a kit with precut walnut, cherry or mahogany parts for the cabinet plus an imported West German clock movement for about two to three hundred dollars.

The popular model shown on these pages has an eight-day, weight-driven movement that strikes hours and quarter hours, has the 16-tone Westminster chimes, and even shows the phases of the moon. The cabinet measures 74" × 16¾" × 10".

One you have received the kit, which consists of two large boxes, one containing the clock movement and the other the cabinet parts, the assembly instructions should be removed, read and reread several times.

Identifying Parts

The first step is to identify the cabinet parts with the aid of the numbered drawings in the instruction booklet. All these parts are easily recognized from the drawings in the instruction booklet. Where you are in doubt note that each piece is listed in the

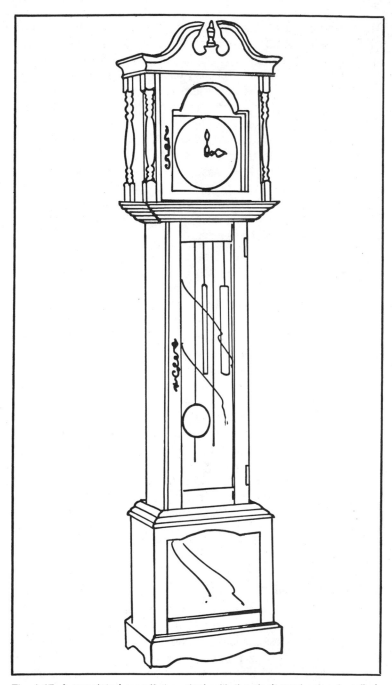

Fig. 4-47. A completed grandfather clock with the clock mechanism installed.

instructions by name, number and all three dimensions—length, width and thickness. By measuring any piece about which you are uncertain and checking to see if the dimensions correspond to those in the instructions, you can easily identify it. Each part should then be marked with its number.

The parts should be segregated into three piles—those that belong to the base, those used in the waist (the central section where the pendulum hangs) and those used to make the hood which houses the clock mechanism (Fig. 4-48). This makes it easier to locate the parts needed in the assembly of the three main sections of the cabinet. The exact details of how the various parts fit together are carefully explained in the instruction manual.

Assembling Base, Waist and Hood

The base is assembled first using white glue, clamp nails (supplied) and flat head screws (Fig. 4-49). The white glue, flat head wood screws, sandpaper, 1″ brads, and glass for two doors are provided by the buyer of the kit. Adjustable screws in the corners of the base permit easy leveling of the cabinet. All exterior surfaces of the base are then carefully sanded first with 100 and then 150 grit garnet or aluminum oxide paper.

The waist or middle section comes next (Figs. 4-50 and 4-51). This section has a glass door. The door frame is fully assembled and the glass behind it is kept in place by flexible plastic strips fastened with small brads. A hammer and nail set are used to drive the brads to avoid breaking the glass. The hardware for the door including the hinges, handle and magnetic catch are all supplied by the manufacturer. All wooden parts are then sanded.

The top section or hood is put together with white glue, 1″ brads, and 1½″ flat head wood screws (Fig. 4-52). Like the middle section, the hood also has a glass door and an assembled door frame. The hardware for the door comes with the kit. There is a removable back which is not installed until the clock movement is in place.

Staining and Finishing

After all three sections are joined together and sanded, the assembled cabinet is stained and finished (Fig. 4-53). The manufacturer makes no recommendations about finishing but this should pose no special problems for the do-it-yourselfer. Use the appropriate stain for the kind of wood you have chosen. Oil stains are the easiest to handle.

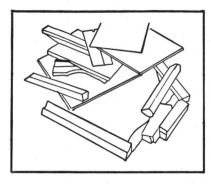

Fig. 4-48. Parts for the grandfather clock.

Allow enough time for the stain to dry according to the manufacturer's directions. A clear furniture type varnish can then be applied and smoothed with fine steel wool, very fine sandpaper or pumice and water.

Clock Movement

The clock movement with its chimes, weights, and pendulum come in a separate box along with a booklet of instructions on how to mount the movement and adjust it. The clock is installed in the hood through the open back and fastened in place with screws.

There are three polished brass cylinders which you fill with weights in the form of metal disks. The cylinders hang from chains attached to the clock movement. The left cylinder operates the chimes, the right cylinder works the mechanism that strikes the hours, and the weight in the center operates the time. If you prefer to have the clock operate silently, remove the weights in the right hand cylinder. The time mechanism is not affected by silent operation.

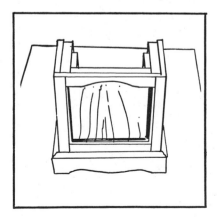

Fig. 4-49. Assemble the base first.

Fig. 4-50. The waist or midsection where the pendulum and weights hang. Preassembled front door frame is shown here without glass or hardware.

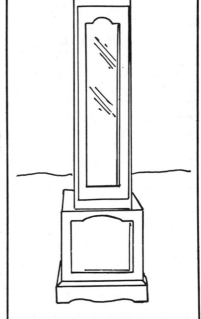

Fig. 4-51. Waist section mounted on its base. Sides and front of waist are checked with carpenter's square to see if they are parallel with the base.

Finally, the pendulum stick and its brass disk are hung in place. There is a threaded brass fitting under the disk that regulates the timing.

Fig. 4-52. Hood or top section which houses completed clock mechanism.

The leveling feet in this clock are very important because if the pendulum bob (disk) strikes the innersides of the case the cabinet is not level and, of course, the clock will not operate if the pendulum cannot move freely. The leveling feet must then be used to raise one side or lower the other until the pendulum can swing back and forth without touching the sides.

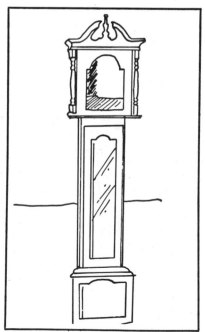

Fig. 4-53. A fully assembled cabinet ready for installation of glass, staining of moldings, door hardware and the final varnish finish.

One note of caution—make sure that your tools are good and sharp. While there is only a little bit of trimming and mitering to be done, the wood in these kits is dense, heavy and very hard. Using a dull saw will make a relatively easy job into one that is slow and laborious.

Chapter 5
Tables

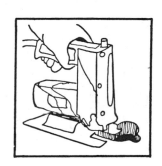

If there is a shortage of tables in your house or apartment, this chapter offers ways to make beautiful, high quality tables in easy fashion. Pieces range from Shaker tables to an unique iron coffee table.

SHAKER TABLES

Shaker furniture is simple to build, yet sturdy and useful. Pieces of furniture that serve beautifully to illustrate these characteristics are the two Shaker tables described here.

Building a Shaker Table

Made about 1880 in Alfred, Maine, the table shown in the Sabbathday Lake Shaker Community in Maine, would make an excellent writing desk, a sewing table or simply an extra table for occasional use (Fig. 5-1). See Table 5-1 for materials.

Solid maple and pine stock were used to build this table although you could use any other wood. Most of the construction of the table is obvious, but there are some not so obvious construction details that should be pointed out. With the exception of the drawer and the corners of the table, butt joints are used. The corners of the table are rabbeted together and the sides, front and back of the drawer are dadoed or grooved to fit over the drawer bottom.

Fig. 5-1. This table is ideal for writing or sewing.

The legs for the table are turned on a lathe using the pattern in Detail 1 of Fig. 5-2. Since the legs are joined to the table at an angle, their upper and lower ends will have to be cut so that they fit flush under the table top and on the floor. The top itself is joined to the sides using dowels and glue.

Table 5-1. Materials for the table in Fig. 5-1.

A. Four pieces, each: 29 × 1½ × 1½"
B. Two pieces, each: 13 × 5½ × ¾"
C. Two pieces, each: 13½ × 5½ × ¾"
D. Two pieces, each: 11¼ × 1½ × 1½"
E. One drawer: one front, 9 × 3½ × ¾"
    two sides, 11¾ × 2⅝ × ½"; one back,
    6½ × 2⅝ × ½"; one bottom, 11¾ × 6½ × ¼"
F. One piece, 25½ × 19½ × ¾"

142

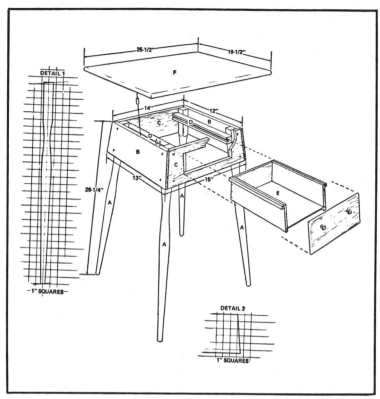

Fig. 5-2. Construction details for the table in Fig. 5-1.

The sides of the table slope as shown in Detail 2 of Fig. 5-2. Because both the sides and the legs slope, the backs of the drawer guides (D) have to be planed at an angle to fit flush against the insides of the legs. Although the legs are joined to the sides in the original using screws and glue, you could also use ½" pegs or countersunk flathead screws and fill in the holes with plugs. Plug cutters made by Stanely can be obtained in hardware stores. The finish is optional, but the original stock had a reddish stain.

Constructing Another Shaker Table

It's relatively easy to imagine one of the residents of the Shaker Dwelling House in Enfield, New Hampshire sitting at this table in their library poring over some book or writing in the 1840's (Fig. 5-3). It would be equally as easy to imagine yourself or your child sitting at the same table today since it remains as useful as it was then. This writing table reflects all the charm characteristic of

143

Fig. 5-3. This table would go well with the most modern decor.

Table 5-2. Required Materials For the Table in Fig. 5-3.

A. Two pieces, each: 25 × 6 × 1"
B. Four pieces, each: 17 × 2 × 1" (one not shown)
C. One piece, 18 × 6 × 1"
D. Four legs, each: 28 × 2 × 2"
E. One piece, 25 × 1 × 1
F. Two pieces, each: 25 × 1½· × 1½" (one not shown)

G. Eight pieces, each: 3 × 3 × ½."
H. Two drawers, each: one front, 15⅞ × 2⅝ × 1"; two sides, 11½· × 2½· × ½"; one back, 13⅞ × 2½· × ½"; one bottom, 12⅜ × 11½· × ¼"
I. One piece, 36 × 25 × 1"
J. Two drawer pulls
K. ¼" pegs

Shaker furniture with its lightness, sturdiness and simplicity. Because of its simple lines this table would blend in easily with the most modern decor. Table 5-2 lists materials.

Solid stock is used throughout with the exception of the plywood bottom of the drawer (H) (Fig. 5-4). Although the original was made of maple, you could also use butternut, cherry, or any other wood that compliments your decor. One factor to consider in choosing the wood to be used is that maple is the more easily obtained of the the hardwoods that are available.

Construction of the table is obvious from Fig. 5-4. The legs are joined to the skirt with ½" rabbet and groove construction and pinned with ¼" pegs on the front and sides. As for the interior construction of the table, pieces such as C, E, F and G are joined to the table using brads to hold the pieces in place while the glue dries. The back and bottom of the drawer are joined using ¼" dadoes with brads and glue. The groove into which the bottom of the drawer fits is located ⅜" up from the bottom—the material for the bottom itself may be either plywood or hardboard.

Refer again to Fig. 5-4. The legs of the table should be turned from solid stock using the pattern on the left side of the drawing labeled Detail 1. Detail 2 shows a cross-section view of the drawer guides (F) which, together with piece E, serve not only as guides for the drawers (H) as shown in Detail 3 but which also contribute to the strength of the table. The finish and the color of the table are optional, but the original had a natural finish.

SHAKER CANDLESTAND

A candle can give a room a softly elegant charm—if the occasion isn't a power blackout. And even if you don't use candles often enough to justify building this 1820 Shaker candlestand, you could still find wide use for it as an occasional table that could blend in easily with early American or colonial decors (Fig. 5-5).

The original of this candlestand, used in the Sabbathday Lake Shaker Community in Maine, differs from most of the ones you 'd

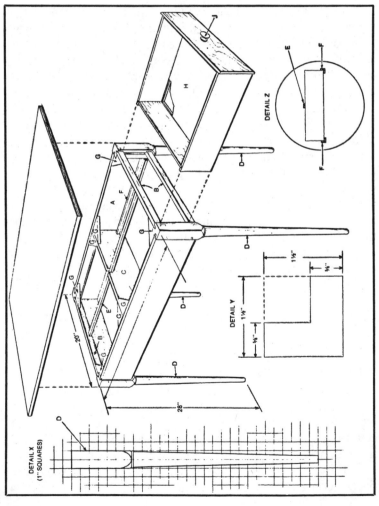

Fig. 5-4. Construction details for the table in Fig. 5-3.

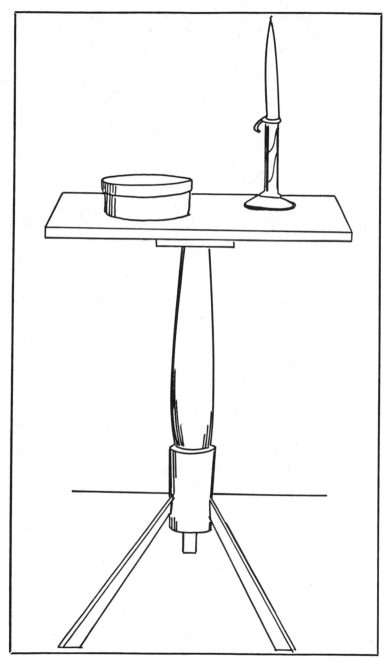

Fig. 5-5. This Shaker candlestand blends in easily with early American or colonial decors.

find later because of its stick or peg legs and its unusual rectangular top. Table 5-3 lists materials. But despite the fact that the legs are tapered, the actual building of the candlestand is quite easy. It's so easy that you may be able to do it in only a few hours—assuming, of course, that you have the necessary lathe on which to turn the tapered legs (B) and the central column (A) (Fig. 5-6).

No nails were used in building this candlestand which with the exception of the maple top, (D) is made from pine. Piece C has a 3″ hole drilled through its center. It is suggested the top (D), be joined to piece C using four screws and glue before piece A is attached as shown in Detail 3 of Fig. 5-6. The central column (A) is joined to piece C with glue.

After the three legs are turned using the pattern in Detail 1 of Fig. 5-6 they are cut off at a 45° angle as indicated. The top dotted line in Detail 1 of Fig. 5-6 shows the angle of the leg holes in piece A shown in Detail 2 of Fig. 5-6. Next, holes are drilled in piece A at a 45° angle to receive the three legs which are attached with glue. Although the way you finish this piece is optional, the original piece had a red stain.

SHAKER SEWING TABLE

Made around 1850 in the Sabbathday Lake Shaker community in New Gloucester, Maine, this combined chest of drawers and sewing table has the simplicity and functional utility characteristic of Shaker furniture (Fig. 5-7). Table 5-4 lists materials.

The table top is made up of three random width solid planks glued together at the edges to form a 20″ width and is nailed and glued to the frame beneath it. The framework is made up of 1 × 2s (B-C-D-E) which are joined to the legs (A) with shallow mortise and tenon joints as shown in Detail 1 of Fig. 5-8. An alternate method of joining the horizontals (B) to the legs is shown in Detail 2 of Fig. 5-8 using two 1″ right angle braces with screws and glue. The ⅛″ pegs (R) are used to pin the mortise and tenon joints as

Table 5-3. Materials needed for the candlestand.

LIST OF MATERIALS
A. One piece, 19¾″ × 3″ (diameter) B. Three pieces, each: 15″ × 1″ (diameter) C. One piece, 6 × 6 × 2″ D. One piece, 20 × 14½· × 1″

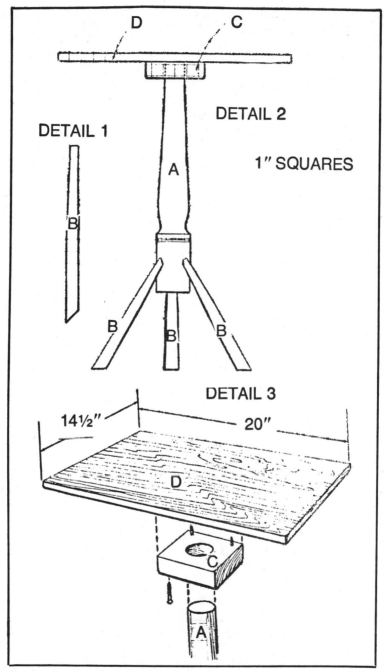

DETAIL 1

DETAIL 2

1" SQUARES

DETAIL 3

14½"

20"

Fig. 5-6. Construction details for the candlestand.

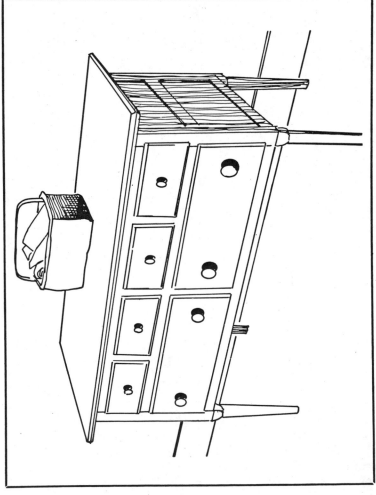

Fig. 5-7. This sewing table has a chest of drawers.

Table 5-4. Necessary Materials For the Shaker Sewing Table.

LIST OF MATERIALS

A. 4 pcs, 2 × 2 × 31¼" (see pattern)
B. 5 pcs, 1 × 2 × 46½" (incl. tenons)
C. 6 pcs, 1 × 2 × 16" (incl. tenons)
D. 1 pc, 1 × 2 × 13¾" (incl. tenons)
E. 2 pcs, 1 × 2 × 5⅞" (incl. tenons)
F. 36 pcs, ½ × ½ × 17"
G. 3 pcs, 1 × 2 × 17¼"
H. 1 pc, 20 × 56½ × ¾"
K. 4 pcs, 4 × 4 × 2"
L. 2 pcs, 15 × 17½ × ¼"

M. 1 pc, 46½ × 17½ × ¼"
N. 4 pcs, 10¾ × 5⅜ × ¾"
O. 2 pcs, 22½ × 8⅜ × ¾"
P. 8 pcs, 4⅞ × 16 × ½"
Q. 6 pcs, ¼-round 15½ × ½"
R. 22 pcs, 1 × ⅛" dowel
S. 4 pcs, 8½ × 4⅞ × ½"
T. 2 pcs, 20½ × 7⅞ × ½"
U. 4 pcs, 16 × 7⅞ × ½"
V. pcs, 9¼ × 16 × ⅛"
W. 2 pcs, 21¼ × 16 × ⅛"

shown in Detail 3 of Fig. 5-8. The verticals (D-E) of the front frame are joined to the horizontals (B) with mortise and tenon joints but the mortises are simply open notches in the backs of the horizontals. Note, however, that the joint where D joins the center rail (B) is a half lap.

The back (M) and sides (L) are covered with ¼" plywood from the inside and fastened to the frame with nails and glue. Since these plywood sheets (L-M) do not overlap the legs but only butt against them, ½" quarter round strips (Q) fastened with brads and glue are used to anchor the plywood to the legs.

The back is constructed like the sides with three horizontal rails like B. There are four triangular wooden braces (K) in each corner at the top which are fastened to the rails (C-B) with long screws and glue. To fit around the corner of each leg, these braces have a notch.

The drawer guides (F) are simply ½" strips which would be waxed for easy operation. The verticals (G) in the back are there to support the ends of drawer guides.

The finish of the original was a dark red stain on the top, sides, back, and drawer fronts. The three front rails (B) and fronts of the legs have a clear natural finish.

SHAKER SIDE TABLES

Following are directions for building two Shaker side tables. The first table has one drawer and the second has two drawers.

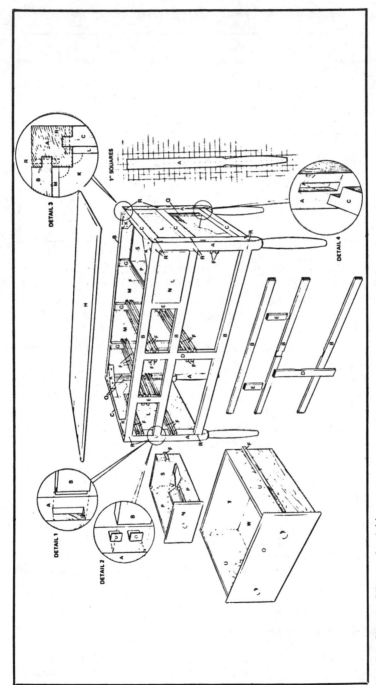

Fig. 5-8. Sketch of the sewing table.

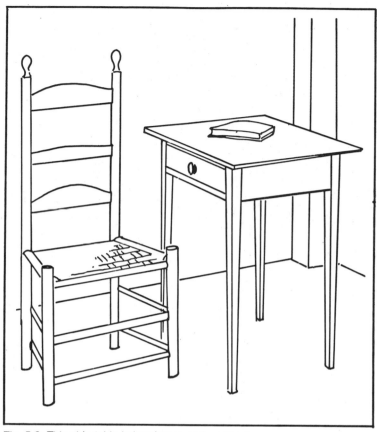

Fig. 5-9. This side table is handsome and practical.

Making the One-Drawer Table

This is a marvelously simple side table that's really very easy to build. Made in the Shaker community of Alfred, Maine, around 1840, it is both practical and good looking and will fit in any room furnished with early American or colonial furniture (Fig. 5-9). Table 5-5 gives materials.

The table top is of the breadboard type which has two separate piece at the ends to conceal the end grain of the wood. The width of these pieces is not specified but they should not be more than 1½". Use nails and glue to attach them to the single board of the top. If you have difficulty finding a ¾" pine board 19½" wide, you can glue two narrower pieces edge to edge.

The back (C), sides (B), and two front strips (D and E) are fitted to the legs with glued mortise and tenon joints pinned with

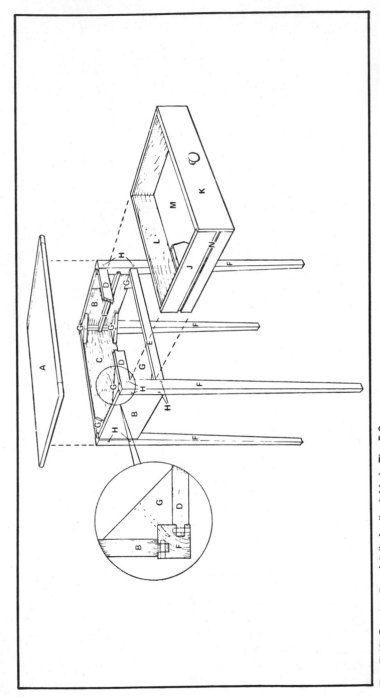

Fig. 5-10. Construction details for the table in Fig. 5-9.

Table 5-5. Materials Needed to Make the Table in Fig. 5-9.

LIST OF MATERIALS	
A. 1 pc, 24 × 19½ × ¾"	F. 4 pcs, 1½ × 1½ × 27¾"
B. 2 pcs, 5½ × 13½ × ¾"	(taper inside to ¾" sq. at bottom)
(including ½" tenons each end)	G. 8 pcs, 1¾ × ¾ × 4½"
C. 1 pc, 5½ × 18 × ¾"	H. 16 pcs, ¼ × 13/16" dowel
(including ½" tenons each end)	I. 2 pcs, ½ × 1 × 13½"
D. 1 pc, 1¼ × ¾ × 18"	J. 2 pcs, 3¼ × ½ × 13½"
(including ½" tenons each end)	K. 1 pc, 3¼ × ½ × 17"
E. 1 pc, 1 × ¾ × 18"	L. 1 pc, 3¼ × ½ × 16"
(including ½" tenons each end)	M. 1 pc, ¼ × 16⅜ × 13⅛"
	N. Groove, 9/16" high × 5/16" deep

¼" dowels (Fig. 5-10). The four triangular wooden braces (G) are notched to fit around the legs and are fastened with a single screw and glue.

Note that the legs are tapered to a ¾" square at the bottom. However, the outside edges are straight and only the inner sides of the legs are tapered. Also note that the tapering begins at the bottom of the sides, back and front.

The drawer has butt joints at the back but the sides (J) are fitted to the front (K) with rabbets. Use finishing nails and glue to fasten the drawer together, but drive the nails through the sides so that there are no nail holes to mar the front.

The drawer runners (I) are ¼" thick and protrude only ¼". The drawer groove which rides on these runners should be made to allow 1/16" clearance (9/16 × 5/16) to permit easy movement. Lubricate the runners with paraffin or silicone spray.

The original finish was a clear varnish. If a clear finish on a test piece of pine makes it look too white, you can use a light birch stain to impart more "age" to the wood before applying clear lacquer, varnish, penetrating finish or just plain linseed oil.

Building the Two-Drawer Table

Made around 1875 in the Sabbathday Lake Shaker community in Maine, this little side table has the rustic simplicity of Shaker furniture (Fig. 5-11).

The construction is relatively easy. In the original all parts are made of solid pine except the two drawer fronts which are maple. The table top is ¾" thick solid pine. If you have difficulty getting an 18½" piece of pine, you can use plywood.

The legs are very slightly tapered on the two inner surfaces beginning at the point where the legs protrude beyond the lower edges of the sides and back (E-D) (Fig. 5-12). Note that the three front rails (C) are deeply notched to fit around the corners of the legs as shown in Detail 1 of Fig. 5-12. The notch is 1½″ deep and has a ⅜″ × 1″ dowel (H) in it to fasten the leg in place. Additionally, these rails (C) are fastened with a screw through the tongues at the ends that goes into the leg. Of course, glue is used in addition to the dowel and screw.

The drawer guides (F) are notched at the ends to fit around the leg corners. Depth of the notch is ⅝″ leaving ⅜″ to engage the groove in the sides of the drawers (J).

The sides and back (D-D-E) are recessed ⅛″ from the outer corners of the legs. Note that the sides and back have rabbeted

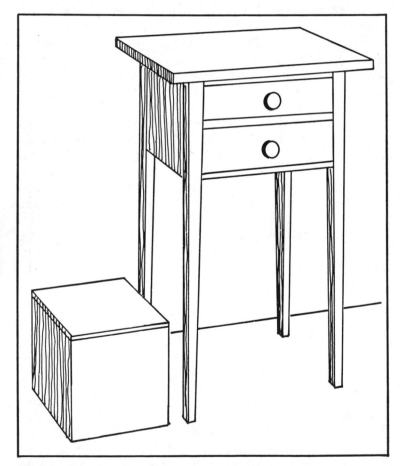

Fig. 5-11. This table has two drawers.

ends that fit into grooves in the legs as shown in Detail 1 of Fig. 5-12.

Two wood corner braces (G) are fastened to each leg, back and sides with screws and glue. The top (A) can be fastened with glue spread on the corner braces, glue blocks (M) and the tops of the legs as well as the top edges of the back and sides (D-D-E).

The drawers have rabbeted joints and are assembled with brads and glue. Note that the dimensions for the small upper drawer are designated with double letter callouts in Table 5-6 but are not shown in Fig. 5-12. The double letters correspond to the single letters on the drawing of the drawer. Thus, II is the front, JJ the sides, KK the back, etc.

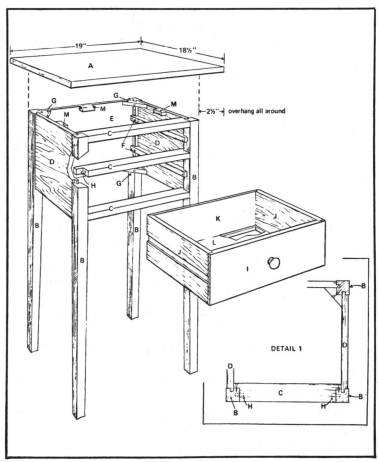

Fig. 5-12. Construction details for the table in Fig. 5-11.

Table 5-6. Materials For the Table in Fig. 5-11.

A. 1 pc, 19 × 18½ × ¾"	L. 1 pc., 11¾ × 10¼ × ¼"
B. 4 pcs, 1½ × 27¾ × 1½"	M. 3 pcs., 1 × 3 × ¾"
C. 3 pcs, 2 × 12¼ × ¾"	Smaller Drawer
D. 2 pcs., 8½ × 11¼ × ¾"	II. 1 pc., 2¾ × 11 × ¾"
E. 1 pc., 8½ × 11¾ × ¾"	(not shown)
F. 4 pcs., 1 × 11⅞ × ¾"	JJ. 2 pcs., 2¾ × 11⅞ × ¾"
G. 4 pcs., 1½ × 3 × ¾"	(not shown)
H. 6 pcs., 1 × ⅜" dowel	KK. 1 pc., 2¾ × 10¼ × ¾"
I. 1 pc., 3½ × 11 × ¾"	(not shown)
J. 2 pcs., 3½ × 11⅞ × ¾"	LL. 1 pc., 11¾ × 10¼ × ¼"
K. 1 pc., 3½ × 10¼ × ½"	(not shown)

SHAKER DROP LEAF TABLES

If you are a lover of Shaker furniture, you can make two Shaker drop-leaf tables. The first is quite large and is based on a Shaker original made about 1830 at the Hancock, Massachusetts, Shaker community. It has long rectangular top and broad side leaves and takes up little space when closed. The table opens up to a width of 38" when the leaves are raised.

The second table can be used as a breakfast table in the kitchen, an odds-and-ends table in the hallway or a game table in the recreation room. Originally built in the Shaker community of Sabbathday Lake, New Gloucester, Maine, around 1835, its two leaves fold down for convenient space saving and fold up to enlarge the work, eating and playing surface.

Assembling the Large Drop-Leaf Table

You can make this table by cutting all the pieces as shown in Table 5-7 or you can make the whole table from a kit with precision cut parts (Fig. 5-13). The kit is supplied by Shaker Workshops, Inc., Box 710, Concord, Massachusetts 01742 (Fig. 5-14).

Assemble the legs and skirts first. Select a right leg and a left leg and place them so that they face each other. Apply glue to the slots (mortises) in each leg. Do not apply glue to the tenons (tongues) of the skirts as they may swell rapidly and make it impossible to get them into the mortises. Line up the holes bored through mortise-and-tenon joints; then glue and insert the ¼" pegs (Fig. 5-15). Start with one of the short skirts. Repeat this procedure with the remaining short skirt and the other two legs. Then add the long skirts to the remaining mortises in the legs already glued to the short skirts, pinning them with pegs as described above (Fig. 5-16).

Fig. 5-13. Accommodate eight people comfortably with this table.

Table 5-7. Materials Needed For the Table in Fig. 5-13.

LIST OF MATERIALS	
A. 1 pc, 19 × 72 × ¾″	G. 2 pcs, 2 × 5½ × 1″
B. 2 pcs, 10⅛ × 73 × ¾″	H. 4 pcs, ⅜ dia. × 1¼″
C. 2 pcs, 6⅛ × 14¼ × ¾″	I. 16 pcs, ¼ dia. × 1⅜″
D. 2 pcs, 6⅛ × 57½ × ¾″	J. 6 pcs, #10 × 2″ screws
E. 4 pcs, 1¾ dia. × 28¼″	K. 10 pcs, #10 × 1¼″ screws
F. 4 pcs, 1¼ × 16½ × 1″	L. 36 pcs, #8 × ½″ screws

Note that all of the skirts have screw holes bored at a slant through the upper edges. These edges will be in contact with the underside of the table top. When assembling the skirts and legs, it is very important that all these skirt edges with holes face upward (Fig. 5-17). Also be sure that all these screw holes face inward. Remove all excess glue at once with a dry cloth.

Because of the size of this table it is suggested that the legs-and-skirt assembly, drop leaves, top and support slides be stained and finished before complete assembly (Fig. 5-18). Instructions for finishing are on the labels of the stain cans that come with the kit.

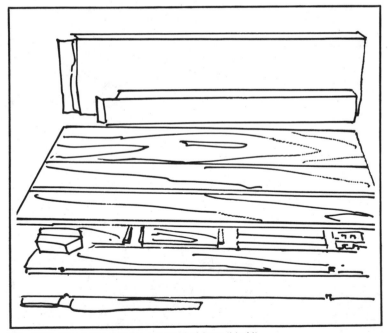

Fig. 5-14. The table can be assembled from this kit.

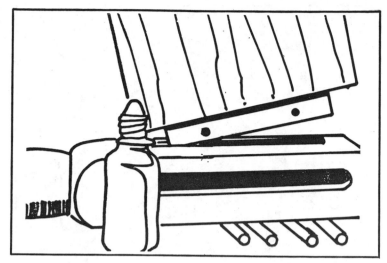

Fig. 5-15. Close-up of mortise-and-tenon joint between skirt and leg shows predrilled holes for dowel pegs.

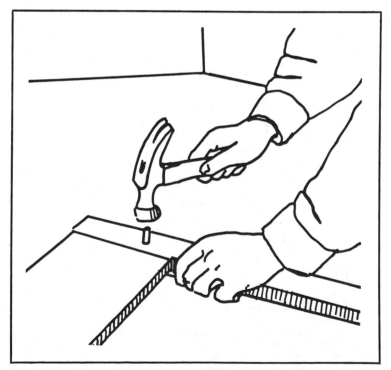

Fig. 5-16. This view shows final dowel peg being driven into table end assembly. Work mat protects the carpeted floor from sawdust and glue staining.

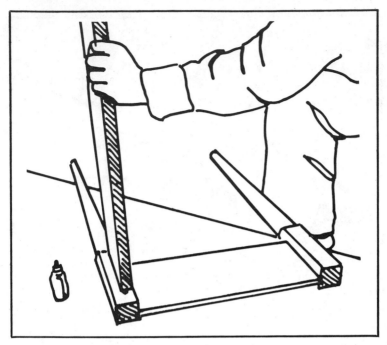

Fig. 5-17. Here the side skirts are being joined to the end assembly. Make sure slide cutouts and screw holes in skirt are facing the tops of the legs.

Fig. 5-18. The table should be stained and finished before the top and leaves are joined to the base.

162

Fig. 5-19. Final assembly begins by attaching the leaves to the top. Hinges and ½" screws aligned to predrilled holes.

Attach the leaves to the table top using three hinges for each leaf (Fig. 5-19). The holes in the hinges should line up with the predrilled pilot holes in the undersides of the leaves and the table top (Fig. 5-20). Use the ½" screws in the kit and be sure to attach the long side of each hinge to the leaves.

Place the assembled table top and leaves face down on the floor. Now place the legs-and-skirt assembly exactly in the center of the underside of the table now facing up toward you.

With a pencil or nail inserted in the holes of the skirts, mark the underside of the table for pilot screw holes. Using a ⅛" drill bit, drill holes not more than ½" deep at the same angle as those in the skirts. Do not drive screws without pilot holes into the bottom of the table top as this may cause it to split. To achieve the proper angle get a ⅛" drill bit which is longer than usual for this size and use the holes in the skirts as guides (Fig. 5-21). The skirts should be fastened with ten 1¼" screws in the kit (Fig. 5-22).

The final job is the installation of the support slides which hold up the hinged leaves and their guides. There are two support slides under each leaf. Insert these slides in the holes in the skirts. The guides for these support slides have three holes in them and

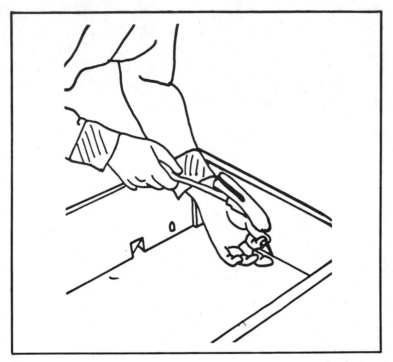

Fig. 5-20. With base assembly centered over open top, a nail or center punch is used to locate pilot holes for joining the two table pieces.

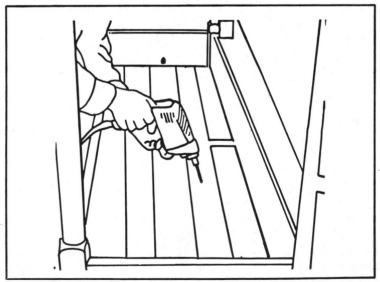

Fig. 5-21. Base assembly is slid aside for pilot hole drilling at 30° angle.

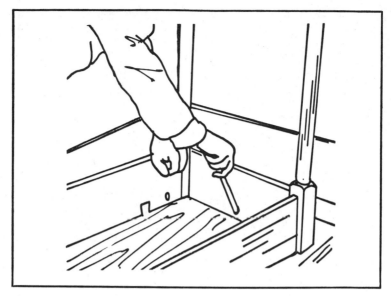

Fig. 5-22. Base and top assemblies are again recentered and fastened using 1½" round head screws. Note angled precountersunk holes in the skirts.

notches that fit the slides. The guides are placed equidistant from the long skirts with their notches or dadoes over the slides. Mark spots on the underside of the table through the holes in the guides. Drill pilot holes at these spots that are no deeper than ½" (Fig. 5-23). Attach the two slide guides with 2" screws. Now glue and insert the ⅜" slide stopper dowels in the holes in the sides of the slide bars (Fig. 5-24). Make certain that these stop dowels face away from each other as shown in Fig. 5-25.

Finish with alcohol and water resistant varnish using two coats on the table top and leaves (Fig. 5-26). An oil finish of boiled lineed oil and turpentine in equal parts can also be used. Finally, use a good grade of paste wax to protect the finish and buff to a soft glow.

Making The Small Drop-Leaf Table

The table top consists of two leaves (B) attached to a center panel (A) with hinges; it (A) is attached to the frame at the front, back, and side skirts (C, D), the top of the legs (F), and the corner braces (H)—all to provide a larger bonding surface (Fig. 5-27). The table top overlaps the skirts (D) by 4½". See Table 5-8 for materials.

Fig. 5-23. Slides and slide guides are held in position while pilot holes are marked carefully.

The skirts (C, D) are slightly recessed in from the legs (F) and are joined by glued mortise and tenon joints as shown in Detail 2 of Fig. 5-27. The framework is further strengthened with corner braces (H) secured with screws and glue to the legs (F). The legs (F) are turnings that are left square at the top and shaped below.

The table leaves' prop mechanisms are simply 10" long strips (E) beveled at both ends (note that the receiving ends in the front

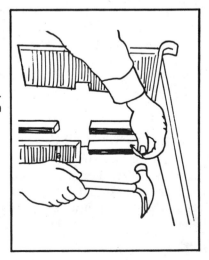

Fig. 5-24. When slide guides are fastened, slide-stop dowels are driven in place.

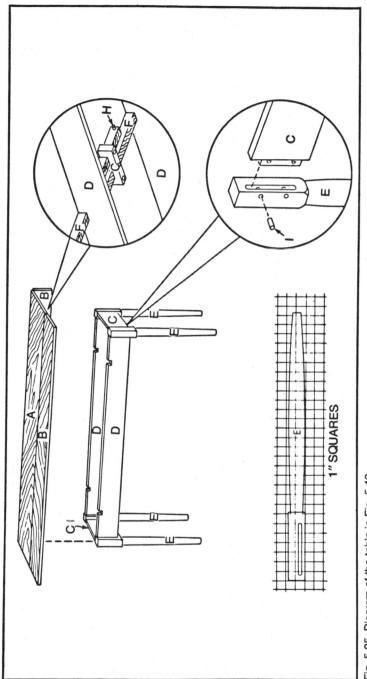

Fig. 5-25. Diagram of the table in Fig. 5-13.

Fig. 5-26. Finishing of top and leaves is the final step in drop-leaf table assembly. Here a final coat of the satin varnish is being applied.

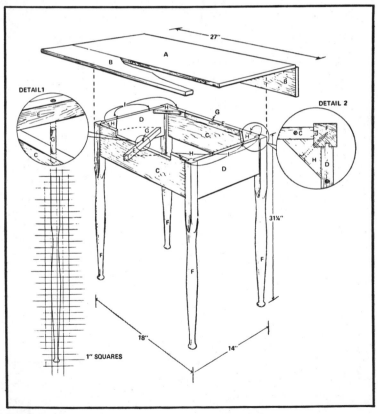

Fig. 5-27. Construction details for the table in Fig. 5-28.

Table 5-8. Materials Needed to Make the Table in Fig. 5-28.

LIST OF MATERIALS	
A. 1 pc, ¾ × 14 × 27″	F. 4 pcs, 1½·× 1½·× 31¼″
B. 2 pcs, ¾ × 6 × 27	G. 2 pcs, ⅜″ hardwood dowel × 1¾″
C. 2 pcs, ¾ × 5½ × 15½″	H. 4 pcs, ¾ × 3½·× 1½″
D. 2 pcs, ¾ × 5½·× 11½.″	I. 8 pcs, ⅜″ hardwood dowel × ¾″
E. 2 pcs, ¾ × 1 × 10″	

and back skirts (C) must also be beveled) and secured with dowels (G) (Detail 1 of Fig. 5-27) to allow for rotation.

The original table was made of maple, was stained red, and had a natural top. The handsome pine towel rack shown in Fig. 5-28 is also a Shaker piece.

SWINGDOWN TABLE

If you have a small kitchen and no convenient space for a refrigerator and no place for a table, you've really got problems. Here's how one young homeowner solved this problem.

He built a booth around the refrigerator with three sides out of ¾″ particle board on which he mounted a white plastic laminate

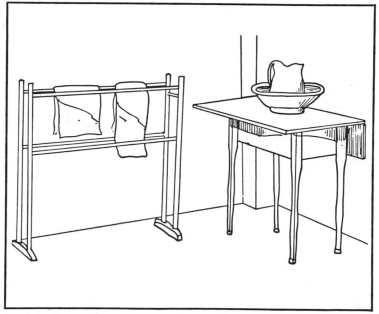

Fig. 5-28. The pine towel rack is also a Shaker piece.

called Melamite with contact cement. The panels were then cleated to the floor and ceiling.

The back of the booth has a recessed space for a telephone message center including a shelf for a Yellow Pages directory, a wall phone and a corkboard back for messages as well as a convenient light under an upper shelf.

The outside wall of the booth has a decorative and clever swingdown table which is a real gem of an idea for a small kitchen with too little space for a table (Fig. 5-29). In its upright position it only protrudes 3″ and looks like a modern wall decoration. When it swings down it can accommodate four people. See Fig. 5-30 and Table 5-9.

The outer frame (A) is made of ¾″ walnut veneered plywood with mitered corners. The top edges of this frame are flush with a ¾″ table top (E) particle board fastened with glue and finishing nails driven through the frame (A) and set, the nail holes being filled with walnut-colored panel wax stick. The top surface is covered with a white plastic laminate called Melamite Solid White Tuft which is attached to the table top with contact cement.

Fig. 5-29. (A). When up on the wall, this table looks like a modern decoration. (B). When it's down, it will accommodate four people.

Table 5-9. Materials Needed to Make the Swingdown Table.

LIST OF MATERIALS	
A. 4 pcs, ¾ × 3 × 35½"	H. Elbow catch
B. 2 pcs, ¾ × 1⅜ × 27¼"	I. ½ × 37" × height to suit
C. 2 pcs, ¾ × 1⅜ × 28¾"	surface with white Melamite
D. 4 pcs, ¾ × 1 × 15¼"	J. 2 pcs, ½ × ½" walnut veneered
E. 1 pc, ¾ × 34 × 34"	plywood, height to suit
top, white Melamite 35½" sq.	K. Hinge ¾ × ¾ × 35½"
bottom, black Melamite 34" sq.	L. 2 pcs, 1½" hinges
F. 1/16 × 28¼ × 28¼" Melamite	M. Folding brace
G. 1/16 × 14¾ × 14¾" Melamite	

The underside of the table is surfaced with three squares of plastic laminate each fitted inside the other. The joints where the edges of the squares meet are concealed by ¾" strips of walnut veneered plywood. The exposed edges of the walnut strips are covered with walnut veneer tape glued on with contact cement.

The horizontal strip (B) above the white square and the two strips (C) at its sides move as the table swings down so that the side strips form a pair of legs (L) hinged at the top. The legs are fastened to B with finishing nails and glue. Both the front and back edges of the legs are kept steady by a folding brace (M) when they are fully extended. A continuous hinge (K) at the back of the outside frame (A) permits the table to swing down easily.

The innermost black square (G) has a textured surface called Solid Black Tuft and is purely ornamental. The mitered strips (D) around it are glued and also fastened with finishing nails which are countersunk and concealed by walnut veneer tape.

An elbow catch (H) suffices to hold the table against the wall or panel when it is in its upright position. Although a table of this type can easily be attached to a wall if the screws of the hinge (K) go through the plasterboard or plaster to the studs, the appearance of the whole assembly will be improved by attaching a white panel to the wall and then fastening the table to the panel.

If this idea appeals to you, make the panel (I) out of ½" particle board and surface it with a white plastic laminate, possibly the same as the one on the table top, using contact cement. Make the plastic laminate about ½" wider than the particle board panel and then trim it to size with a router or fine-toothed saw. To conceal the raw edges of the panel, use walnut strips (J) or walnut-stained hardwood which can be fastened with finishing nails. Conceal the nail holes with walnut-colored panel wax sticks. Attach the panel to the wall with panel cement.

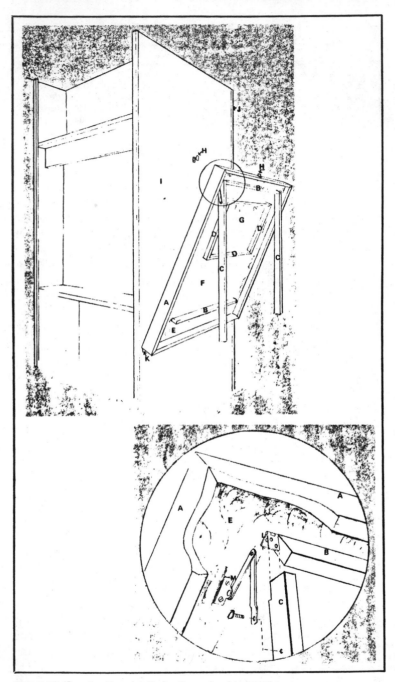

Fig. 5-30. Construction details for the swingdown table.

172

Fig. 5-31. This coffee table is easy to make.

In attaching the table hinge (K) to the panel, be sure to use screws long enough to reach the studs of the wall behind the panel. The height of the panel is a matter for you to decide. However, extending the panel to the ceiling makes a striking effect.

IRON COFFEE TABLE

Here's a very attractive coffee table that can be used in your living room or as part of your patio furniture (Fig. 5-31). Although it looks as if it were strictly a factory job, you can make this yourself and you don't need to be specially skilled to do it. Once you have made this table, you will find it easy to make many other things out of iron such as a divider, chair, wall decoration or planter.

The great thing about making any of these items is that it's so easy. Unlike regular wrought iron, which can only be shaped when cherry-red hot and needs special equipment, this soft iron is formed by hand when cold, with a simple jig. And rather than having to weld the parts, you can rivet them together easily and still achieve strong connections.

The methods for making the coffee table are applicable to other items as well. Table 5-10 lists materials.

Table 5-10. Required Materials For the Iron Coffee Table.

MATERIALS LIST	
Legs—4 pcs. 5/16" dia. round rod 37¼" long Frame—2 pcs. ½" × ½" × 96" angle Brace—2 pcs. ⅛" × ½" × 2" Leg Scroll—4 pcs. ⅛" × ½" × 15" Side Scrolls—12 pcs. ⅛" × ¼" × 15"	End Scrolls—8 pcs. ⅛" × ½" × 13½" Rivets—#44-50 pcs. (for attaching scrolls) Rivets—#48-24 pcs. (for attaching legs) Glass—¼" × 17⅞" × 30⅞"

The scrolls are made with ⅛" × ½" iron and a jig made of two pieces of drill rod set close together in a steel block, which is clamped in a vise (Fig. 5-32). By feeding the iron between the rods and controlling feeding speed and bending pressure you can make the large and small circular sweeps required. To insure accurate shapes, draw a scroll full size, then bend a test piece to match the drawing. Match each succeeding piece against pieces already created.

The framing, made from ½" angle, can be bent to shape by notching, anchoring one end in a vise and pulling on the free end (Fig. 5-33). Do the same for the legs which are made of 5/16" soft iron rod.

When all components are cut and formed, assemble the framing. The joints fall midway at each end of the piece and are held

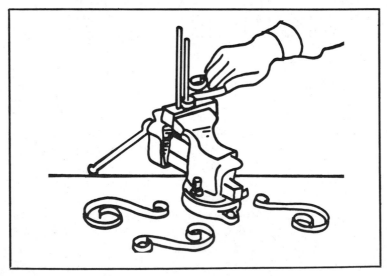

Fig. 5-32. A simple forming jig is used to bend flat iron stock into the decorative curves characteristic of wrought iron.

174

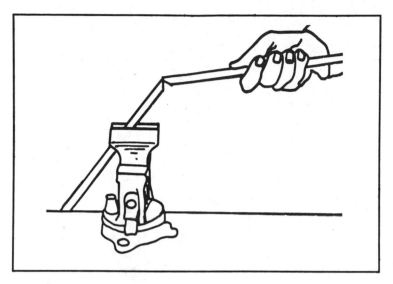

Fig. 5-33. Angle stock for the upper and lower frames of the table is notched with a hacksaw and bent as shown.

together by short sections of iron, which are attached from the inside and won't be noticeable.

Now drill the scroll holes, position the scrolls on the top framing section, and mark where their matching holes fall with a

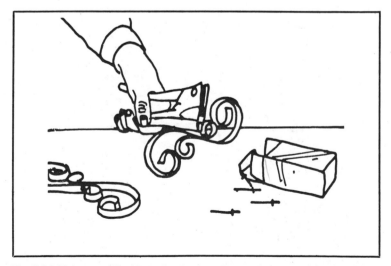

Fig. 5-34. Holes are drilled in the finished scrolls; scrolls are then joined together with steel "pop" rivets.

Fig. 5-35. Scrolls are positioned and riveted to the top framing section. Then they are riveted to the bottom section.

felt pen (Figs. 5-34 through 5-36). Then assemble the scrolls to this framing and repeat the procedure for the bottom section. To avoid confusion, label each scroll and its place on the framing with letters or numbers. Finally, clean the metal, spray on a coat of metal primer and finish with a suitable lacquer preferably white or

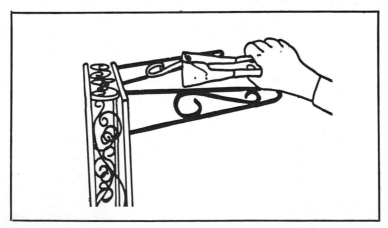

Fig. 5-36. Legs need a size S-48 rivet because of added thickness of predrilled round stock. Scrolls help reinforce legs.

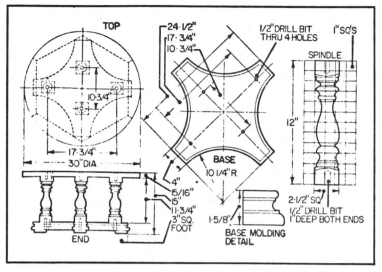

Fig. 5-37. Construction details for the coffee table in Fig. 5-41.

black. Ordinary window glass is used as the top. It need not be fastened.

COFFEE TABLE

You can build this elegantly styled coffee table from ready-made parts, or construct it from "scratch" using Fig. 5-37. The combination of the carved base, turned spindles and beautifully figured walnut veneer face produces a table guaranteed to extract compliments from your friends.

If you elect to assemble this table from ready-made parts, the only tools you'll need will be an electric drill, hammer and screwdriver (Figs. 5-38 through 5-41). The radial matched walnut veneer is purchased completely assembled, and taped, ready to glue to the top. If desired, even the 30″ diameter ¾″ particleboard top may be purchased ready cut. Particleboard is preferred over plywood because the absence of any grain makes it essentially warp-proof, and the smooth flat surface is an excellent base for the veneer overlay. Table 5-11 gives materials.

Assembling Parts

The veneer banding used around the edge of the table may be purchased with the top. This banding is 1″ wide, and we elected to take advantage of the full width by building up the top with seg-

Fig. 5-38. The table can be built from scratch or assembled from ready-made parts.

Fig. 5-39. Base spindles can be arranged in various combinations.

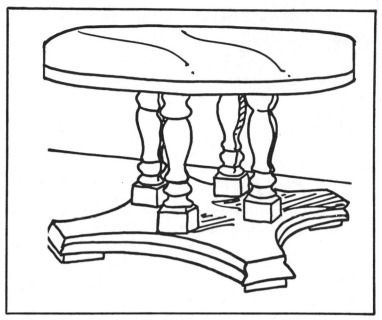

Fig. 5-40. Another arrangement of base spindles.

ments cut from 3/16" plywood. This gives a total thickness of 15/16" which will allow the edge band to be sanded flush with the top if carefully applied. Cut the segments from 3"-wide strips of plywood and glue and nail to the underside of the table. Sand the table edge smooth and square with the top.

Drill the ½" holes in the center of the spindle ends 1" deep, as shown in Fig. 5-37. Locate and drill the ½" dowel holes through the base and top. The two pieces can be clamped into position and

Fig. 5-41. A completed coffee table.

Table 5-11. Materials For the Coffee Table.

MATERIALS LIST	

1—24½" Alder hardwood pedestal base*
4—12" × 2½" sq. hardwood turned
   spindles
1—30" dia. × ¾" particle board table top
4—3" sq. × ¾" pine or hardwood feet
1—30" dia. matched veneer Constantine
   #78C6**
	1—1" × 8' walnut veneer tape
	   Constantine # 160K20* *
	1—pint can veneer adhesive**
	4—# 10 × 1½" flat head woodscrews
	4—# 10 × 2" flat head woodscrews

drilled together if desired to assure perfect alignment. Carefully sand all surfaces of each piece before assembly.

Use spiral grooved dowels to provide a relief passage for the excess glue (Fig. 5-42). Cut four dowels 2⅝" long and four 1¾" long. Sand the dowels so they will slip fit into the drilled holes. Apply a thin coat of glue to the end grain of the spindles, and allow to dry.

When you are ready for final assembly, spread glue onto the long dowels, and drive them into the lower end of the spindles. Apply a second coat of glue to the end grain of the spindles, and drive them tight against the base aligning the spindles square with the base. Wipe off any excess glue from the joint with a damp cloth.

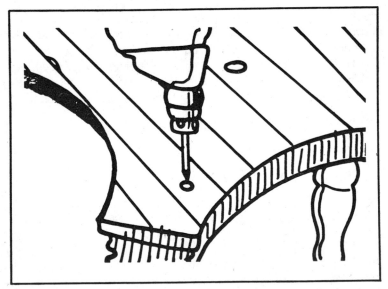

Fig. 5-42. Spiral grooved dowels are glued, driven into spindles, base and top, and then fastened with countersunk screws.

Fig. 5-43. After inserting dowels, sand the dowel ends flush and fill holes and screw heads with filler or water putty.

Assemble the top to the doweled spindles in the same manner. Drill and countersink for a #10 × 1½″ flat head woodscrew through the top into each one of the spindles. Turn the table over, and drill for a #10 × 2″ flat head screw through the top into each of the spindles.

When the glue has set, sand any protruding dowel ends flush with the table top. Fill any holes around the dowels, and the heads of the countersunk screws with a wood filler or water putty (Fig. 5-43). Use a sanding block and carefully sand the filler flush with the top surface. Prepare the feet for the base of the table by cutting four 3″ square blocks from ¾″ scrap lumber (Fig. 5-44). Sandpaper blocks, then glue and nail the feet in place on the underside of the base. Set the block back from the edges ¾″.

Applying Veneer Edge Trim

The veneer edge trim is applied to the table top with contact cement before the face veneer is put on. Read and observe the instructions on the contact cement container label, particularly the cautions to be observed if the solvent is flammable. The temperature of the objects being cemented, as well as the temperature of the cement, is critical with most products.

Coat the inside surface of the edge trim, and the table edge with a sealing coat of contact cement. Allow both surfaces to dry at least 20 to 30 minutes, and apply a second coat. When the second coat is dry, the surface will appear glossy if properly coated. If there are any areas that still present a dull appearance, give them a third coat and again allow to dry thoroughly.

Hold the top of the edge trim parallel with the top of the table and touch the front edge to the table. It will adhere immediately. With a small roller, or block of wood and a hammer, force the trim tight against the edge of the table, working a small area at one time. Make certain the trim remains parallel with the table top. After the trim is applied all around the top, trim the excess end with a razor blade to butt tightly with the starting point. Using a sanding block, sand the upper edge of the trim flush with the table surface.

Remove all dust from the top surface, and apply two or more coats of cement to the table top and to the underside of the veneer. Coat the side of the veneer that is not taped. After the cement has thoroughly dried, check both surfaces again to be sure there are no dull spots indicating a lack of sufficient adhesive.

Get some wax paper, or a piece of Kraft paper large enough to cover the complete table top. Two large grocery bags unfolded and taped together will be adequate. Do not use newspaper or other thin uncoated paper! Lay the paper over the table top completely covering the glued area, and center the veneer carefully on the top.

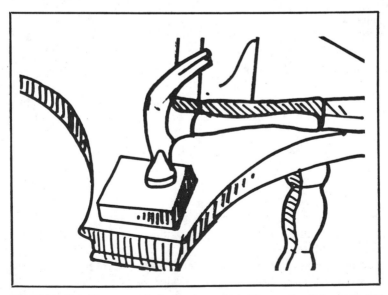

Fig. 5-44. Cut 3″ square blocks for base feet. Glue and nail in place on underside of base, ¾″ back from the edges.

Hold the veneer in position, and slowly pull out the paper exposing a small area of cemented surface. Press the veneer down firmly on the exposed adhesive, again checking the alignment of the veneer with the table top. Continue to slowly pull the spearation paper from under the veneer. Use a rolling pin or a smooth block of wood and hammer to force the cemented surfaces together and work out any entrapped air as the paper is being removed. If there are any blisters, or small areas where the veneer is not completely bonded, the cement may be reactivated by pressing the areas over a piece of aluminum foil with a warm iron.

The next step is to remove the veneer tape from the seams. If an industrial belt sander is not available to you, the tape will have to be removed by moistening and scraping. Soak a small sponge and carefully dampen only the paper tape. Using your fingernails or a dull knife blade, scrape off the tape one layer at a time. Continue to moisten and scrape until all of the paper tape is removed. Allow the areas to dry, and then sand the table top with progressively finer sandpaper until the surface is smooth and free of any scratch marks.

Apply paste filler to all surfaces and stain the base and spindles to match the top. Be very careful not to get any stain on the white band around the outside of the veneer. Finish sanding all surfaces with 320 grit paper, and apply several coats of clear varnish. Carefully sand the surfaces between each coat to remove all brush marks and apply the varnish in a dust free area. For a truly fine finish on the top surface, rub down the final two or three coats on the top with 0000 steel wool and finish with auto body rubbing compound.

CONSTRUCTION GRADE LUMBER TABLES

If you've shopped for low-to-medium priced furniture lately, you know there won't be many heirlooms around for the grandchildren. Thin veneers, quick assembly, and lots of plastic often guarantee the piece you buy will be well worn almost as soon as you've decided on an arrangement.

But if you want sturdy furniture to fit early American or colonial decor that's bullet-proof enough for a rec room where teenagers romp, you can build these pieces yourself from construction grade lumber (Figs. 5-45 through 5-47). We'll guarantee this furniture will last for generations, and you end up with furniture instead of payments.

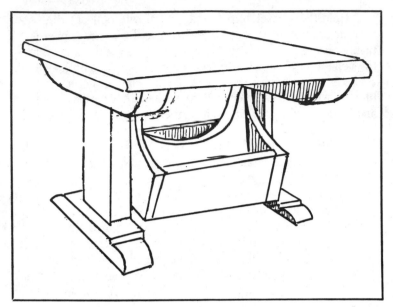

Fig. 5-45. An end table made from construction grade lumber.

This coffee table and end table/magazine rack are of construction grade 2 × 6s, 2 × 8s and 4 × 4s, either fir, pine or hemlock. Tight knots or blemishes can enhance the appearance of these rustic pieces, but lumber must be straight and free of cracks. See Figs. 5-48 and 5-49.

Wood used was bought cut-to-length at a lumber yard. Shaping was done with a saber saw. The only other tools you need are a drill, ¼″, 1″ and 1¼″ bits, wrench to drive lag bolts, belt sander

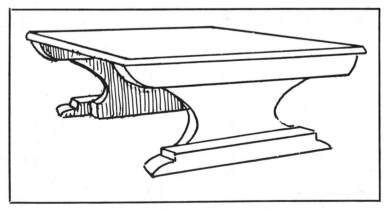

Fig. 5-46. A coffee table made from construction grade lumber.

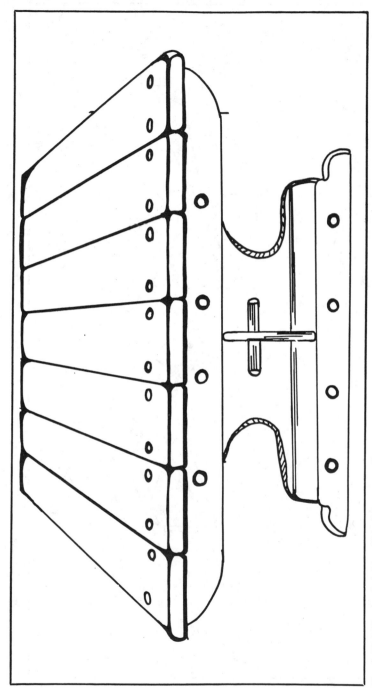

Fig. 5-47. This sturdy table will last for generations.

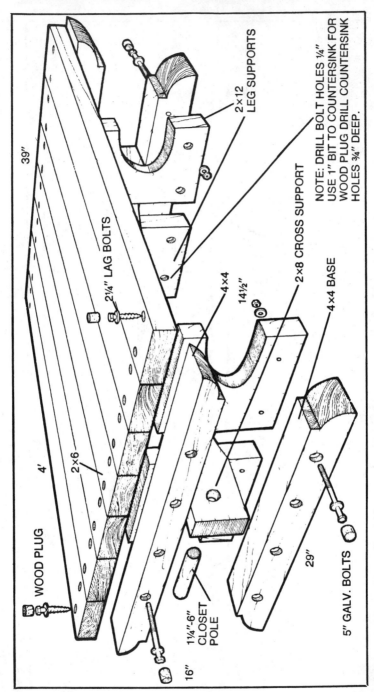

WOOD PLUG

WOOD PLUG DRILL COUNTERSINK HOLES ¾" DEEP.
USE 1" BIT TO COUNTERSINK FOR
NOTE: DRILL BOLT HOLES ¼"

2×12 LEG SUPPORTS

39"

2¼" LAG BOLTS

2×8 CROSS SUPPORT

4×4

14½"

4×4 BASE

2×6

4'

29"

16"

1¼"-6" CLOSET POLE

5" GALV. BOLTS

Fig. 5-48. Diagram of the coffee table.

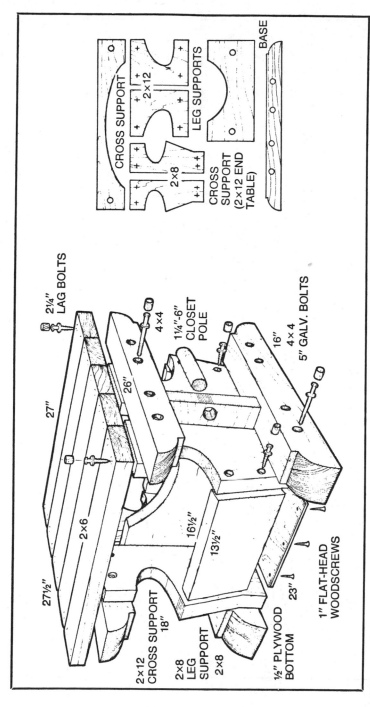

Fig. 5-49. Diagram of the end table, along with a detail pattern for decorative curves on the supports and base.

187

Fig. 5-50. With a socket wrench, drive the lag bolts which fasten the 2 × 6s to the 4 × 4.

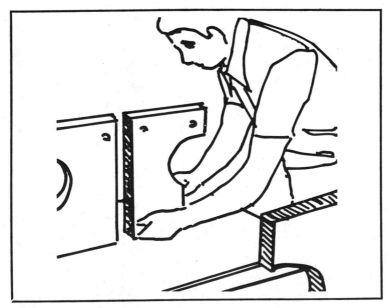

Fig. 5-51. Legs are attached to the 4 × 4s with washers and nuts.

Fig. 5-52. Place 5″ lag bolts through the 4 × 4 to hold the table legs. To drill 4 × 4s, use an extension wood bit.

(which you can rent), and 1½″-round wood shaping file. Here's how to proceed:

Cut 4 × 4s to length and then curve the ends. Decorative curves can be cut with a saber saw, but a bandsaw works better. Lay the two 4 × 4s that join the top of the table across sawhorses, with curved ends down. Place all 2 × 6s over the 4 × 4s, allowing them to overhang on each end an equal amount. Using a ¼″ bit, drill pilot holes on each end of the 2 × 6 at the edge of the table top. Then countersink with a 1″ bit, approximately ¾″ deep, (countersinks will later be plugged with 1″ dowel). Fasten the edge 2 × 6 with ¼″ × 2″ lag bolts through the pilot holes, using white carpenter's glue at each joint (Fig. 5-50).

When the first edge piece is secure and square to the 4 × 4s, place the rest of the 2 × 6s against it. Be sure all are tightly fitted at the joints. Drill, glue and lag screw the other 2 × 6s to the 4 × 4s.

When the top is complete, flip it over and drill pilot holes for ¼″ carriage bolts to fasten the legs to the 4 × 4 (Fig. 5-51). Next shape the curves in the 2 × 8 legs with a saber saw. Attach the cross brace 2 × 8 with glue and 1½″ wood screws. The base 4 × 4s are attached to the 2 × 8 legs with glue and 5″ galvanized lag bolts (Figs. 5-52 and 5-53). Next drill 1¼″ holes through the ends of the 2 × 8 cross support and insert 6″ lengths of 1¼″ closet pole (Fig. 5-54).

Using 1″ dowel, plug all countersink holes by putting glue in the hole, driving in a 1″ dowel with a mallet, then cutting dowels off flush with work surface.

You may leave the cracks between the 2 × 6s on the top and apply the finish. We used a ½″ round file to groove out the seams ⅛″ deep and ¼″ wide. We then filled the grooves with wood filler mixed with stain, and used a belt sander on the table top and all edges. For a distressed look, sand was poured on the table top and pounded with a mallet, then metal objects around the garage were used to give the table even more of a rustic look (Fig. 5-55).

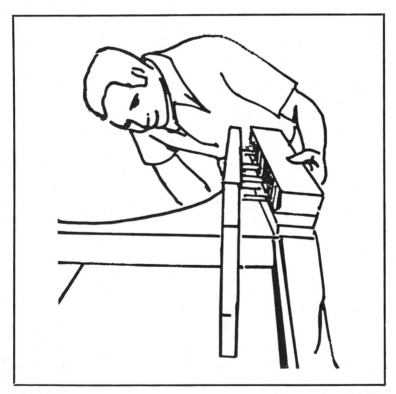

Fig. 5-53. Lag bolts are then threaded through the 4 × 4 base and attached to the legs.

Fig. 5-54. The 2 × 8 cross support is fitted between legs and secured by a 6″ section of closet pole.

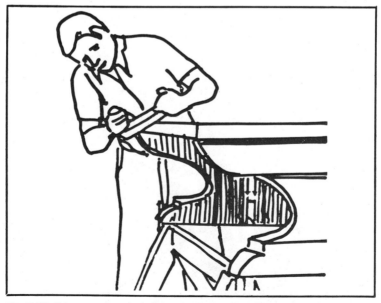

Fig. 5-55. Edges are beveled slightly and the table is distressed to give a rustic appearance.

The table was stained, then received 10 coats of polyurethane at a rate of one coat per day. The finish was left to harden for two weeks, then sanded with 600 grit paper until dull. The table was then cleaned with a tack rag, and given a final coat of polyurethane.

Chapter 6

Bars

This chapter details the procedures involved in building several types of bars—including one for the family room, recreation room, a built-in hospitality cabinet or drink dispenser and a serving bar. And you can make a wine rack to store your favorite beverages.

FAMILY ROOM BAR

Bars are very popular these days and most often plans are wanted for a bar to build in the family room. Structurally simple, this bar resembles an L-shaped bookcase when seen from the rear (Fig. 6-1).

To avoid complex framing, the entire construction consists of ¾" plywood except for the bottom platform which consists of 2 × 4s fastened with white glue and 1½" finishing nails. See Table 6-1. The plywood used here should be good on one side and smoothly sanded. Additional sanding with an orbital sander and 120 grit aluminum oxide is recommended.

The sides and front are fastened with finishing nails and glue in simple butt joints reinforced with triangular glue blocks. The L-shaped shelves are supported by cleats and attached to the front and sides by 1½" finishing nails driven from outside into the shelf edges. Three partitions provide additional support for the shelves and the top.

Make the top in one piece and nail it to the top edges of the sides, front, topmost partition, and rear panel. Countersink the nail heads and fill nail holes with wood putty.

The surface of the bar is a plastic laminate like Formica and can be cut in one piece. Use a good contact cement to glue the plastic laminate to the bar top. The edging (H) all around the skirt of the bar is made up of strips of laminate cut from the remaining piece of the top surface and cemented to a skirt (Fig. 6-2). Plywood strips of ¾ × ¾ clear pine may be used for the skirting. Alternatively, the bar top need not have rounded corners if too difficult for the builder. Figure 6-2 illustrates method of cutting the skirt to allow it to round the corners smoothly.

If fir plywood is your choice for the large surfaces, finish it with a prime coat of Firzite, which will tame the fir grain, followed by sanding and two coats of white alkyd enamel.

RECREATION ROOM BAR

No family rec room is complete without a service bar from which refreshments can be served—whether soft drinks for a teen-age group or more potent concoctions for the adults of the family. In addition to the utility of a bar, it is also a focal point around which group activity may swirl in the course of a social gathering.

These reasons are more than sufficient to make a project of this sort important as well as desirable. In layout and construction, it is almost equivalent to a small kitchen. Figure 6-3 shows two features that give it the kitchen resemblance, but are really options that may be omitted by the prospective builder.

Sink And Plumbing

The first of these is the sink and its plumbing. While a bar cannot really be considered complete without one, it has been deliberately put into the "option" category. A bar that is to be constructed in a basement rec room may produce a problem with drainage of waste water if the existing drain line to which the sink would be tied is not sufficiently low. A homeowner determined to overcome even this handicap may resort to attaching a pump to the sink drain, which will force waste uphill to the drain.

Water supply for the sink is conventional. Tees may be cut into present lines and pipes extended to the new location. Note that pipes may be passed through the wall behind the short ell of the counter, if they cannot be conveniently brought in another way. We will not go into further details, however, since the reader may very well opt to hire a plumber for that aspect of the work. It is

Fig. 6-1. This bar is a great addition to the family room.

195

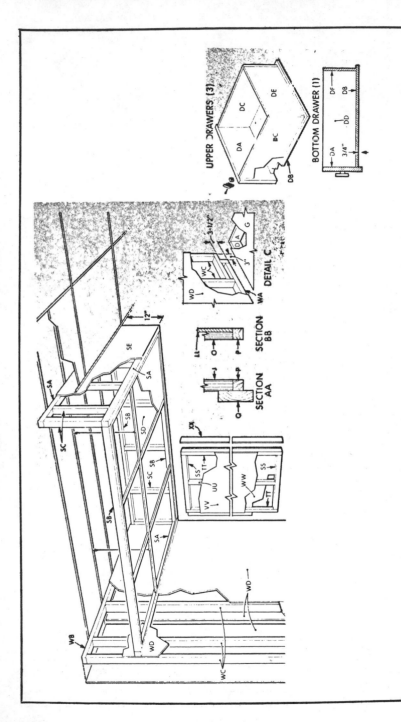

UPPER DRAWERS (3)

BOTTOM DRAWER (1)

DETAIL C

SECTION BB

SECTION AA

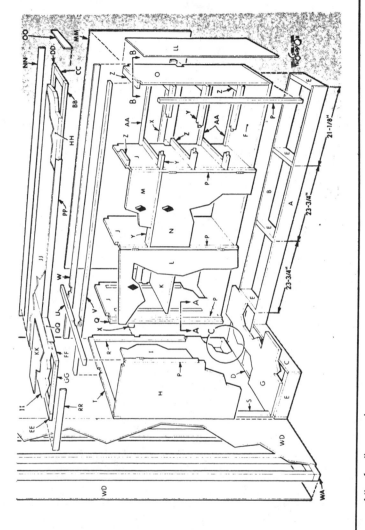

Fig. 6-2. Diagram of the family room bar.

197

Table 6-1. Materials Needed to Make the Family Room Bar.

A. Base Rail, 1 pc, ¾ × 3½ × 89¼"
B. Base Rail, 1 pc, ¾ × 3½ × 90"
C. Base Rail, 1 pc, ¾ × 3½ × 27"
D. Base Rail, 1 pc, ¾ × 3½ × 44¼"
E. Spacers, 5 pcs, 1½ × 3½ × 16½"
F. Bottom, 1 pc, ¾ × 23 × 72½"
G. Bottom, 1 pc, ¾ × 20¼ × 47"
H. Side, 1 pc, ¾ × 20¼ × 36"
I. Door, 1 pc, ¾ × 22½ × 35¼"
J. Dividers, 3 pcs, ¾ × 23 × 35¼"
K. Shelves, 1 pc, ¾ × 22½ × 22½"
L. Door, 1 pc, ¾ × 23 × 35¼"
M. False Drawer, 1 pc, ¾ × 23 × 8¼"
N. Door, 1 pc, ¾ × 23 × 26¼"
O. Side, 1 pc, ½ × 23 × 35¼"
P. Facing Strips, 5 pcs, ¾ × ¾ × 35¼"
Q. Upright, 1 pc, ¾ × 2½ × 35¼"
R. Upright, 1 pc, ¾ × 1½ × 33¾"
S. Upright, 1 pc, ¾ × 1½ × 33¾"
T. Rail, 1 pc, ¾ × 1½ × 47¼"
U. Rail, 1 pc, ¾ × 1½ × 48"
V. Rail, 1 pc, ¾ × 1½ × 92¾"
W. Rail, 1 pc, ¾ × 1½ × 92¾"
X. Rail, 1 pc, ¾ × 1½ × 92¾"
Y. Front Rails, 4 pcs, ¾ – 1½ × 23"
Z. Slides, 8 pcs, ¾ × 1½ × 22¼"
AA. Draw Stops, 3 pcs, ¾ × ¾ × 23"

BB. Counter Base, 1 pc, ¾ × 1½ × 91¼"
CC. Counter Base, 1 pc, ¾ × 1½ × 20½"
DD. Counter Base, 1 pc, ¾ × 1½ × 92¾"
EE. Counter Base, 1 pc, ¾ × 1½ × 46"
FF. Counter Base, 1 pc, ¾ × 1½ × 24"
GG. Counter Base, 1 pc, ¾ × 1½ × 17¾"
HH. Counter, 1 pc, 1" × 23½ × 72"
II. Counter, 1 pc, 1" × 20¾ × 47½"
JJ. Laminate, 1 pc, 24 × 93"
KK. Laminate, 1 pc, 24 × 21"
LL. Hardboard, 23 × 36"
MM. Hardboard, 96 × 36"
NN. Hardboard, 96 × 1¾"
OO. Hardboard, 23½ × 1¾"
PP. Hardboard, 72¼ × 1¾"
QQ. Hardboard, 24 × 1¾"
RR. Hardboard, 20¾ × 1¾"
SS. Frames, 2 pcs, 1½ × 1½ × 17¾"
TT. Frames, 2 pcs, 1½ × 1½" × to suit
UU. Frames, 1 pc, 1½ × 1½" × to suit
VV. ¼" Hardboard, 21" × to suit
WW. ¼" Hardboard, 24" × to suit
XX. ¼" Hardboard, 1½" to suit
WALL
WA. Sole Plate, 1 pc, 1½ × 2½ × 67½"
WB. Header, 1 pc, 1½ × 2½ × 71¾"
WC. Studs, 6 pcs, 1½ × 2½ × to suit

WD. 3 pcs, ¼ × 48 × 96" sheets
SOFFIT
SA[1] 1½ × 1½" Framing, 3 pcs, 71¾"
SB[2] 1½ × 1½' Framing, 3 pcs, 68¾"
SC[3] 1½ × 1½" Framing, 11 pcs
S4 ¼" Hardboard, 1 pc, 72"
S5 ¼" Hardboard, 1 pc, 71¾"
SC[3], S4, S5 Height to suit

CEILING PANELING
24 ft. of Wall Angle
1 pc, 72" Main Runner
4 pcs, 48" Cross Piece
3 pcs, 24" × 48" Panels
3 pcs, 24" × 24" panels

DRAWERS
DA Front, 4 pcs, 8⅛ × 22⅞ × ¾"
DB Bottom, 4 pcs, 22¼ × 22⅞ × ½"
DC Sides, 6 pcs, 7 11/16 × 21¾ × ½"
DD Sides, 2 pcs, 6 15/16 × 21¾ × ½"
DE Back, 3 pcs, 7 11/16 × 21 × ½"
DF Back, 1 pc, 6 15/16 × 21 × ½"
3 Magnetic catches for doors
3 Sets of 1½" Butt Hinges
4 Adjustable Shelf Strips, 14"
Clips for above

suggested, though, that if you plan to do so, consult with him before beginning any construction.

Refrigerator Space

The second optional feature, more easily provided and just as easily eliminated, is space for a small refrigerator. There is no doubt that to have one handy is a great conveneince. It is another matter to consider it a necessity. In the event that floor space for the bar area is limited, but a refrigerator is still desired, we suggest investigation of a built-in under-the-counter type. Information on these can often be obtained at larger appliance dealers. To include such a unit would, of course, require a change in the layout of the cabinets. In the same manner, a dishwasher could also be built in, for a truly deluxe bar.

In this project, refrigerator space was provided by the simple expedient of placing the counter and cabinets at an appropriate distance from the wall adjacent to the stairway, creating a nook of the correct width. It would have been possible to simply eliminate the space—and the refrigerator—allowing the unit to be moved that much closer to the stairwell, a consideration to be remembered when floor space is at a premium.

Other Options

As another option, especially useful when the refrigerator is omitted, the wall-and-a-half partitition may be dropped too. Actually, the reader may want to eliminate this even when a refrigerator is included. It will depend largely on room layout and personal needs. The wall can be most useful in certain layouts; as an example, it may hide from view an unfinished portion of the basement, or provide privacy on the path to a lavatory, or act as a vestibule of sorts when there is direct access from outdoors to the room.

Another option is the overhead soffit which has the effect of setting the bar area off from the rest of the room—in feeling creating a room within a room. Visually strong, it has no real function but in one way, is an asset. By creating a dropped ceiling area, it is possible to recess lighting fixtures as desired. If you decide to add a dropped ceiling to your plan, by all means use a ceiling material that will match the rest of the room. Otherwise the contrast may be so strong it will destroy the intimate feeling of the bar.

Fig. 6-3. You can unwind at the bar in your recreation room.

Building the Bar

The construction of the unit may be considered in three sections: the cabinet with its base, the partition, and the soffit.

The base of the cabinet is constructed first using the rails (A-D) and the spacers (E), and the rest is built on top of it. Follow Figure 6-4 and Table 6-2 for dimensions and attachments. To insure the strongest support for the base and for the entire structure, joints should be glued as well as nailed. Three-inch baseboard should be attached to the base after the cabinet is built.

The interior of the cabinet has four storage sections. In Fig. 6-4 the section to the far right is composed of four drawers for smaller items. The other three areas are arranged differently and are closed by hinged doors (N, L and I) and magnetic door stops hold the door in place when closed. The door of the closest section to the drawers is shorter than the other two due to the false drawer (M) located between it and the countertop. This is needed in case of plumbing repairs to the sink located directly above it and can be omitted should you choose not to have a sink. The next section has a shelf (K) dividing the storage area in half. The last section has been deliberately left blank for the builder to do with what he wishes and is much larger than the others.

This is just one way of modeling the interior of the cabinet. There are many variations you can choose from to suit your own needs. For instance, you may wish to use two of the sections for drawer space instead of just one. Figure 6-4 gives a basic idea of what can be done, rather than what must be done.

The countertop (JJ) shown is plastic-laminate surfaced, attached to chipboard with contact cement. The chipboard is nailed to

Table 6-2. Required Materials For the Recreation Room Bar.

LIST OF MATERIALS	
A. 1 pc, ¾ × 45 × 72″	M. 1 pc, ¾ × 11¼ × 44¼″
B. 1 pc, ¾ × 16½ × 44¼″	N. 2 pcs, ¾ × 1½ × 44¼″
C. 1 pc, ¾ × 30½ × 44¼″	O. 1 pc, ¾ × ¾ × 110″
D. 1 pc, ¾ × 38 × 72″	P. 1 pc, ¾ × ¾ × 60″
E. 3 pcs, ¾ × 30½ × 70½″	Q. 1 pc, ¾ × ¾ × 14″
F. 3 pcs, ¾ × 14 × 17¼″	R. 1 pc, ¾ × ¾ × 10½″
G. 1 pc, 1½ × 3½ × 68″	S. 2 Triangular Blocks, ¾ × ¾ × 14″
H. 1 pc, 1½ × 3½ × 61½″	T. 7 Triangular Blocks, ¾ × ¾ × 13¼″
I. 1 pc, 1½ × 3½ × 11″	U. 2 pcs, ¾ × ¾ × 16½″
J. 1 pc, 1½ × 3½ × 26½″	V. 2 pcs, ¾ × ¾ × 10½″
K. 1 pc, 1½ × 3½ × 14″	W. Plastic Laminate
L. 1 pc, 1½ × 3½ × 5″	X. 1½″ wide Plastic Laminate

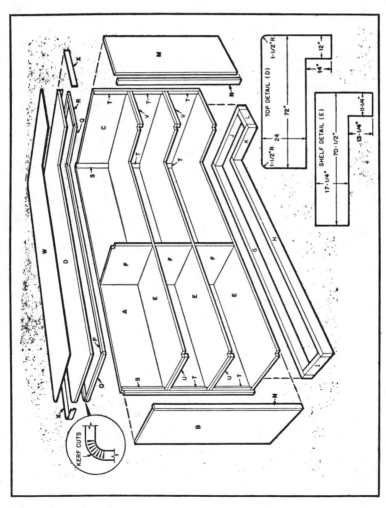

Fig. 6-4. Construction details for the recreation room bar.

the frame of the cabinet. Many other materials can be used for the countertop including butcher board, tile and linoleum.

Build a partition wall between the cabinet and the soffit, nail up the studs and then nail ¼" hardboard to them. The wall covers one side entirely (left, in Fig. 6-4) and turns into a part of the other side, directly in line with the largest storage area.

The soffit framing is nailed to the studs in the wall and the beams in the ceiling. The ceiling paneling on the underside of the soffit is regular acoustical ceiling paneling that was picked to match the paneling on the ceiling of the room. Individual panels fit into grooves in the channels on the underside of the soffit that are hung by wires from the frame; ¼" hardboard is nailed to the frame on the outside of the soffit.

HOSPITALITY CABINET

This attractive built-in wall cabinet is basically an oversized box, 8' long and 18" from front to back (Fig. 6-5). It is made of birch veneered plywood stained to look like walnut. The four corners formed by E-D-E-D are mitered and fastened with glue and three 2" countersunk angle braces on the inside (Fig. 6-6). The central partition is fastened in the same way as the corners with the braces in the shelf compartment behind the sliding doors. Table 6-3 lists materials.

All the forward edges of the plywood are covered with birch veneer tape stained to match the top and sides as well as the front of the swingdown door (B). The insides surface of this door is covered with white Formica (A) as is the shelf behind it (G). This shelf is the top of a dummy compartment and rests on cleats or small angle braces. The front of this compartment is covered by a dummy panel of the same construction as the sliding doors (H).

The shelf (F) with the deep cutout is adjustable and can be moved up and down. The odd looking thing above the cutout of the shelf is a fluorescent lamp. The fabric on the doors is glued to ¼" hardboard held in position by ⅜" quarter rounds glued and nailed to the inner sides of the frame (I-I-J-J). The tops and bottoms of the door frames (J-J) are slotted to fit on the ridges of the metal tracks on which they slide. The back of the cabinet (C) is ¼" birch veneered plywood glued and nailed with brads to the rabbeted back edges of the top, bottom and ends (D-D-E-E).

The entire cabinet rests on six 5" angle braces whose vertical arms go up behind the cabinet and are fastened to the studs behind

Fig. 6-5. Dispense drinks from this easily made wall cabinet.

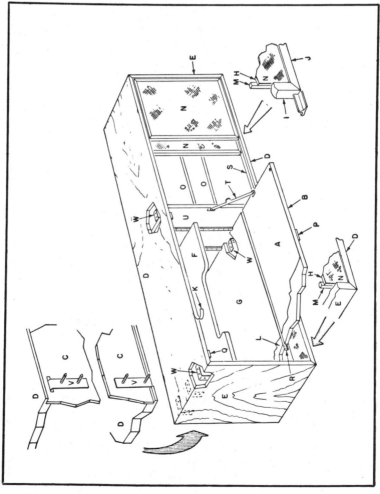

Fig. 6-6. Diagram of the hospitality cabinet.

205

Table 6-3. Materials For the Hospitality Cabinet.

A 1/16 × 28½ × 46⅞" Formica B 1 pc, ¾ × × 28½ × 46⅞" C 1 pc, ⅜ × 94½ × 34½" D 2 pcs, ¾ × 18 × 96" E 2 pcs, ¾ × 18 × 36" F 1 pc, ¾ × 12½ × 46¼" G 1/16 × 16½ × 46⅞" Formica H 2 pcs, ⅛ × 23 × 33⅜" I 4 pcs, ¾ × ½ × 34⅜ " J 4 pcs, ¾ × ½ × 24" K 30 ft. of ¾" wood tape L 1 pc, ¾ × 16½ × 46⅞"	M 38 ft. of ¼" Quarter Round N Fabric, 7 sq. ft. O 2 pcs, ¾ × 15⅞ × 46½" P 1 pc, Handle Q 2 pcs, Magnetic Catches R 1 pc, Piano Hinge, 48" S 1 pair Tracks, each 24" t 1 pair Hinges U 1 pc, ¾ × 18 × 34½" V 8 Braces ¾ × 5" W 24 Braces ½ × 3"

the wall paneling with 3" flathead screws. Smaller angle braces (3") are fastened to the studs and the underside of the top (D).

The finish can be several coats of paste wax applied after staining and buffed to a soft glow or two coats of varnish each of which has been sanded and the top one waxed.

SERVING BAR

The attractive built-in serving bar shown should offer no difficulties to the home handyman (Fig. 6-7). The woodgrain paneling on the walls is the standard ¼" material applied with usual panel adhesive. However, the paneling on the cabinets is laminated to ½" plywood with contact cement. Perhaps the easiest way to cut the cabinet doors and their surrounds is to glue a 4 × 8 sheet of paneling to a 4 × 8 sheet of plywood and then cut the doors out with a saber saw. See Table 6-4 for materials.

The floor cabinets have a single framework mounted on a pair of 2 × 4s (Q), one of which is fastened to the wall behind the cabinets (Fig. 6-8) The lower and upper shelves in the base cabinets are ¾" plywood (M) notched to fit around the front posts (N). Magnetic catches on the front edges of shelves are the easiest way to hold the doors in place.

Table 6-4. Materials Needed to Build the Serving Bar.

A. 4 pcs., 1½" × 1½ × 8' B. 5 pcs, 1½ × 1½ × 5" (2 pcs. not shown) C. 5 pcs, 1½ × 1½ × 46½" D. 8" × 8" × ½" (plywood) E. 4' × 8' × ⅜" (gypsum board) F. 16 ft. of 2" cove molding G. 8 ft. of ½" quarter round H. 3 pcs., 10 × 47 × ¾" I. 2 pcs., 1½ × 1½ × 47" J. 2 pcs., ¾ × 1½ × 10" K. 2 pcs., 10½ × 37 × ½" (plywood) L. 46 × ½" (plywood) M. 2 pcs., 25" × 8' × ¾ " N. 4 pcs., 1½ × 2½ × 31¾". O. 4 pcs., 1½ × 2½ × 24¾" (2 pcs., not shown)	P. 1 pc., 8 × 26½" × ¾" Q. 2 pcs., 1½" × 3½" × 8' R. 6 pcs., 1½ × 1½ × 28⅝" (2 pcs. not shown) S. 4 pcs., 1½ × 1½ × 24" T. 1 pc., 1½" × 8 U. 1 pc., 1½" × 2½" × 7' 9½" V. 2 pcs., 1½ × 2½ × 22½" (1 pc., not shown) W. 1 p., 1' × ¾" × 8' X. 1 pc., Formica edging, 1½" × 8' Y. 1 pc., Formica top, 26½" × 8' Z. 12 ft. of 2" cove molding AA. 34 × 21 × ¾" BB. 31¾" × 14-5/16 × ¾" CC. 4 pcs., 3" angle irons

Fig. 6-7. This serving bar should present no major problems for the do-it-yourselfer.

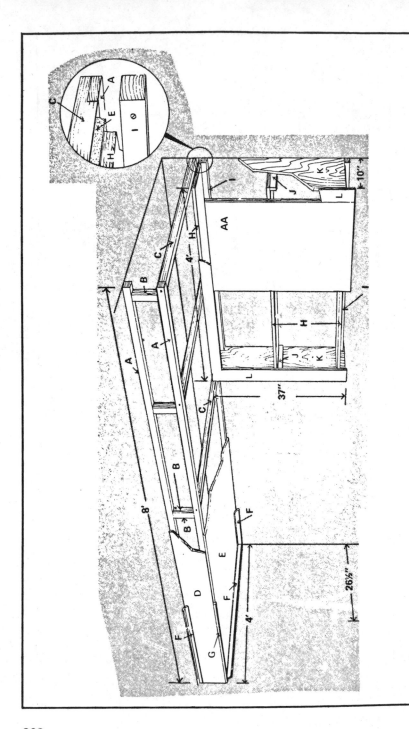

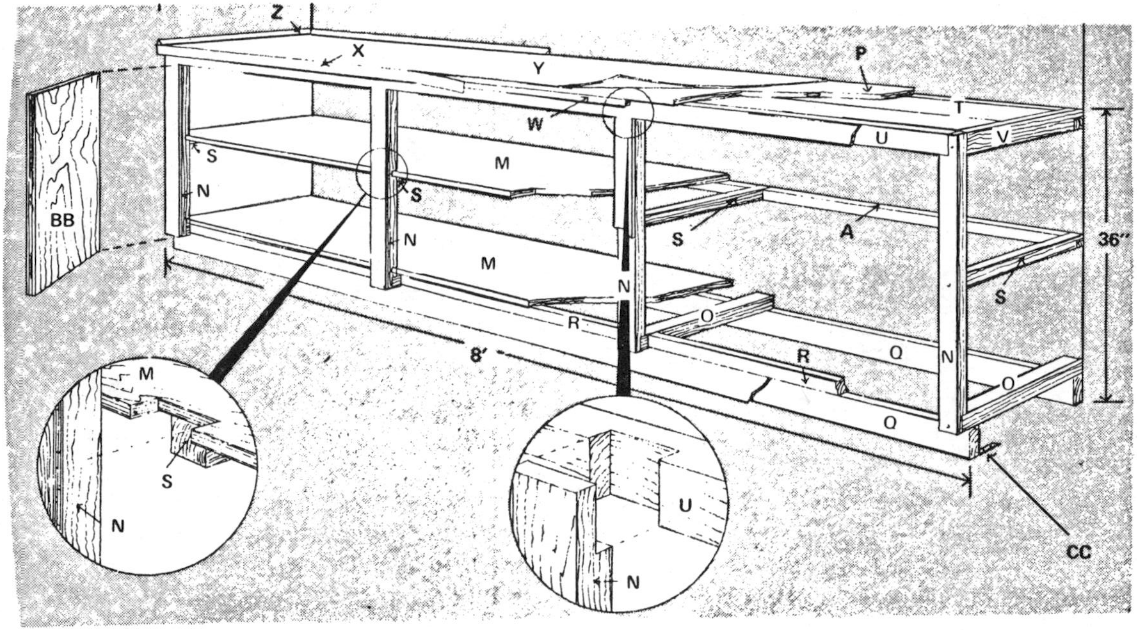

Fig. 6-8. Diagram of the serving bar.

209

The dropped ceiling is a framework (A-B-C) of 2 × 2s fastened to studs at the back and to ceiling joists. The strip of paneling at the front of the dropped ceiling is glued to ½″ plywood. The recessed lights in the ceiling that show through the plasterboard of the dropped area are optional. If you prefer something lighter than the plasterboard (E), use ¼″ hardboard painted white.

The wall cabinet has no framework and is made of ½″ plywood to which the paneling is glued. Two long celats (I), one under the top of the cabinet and the other underneath the bottom shelf, support the cabinet and are screwed to the studs of the wall. Nails and glue are used to fasten the cabinet to the cleats. Shelves of the wall cabinet are made of ¾″ plywood supported at the ends by cleats (J). Here, too, magnetic catches are recommended to hold the doors in place. Forward edges of the shelves should be painted to harmonize with the color of the paneling.

The countertop of the serving bar is a lustrous black plastic laminate glued to ¾″ plywood of the top with contact cement.

WINE RACK

With its slim functional lines, this wine rack will fit almost any decor (Fig. 6-9). The wine bottle themselves, with their different labels, colors and shapes, provide the decorative appeal of this simple rack. It is held together with dowels and glued joints; no nails or screws are used.

The original was made of white oak, with darker walnut plugs concealing the exposed dowel holes used to provide a decorative contrast. Although the ¾″ oak material is usually fairly easy to find, you will probably have to order the 2 × 2s from a larger building supply center, or a woodworking specialty house.

Making Crosspieces

First make the crosspieces that hold the bottles. See Fig. 6-10. Although you can use a saber saw on the cutouts, a simpler way is to use a flycutter in a drill press. With it, you can cut the arcs very smooth so they won't require any additional sanding. Mark the center line on a 5″ wide board, then use the flycutter to cut complete circles 3″ in diameter. Rip the stock down the middle to make two crosspieces. Use the same method to make the front crosspieces with their 1½″ diameter holes.

When you use a flycutter, make sure you have the stock clamped tightly to the drill press table (Fig. 6-11). If the stock whirls loose, it can be dangerous.

Fig. 6-9. This rack has room for a lot of bottles.

After you have made four sets of crosspieces, sand them thoroughly. Then cut the end support posts to the proper size. Lay the two back end posts on a flat work surface and position the back crosspieces in place. Mark their locations and mark for the dowel holes (Fig. 6-12).

It's a good idea to number each piece. For example, mark "A" on the top corner of a post and "A-2", "A-3", and so on for the ends

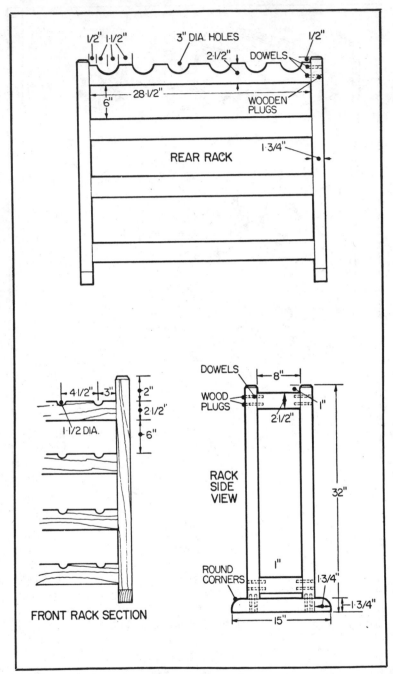

Fig. 6-10. Construction details for the wine rack.

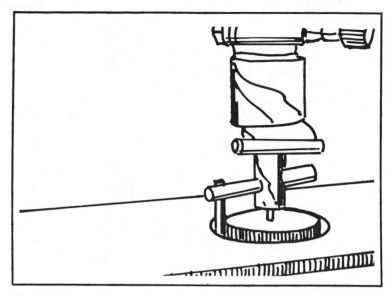

Fig. 6-11. Cutouts for wine bottles are made with circle cutter or flycutter in a drill press. Then the piece of stock is split down the middle on a table saw. Do it twice to make four back crosspieces.

of the back crosspieces that fit against that post. With as many pieces as this unit has, and with all the dowel holes, you can easily get a mismatch. Imagine glue running everywhere as you try to bang the pieces apart and find the right piece to fit in place.

Use a doubling jig to drill the dowel holes. This assures the holes will be bored in the proper location for each piece. Although the doweling jig also can be used to bore the holes in the uprights, you can do it an easier way. Locate a center line, mark locations of the dowels just as you would for the doweling jig—but bore the holes with a Forstner bit in a drill press (Fig. 6-13). Drill from one side until the point of the bit protrudes through the opposite; then turn the stock over and finish the hole from that side. This prevents splintering out the stock on the finished side.

Cut dowels 2″ in length from a ⅜″ dowel rod. Round off ends and cut a glue channel down one side, using a grinder or sanding disc. You can also buy precut dowels with a spiral glue slot already made.

Assembling The Rack

To assemble the rack, begin doweling and gluing, starting with the back part. Squirt a little glue into a dowel hole and tap a

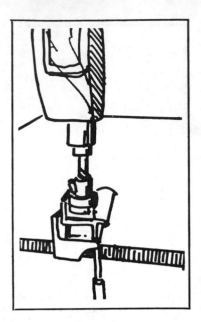

Fig. 6-12. Mark locations of dowels after all pieces have been cut to size and, using a doweling jig, position the drill bit for boring holes.

dowel in part way. Position the first crosspiece, tap the dowel again gently to hold it and then start another piece.

When all the pieces have been started in one end post, put glue in the holes in the opposite end post and place it in position, until all

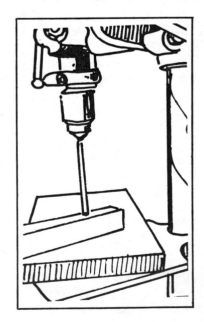

Fig. 6-13. Cut holes in side supports on a drill press fitted with a Forstner bit, first from one side and then from the other.

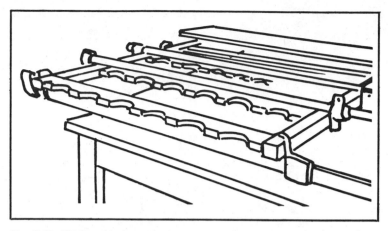

Fig. 6-14. Fill dowel holes with glue, tap the dowels in and clamp the frame together. After cleaning off excess glue carefully, reset clamps and begin tightening them evenly until the frame has been squared.

dowels have been started in place (Fig. 6-14). Position two clamps on the work surface, one for the top crosspiece and one for the bottom one. Place unit on top of clamps and position two more clamps on top. Gently draw the unit together, turning each clamp equally.

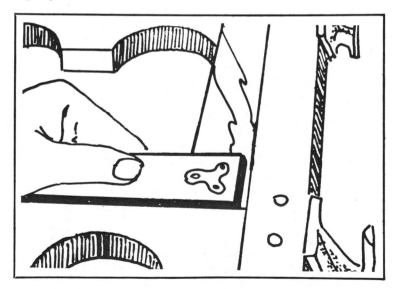

Fig. 6-15. Square up frames before you allow the glue to set. Shift it around a bit to get it perfectly square in the clamps due to the number of long, thin pieces involved.

215

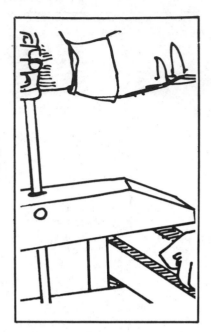

Fig. 6-16. Bottom pieces are cut on a band saw and sanded smooth. Then they are doweled in place.

When it has been drawn together, remove it from the clamps and, using a cloth with warm water, immediately wash away excess glue. White glue or carpenter's glue will stain oak blue or black if any comes in contact with metal, such as the clamps.

Place the unit back in the clamps, check to make sure it is square, and snug up clamps to hold it securely (Fig. 6-15). Allow it to cure thoroughly, then remove it from the clamps and do the front in the same way. Then position the side stretchers in place and dowel, glue and clamp them as you did the front and back.

When the unit has cured properly, cut ⅜" walnut plugs using a plug cutter in a drill press. Place a bit of glue in each dowel hole and tap the plugs in place. Allow the gluing to cure properly, then use a belt sander to cut plugs down flush with the wood surface, blending all surfaces smooth. Cut bottoms to proper size and shape, glue and dowel them in place (Fig. 6-16). Bevel the top ends of the unit, sand it thoroughly and finish it to suit.

The wine rack shown was given several coats of lacquer, sprayed on. However, you might prefer a hand-rubbed oil finish, which will make this style of furniture particularly beautiful.

Chapter 7
Bedroom

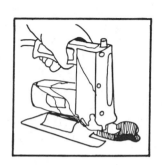

You can brighten up a dull bedroom with some beautiful furniture projects. A Shaker bed, bedroom table, and plans for twin beds, shelves and bookcases are some of the possibilities.

SHAKER BED

This Shaker bed, the original of which is in the Shaker Museum in Chatham, New York, is extremely simple in its basic structure (Fig. 7-1). The side rails (D) and cross pieces (C) are joined to the legs (A-B) in simple butt joints reinforced with strong steel bolts 6″ long and ½″ thick. See Table 7-1 for materials.

Holes for the bolts are drilled through the square part of the legs and into the end grain of the side rails and cross pieces. Another hole is then drilled at right angles to the lengthwise hole to provide space for the insertion of the nut and its washer as shown in Fig. 7-2. Of course, you can simply use a long lag bolt which requires no nut, but a machine bolt and nut has more holding power than a lag bolt.

The head of the bolt must be countersunk and the round opening enlarged with a chisel or router to form a rectangular shape for a plug to cover the hole in the leg. The plug need only be about ¼″ thick and should be cut from end grain so that it will stain darker than the surrounding wood and look like a plug.

The little pegs on the top of the bed frame were originally used to anchor ropes that were laced back and forth across the width and

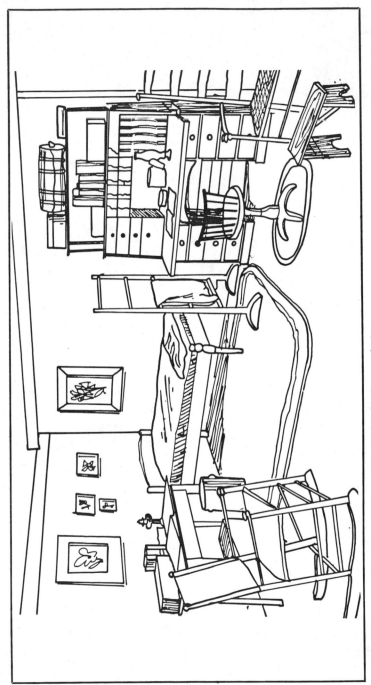

Fig. 7-1. This delightful bed is one of many fine Shaker furniture projects.

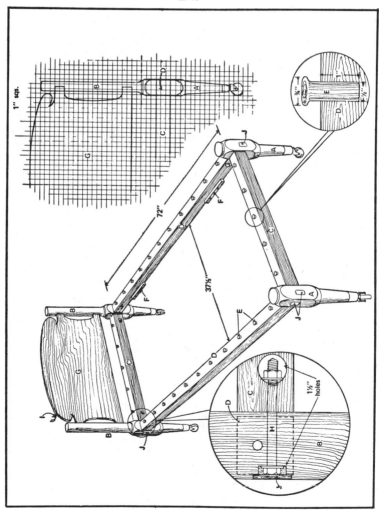

Fig. 7-2. Construction details for the Shaker bed.

down the length of the frame. The ropes, of course, functioned as "springs" for the mattress.

The cleats (F) on the inside of the rails (D) are supposed to support a bedspring. The usual box spring which is about 6" high should not be used here because it will raise the mattress too far above the rails. The flat type of spring commonly used in metal folding cots is best for the purpose.

The headboard (G) should be cut from a piece of ¾" plywood, preferably with a birch veneer facing. Use birch veneer tape to conceal the edges of the plywood. Note the two points on each side of the headboard which form tenons that engage slots in the upper parts of the adjacent legs. Note also that the legs at the foot of the bed are really the same as those next to the headboard except for the round upper extensions. (See Fig. 7-2.) Since the casters cannot be duplicated, use modern 4" casters instead.

SHAKER BEDROOM TABLE

Made of pine, this little bedroom table has all the simplicity of line so characteristic of Shaker design (Fig. 7-3). This simplicity also extends to its construction, so you'll find it an easy project to make. Table 7-2 lists materials.

The top (A) is a solid piece of pine which overhangs the sides by 3" on each end and at the front and back. The back (D) and sides (C) are rabbeted and fit into grooves cut into the upper parts of the legs (B). The three front rails (E-F-G) are half-lapped at each end and, like the sides and back, fit into grooves in the upper parts of the legs and are pinned with ⅛" dowels or pegs.

Pine corner braces (I) are used to reinforce the corners. Glue is applied to the ends of the braces before the center screw is

Table 7-1. Materials Required to Make the Shaker Bed.

A-2 pcs. 3½ × 3½ × 18"
B-2 pcs. 3½ × 3½ × 39"
C-2 pcs. 3 × 3 × 37½"
D-2 pcs. 3 × 3 × 72"
E-32 dowels ¾ × 1½"
F-4 pcs. 1 × 1 × 8"
G-¾ plywood 41 × 21"
H-8 bolts ½ × 6', 8 nuts, 16 washers
I-¾" veneer strip
J-8 pcs. ¼ × 2 × 1¼"

Fig. 7-3. This little bedroom table is made of pine.

driven home. Note that the inside corner edge of the legs is cut back where the brace crosses them so that the screw can go in straight.

The braces provide additional gluing surface when fastening the top (A) to the front rail (E), back and sides. Of course, glue should also be applied to the tops of D, C, and E. Two screws should be driven through each of the four top braces (I) into the underside of the top.

The legs are tapered on the inner sides. Note the curve in the two front legs where they meet the front bottom rail (G) as shown in the leg detail.

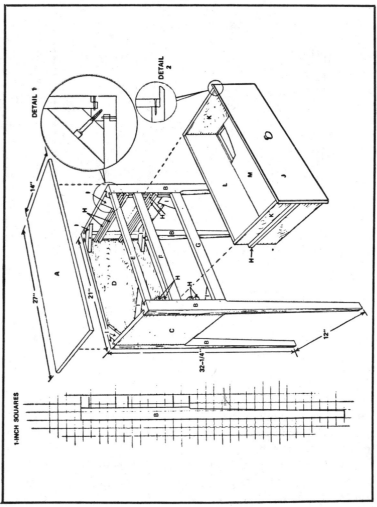

Fig. 7-4. Diagram of the Shaker bedroom table.

Table 7-2. Required Materials For the Shaker Bedroom Table.

A. 1 pc, ¾ × 14 × 27″	J. 1 pc, ¾ × 18½ × 6″
B. 4 pcs, 1½ × 1½ × 32¼″	K. 2 pcs, 1½ × 5½ × 11¼″
C. 2 pcs, ¾ × 9¾ × 13¼″	L. 1 pc, ½ × 5½ × 16″
D. 1 pc, ¾ × 18¾ × 13¼″	M. 1 pc, 3/16 × 16½ × 11¼″
E. 1 pc, ¾ × 18¾ × 1″	Top Drawer (not shown)
F. 1 pc, ¾ × 18¾ × 1½″	JT. 1 pc, ¾ × 18½ × 3¾ (front)
G. 1 pc, ¾ × 18¾ × 2″	KT. 2 pcs, ½ × 3¼ × 11¼″ (sides)
H. 12 pcs, ½ × ½ × 11¼″	LT. 1 pc, ½ × 3¼ × 16″ (back)
I. 8 pcs, ¾ × 1½ × 4¾″	MT. 1 pc, 3/16 × 16½ × 11¼ (bottom)

The drawer fronts are ¾″ thick and are deeply rabbeted to receive the sides (K and KT) which are fastened to the fronts (J and JT) with nails and glue as shown in Detail 2 of Fig. 7-4. The drawer guides (H) are simply ½″ square strips inside. The drawer guides should be rubbed with paraffin (candle wax) or sprayed with a silicone lubricant. Finish can include a light birch stain and a shellac or clear varnish coating.

TWIN BEDS AND SHELVES

These modernistic twin beds are extremely simple and it shouldn't take you long to put the parts together (Fig. 7-5). In fact, the whole project is pretty much of a hammer-and-nail job once the lumber is cut. Refer to Fig. 7-6 and Table 7-3. Each bed is supported at both ends by a rectangular frame (C-D) which has simple butt joints that are joined with 2½″ finishing nails. The two braces (E-E) are also attached with nails. Note that the ends of these braces (E) cover only half of the thickness of the frame sides (D); the other half is covered by the ends of the sides (F). These sides are supported by 3″ angle braces (I) at the bottom and nailed to the ends of the braces (E) with counterset finishing nails. The sides should also be toenailed to the verticals (D).

The bottom of the bed (G) is a piece of ½″ plywood and is supported by cleats (H) along both inner sides of F-F. The upper surface of these cleats (H) should line up with the bottom edge of the top brace (E). Note that there are four angle braces (J) along the bottom edge of the top brace (E) on which the ends of the bed bottom (G) rest. These angle braces must line up with the top surfaces of the side cleats (H) to assure that the bed bottom will be evenly supported all around.

The bed bottom is rather high inside the sides and is made for a 4″ foam rubber or urethan mattress. The shelves (B) between the

Fig. 7-5. Shown are two handsome beds and a simple set of shelves for your kids.

beds reach from ceiling to floor. They are simply nailed through the sides (A-A) with finishing nails that are counterset and puttied. The side against the wall should be nailed through the plasterboard to a stud behind the wall. A cleat (K) anchors the front to the floor.

TWIN BEDS, BOOKCASES AND DESK

This is one of those projects that makes the average homeowner feel that it's a job for a professional carpenter (Fig. 7-7). Yet, if you analyze the plan on the opposite page you'll see that it's much simpler than you think and that you really don't need any great professional skill to make it.

Practically all of it is made of ¾" plywood stained brown to simulate walnut (Table 7-4). The beds are simply boxes joined at

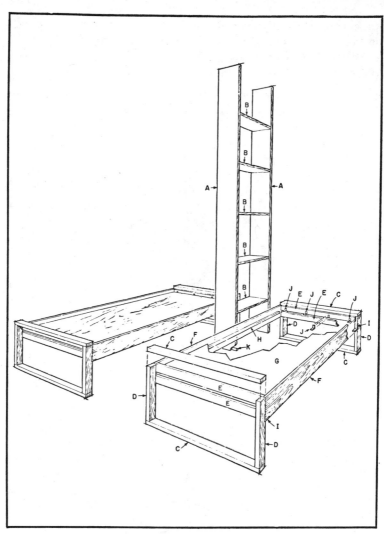

Fig. 7-6. Sketch of the twin beds and shelving.

Table 7-3. Materials Needed to Make One Bed.

A. 2 pcs, ¾ × 9½ × 96"	G. 1 pc, ½ × 37½ × 70½"
B. 5 pcs, ¾ × 9½ × 30"	H. 2 pcs, 1 × 1 × 88½"
C. 4 pcs, 1⅝ × 2⅝ × 39"	I. 4 pcs, angle irons 3"
D. 4 pcs, 1⅝ × 2⅝ × 19"	J. 8 pcs, angle irons 1½"
E. 4 pcs, ¾ × 2½ × 37½"	K. 1 pc, quarter round 9½"
F. 2 pcs, ¾ × 6 × 72"	

the corners with finishing nails and white glue. Although not shown in the plan, each corner is reinforced inside with 3″ right angle steel braces, three to a corner. Each bed is also reinforced by cross pieces G and a central partition (E) (Fig. 7-8).

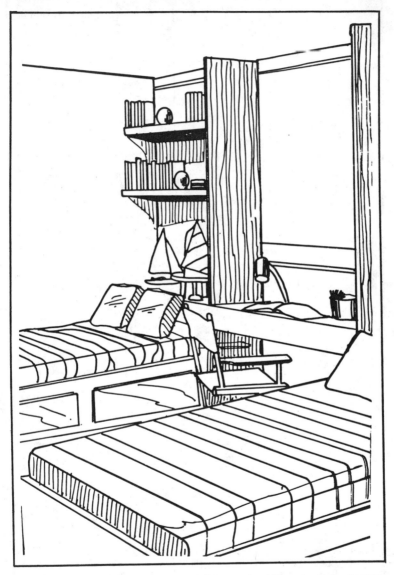

Fig. 7-7. It's not as hard as you may think to construct these beds, bookcases and desk.

The cross pieces, the partition, and the cleats (F) all around the inside of the bed support the big sheet of plywood (I) on which the 6″ foam mattress will rest. It is fastened down with finishing nails and glue.

Note the large sheet K which unites the bed and the bookcase in one unit. Not only does this sheet provide a headboard for each bed, but it also stiffens and reinforces the lower part of each bookcase.

The bookcases are further strengthened by shelves (J) nailed through the sides (A) with finishing nails, and even further strengthended with white glue.

The two drawers under the bed ride on the cross bars (H) and are kept in line by the guide bars (W) which move inside the cross bars mentioned above. Note the detail of the drawer fronts (V), which have no knobs but instead have finger grooves under the lower front edges.

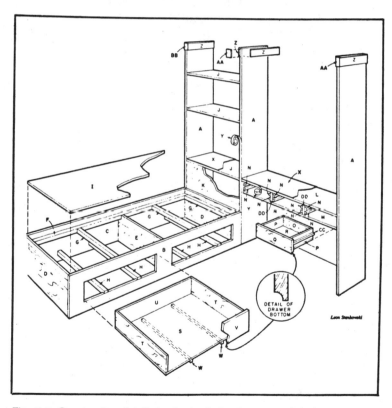

Fig. 7-8. Construction details for the beds, bookcases and desk.

Table 7-4. Required Materials For the Beds, Bookcases and Desk.

A. 4 pcs, ¾ × 18 × 96"	K. 2 pcs, ¾ × 29 × 40"	U. 4 pcs. ½ × 6¾ × 31"
B. 2 pcs, ¾ × 17 × 77½"	L. 1 pc. ¾ × 18 × 39"	V. 4 pcs. ¾ × 9 × 33"
C. 2 pcs, ¾ × 17 × 77½"	M. 1 pc. ¾ × 17¼ × 39"	W. 8 pcs. ¾ × ¾ × 30"
D. 4 pcs, ¾ × 17 × 40"	N. 12 pcs. ¾ × ¾ × 17¼"	X. Plastic Top
E. 2 pcs, ¾ × 15¼ × 40"	O. 3 pcs. ½ × 4 × 10½"	Y. Edge STrips
F. 4 pcs, 1½ × 1½ × 76"	P. 6 pcs. ½ × 4 × 17"	Z. 6 pcs. ¼ × 2½ × 18"
G. 4 pcs, 1½ × 1½ × 37"	Q. 3 pcs. ¾ × 5½ × 13"	AA. 2 pcs. ¼ × 1¼ × 2½"
H. 8 pcs, 1½ × 1½ × 40¾"	R. 3 pcs. ½ × 11½ × 17"	BB. 2 pcs. ¼ × 1 × 2½"
I. 2 pcs, ¾ × 40 × 76"	S. 4 pcs ½ × 30 × 31"	CC. 6 pcs. ¾ × ¾ × 17"
J. 6 pcs, ¾ × 18 × 40"	T. 8 pcs. ½ × 6¾ × 30"	DD. 2 pcs. ¾ × 4½ × 17¼"

The verticals of the bookcases (A) are attached to the walls with 3" right angle braces and screws. The shelves DD and J are dadoed into the verticals (A) and the edges of the joints are covered with thin strips of wood tape (Y).

Unless you are using stain on plywood with a hardwood veneer, your best finish is paint. Seal the wood with a shellac diluted 50-50 with alcohol. When dry, apply a primer or undercoat for enamel. Sand the primer lightly and remove all dust with tack rag. Then apply the enamel, sand lightly and remove the dust and then apply the final coat of enamel.

Chapter 8
Built-In Units

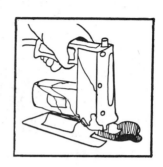

Built-in units are becoming increasingly popular these days. On the following pages are instructions for making desk and cabinet combinations, bunk beds, study centers, closet and bunk bed combinations and a host of others.

SUPERDESK AND STORAGE CABINET COMBO

If you've got two boys in a room you'll find this project a very satisfying way of providing ample storage space for their clothing, toys and athletic equipment as well as splendid desks for school-work (Fig. 8-1).

Desk Tops

The desk tops are extremely easy to make and call for no special skill. See Fig. 8-2 and Table 8-1. The tops (C) consist of the two halves of a standard, hollow, birch veneer door cut down its length with a saw. Each half was laid on top of a pair of cabinets (B and H, D) as shown in Fig. 8-2. The desk tops are fastened to the cabinets by screws driven through the undersides of the cabinet tops into the framework of the hollow door (C).

You may find it necessary to insert some wood blocks between the veneered sheets of the door halves along the edges that touch the wall in order to stiffen the surface at these points because there is no framing left along these back edges. If you find this necessary,

Fig. 8-1. The cabinets and desks are ideal for storage and schoolwork, respectively.

fasten the blocks in place with glue and clamps instead of nails to avoid marring the surface of the top.

Center and Wall Cabinets

The two center cabinets (B) are unfinished furniture purchased at a department store. They are also available from mailorder houses and stores which specialize in unfinished furniture. The overhang of the tops of these two cabinets were cut flush with the sides and fronts. Both cabinets are screwed to each other through the two sides that butt together.

The cabinets at the far ends are made of ¾" plywood with the tops and bottoms rabbeted to the sides and fastened with nails and glue. The sliding doors (H) of these cabinets are made of tempered, perforated harboard and slide in grooves cut into the tops, bottoms and sides (Fig. 8-2). The doors must be slipped into their grooves when the cabinet is assembled. The two wall cabinets, like the two

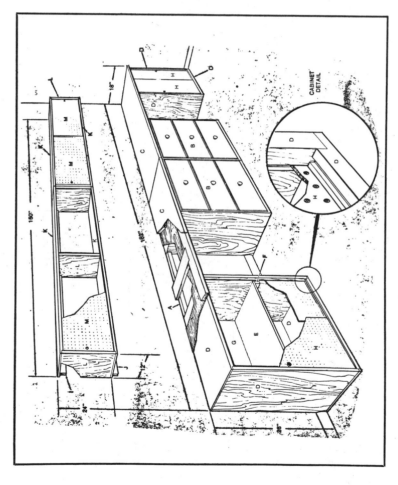

Fig. 8-2. Construction details for the desks and cabinets.

Table 8-1. Materials Needed For the Desks and Cabinets.

A. Two pieces. each: 79 × 2 × 1" (one not shown)	H. Four pieces. each: 26 × 15 × ⅛"
B. Two chests of drawers. each: 28 × 28 × 18"	I. Two pieces. each: 73 × 2 × 1" (one not shown)
C. One standard hollow birch veneer door. 81 × 36 × 1"	J. Two pieces. each: 75 × 2 × 1" (one not shown)
D. Eight pieces. each: 28 × 18 × 1" (one not shown)	K. Four pieces. each: 75 × 12 × 1"
E. two pieces. each: 26 × 16 × ¾" (one not shown)	L. Six pieces. each: 24 × 12 × 1"
F. Four pieces. each: 16 × 2 × 1" (three not shown)	M. Four pieces. each: 38½ × 22 × ⅛" (one not shown)
G. Two pieces. each: 28 × 28 × ⅛" (one not shown)	

end cabinets below them, have no backs and are assembled with rabbet joints and fastened with nails and glue. Both wall cabinets are nailed to cleats (I,J) which are screwed to wall studs. The upper cleat (I) is inside the cabinets. The center partition (L) is nailed through the top and bottom. Both sliding doors (M) are made of perforated hardboard and slide in tracks as shown in Fig. 8-2.

CABINET-DESK COMBO FOR A STUDENT

Here is an attractive combination cabinet and desk (Fig. 8-3). The upper section (A-B-A-D) is made separately with simple butt

Fig. 8-3. This cabinet-desk combination is easy to make.

Table 8-2. Required Materials For the Cabinet-Desk Combination.

A. 4 pcs, ¾ × 9½ × 53¼"	Q. 1 pc, ¼ × 54 × 57"
B. 1 pc, ¾ × 9½ × 57"	R. 2 pcs, ¼ × 16½ × 30"
C. 9 pcs, ¾ × 9½ × 18"	S. 2 pcs, ¾ × 1½ × 15"
D. 3 pcs, ¾ × 1½ × 18"	T. 12 pcs, ¾ × ¾ × 15¼"
E. 6 pcs, ¾ × 1½ × 8¾"	U. 4 pcs, ¾ × ¾ × 12"
F. 3 pcs, ¾ × 18 × 28"	V. 6 pcs, ½ × 4¾ × 8¾"
G. 3 pcs, ¾ × 5 × 18'	W. 3 pcs, ½ × 4¾ × 17"
H. 4 pcs, ¾ × 15 × 9"	X. 3 pcs, ¼ × 9¼ × 18"
I. 2 pcs, ¾ × 5¾ × 15"	Y. 4 pcs, ½ × 4¾ × 15¼"
J. 4 pcs, ¾ × 16 × 29¼"	Z. 2 pcs, ¼ × 15 × 15½"
K. 12½ × 61" Formica	AA. 2 pcs, ¼ × 15 × 15½"
L. 1 pc, ¾ × 22 = 57"	BB. 8 pcs, ½ × 8 × 15¼"
M. 1 pc, ¾ × ¾ × 57"	CC. 4 pcs, ½ × 8 × 14"
N. 2 pcs, ¾ × 4 × 4"	DD. 4 pcs, ¼ × 15 × 15½"
O. 1½ × 65" Formica	EE. 60" moulding
P. 2 pcs, ¾ × 4 × 16½"	FF. 6 pcs, ¾ × 8¾ × 18"

joints fastened with glue and finishing nails (Fig. 8-4). The shelves (FF) behind the doors are joined to the verticals (A) with finishing nails driven through the sides of these uprights. See Table 8-2 for materials.

Parts Information

However, the two top shelves in the center section (FF) are adjustable and have movable shelf supports at each end. The bottom shelf and the two drawer separators (C) in the center section are supported by small angle braces screwed to the inner sides of the two central verticals (A).

The bottom brace of the upper structure (D) has been divided into three pieces in Fig. 8-4 for ease of construction. If you prefer to have this part in one piece as shown in Fig. 8-3 make it 55½" long and notch the two central verticals (A) at the bottom to fit.

The flush cabinet doors (F) are made of ¾" plywood. The entire upper structure is anchored to the desk platform (L) with 2½" flathead screws driven through the six pieces (E) on which drawers G-V-W-V ride. In addition, screws of the same length are driven through the back (Q) near the top into the studs of the wall.

In the original project, the desk shelf (L) is covered with Formica on top (K) and along the edge (O). In fact, all the front surfaces of the drawers and the three cabinet doors are covered with Formica since they are made of ¾" plywood with factory bonded Formica facings. All the forward edges are covered with 1/16" strips of this same facing material which is attached with contact cement.

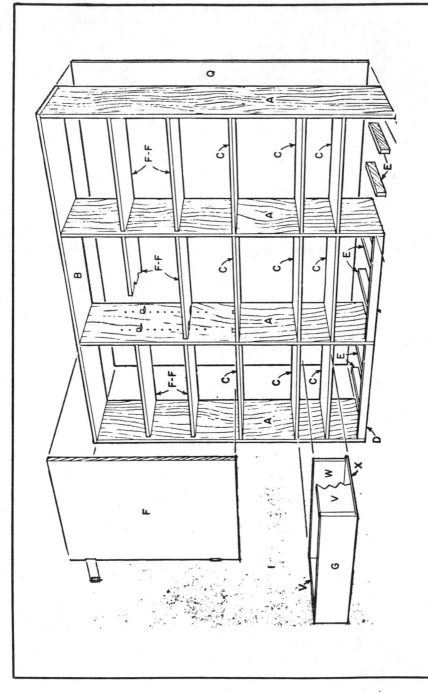

234

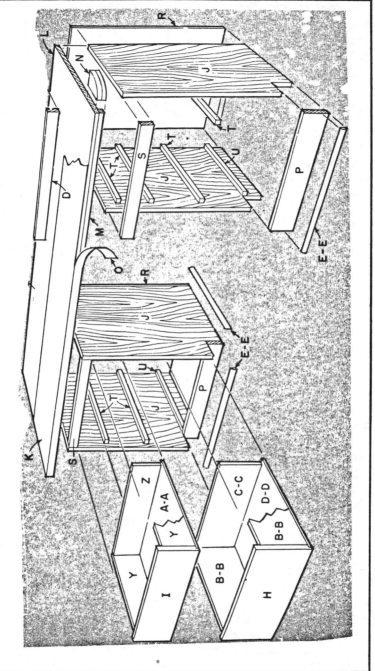

Fig. 8-4. Diagram of the cabinet-desk combination.

You may find it much easier and less expensive to build this project by using Formica only on the desk top and edge and finishing the rest of the front surfaces with a good grade of interior enamel of a matching or contrasting color.

Making Modifications

If you like this project but don't happen to have an alcove which conceals its sides, you can still make it with only a few modifications. One of these is to make the two sides in one piece by joining the upper outside verticals (A) to the outer sides of the bottom drawer cabinets (J). Allowing for the thickness of the desk shelf (L), the side pieces are then 83¼" long and as single pieces greatly strengthen the structure of the project. The length of the desk shelf (L) is then shortened by 1½" and its ends are attached to the sides with glue and finishing nails driven through the new side pieces (A-J). The nail holes are puttied and concealed by a paint finish. The two combined sides (A-J) are easily cut out of ¾" plywood.

The only other modification is not to make the rounded section labeled N and to paint the exposed sides of the desk shelf the same color as the sides.

BUILT-IN BUNK BEDS

Here's an attractive project for the homewoner who likes built-in bunk beds (Fig. 8-5). They are easy to make and have a neat, clean, uncluttered look about them. While the dimensions given are for a mattress and box spring 6' long and 3' wide, the design will accommodate narrower or longer springs and mattresses with a few changes in the measurements.

Basically, the bunk beds consist of a framework, a shell and a storage drawer. Table 8-3 lists materials. The framework is made up of two parallel frames of 2 × 3s, one above the other (A), connected to each other by short lengths (G) of 2 × 3 lumber (Fig. 8-6). The crossbars of the upper and lower frames are connected to the longer members with half lap joints. In the upper frame, midway between the central crossbar and the end crossbars, there are additional supports (D). These are 1 × 3s (one each side of the central crossbar) dadoed into the sidebars (B) of the frame. They provide the extra support that prevents the dust cover (E) from sagging. The dust cover is a ⅛" sheet of tempered hardboard and while it is not absolutely necessary, it's a good idea to have one because it keeps dust from accumulating under the bed or getting into the storage drawer. The frames should be made 1" larger on all

Fig. 8-5. These built-in bunk beds have a neat look about them.

four sides than the box spring and mattress to allow room to tuck blankets and covers inside the upper edges of the shell.

The shell is made of ¾″ plywood and is nailed and glued to the framework. The two ends (K) are each plywood pieces nailed to

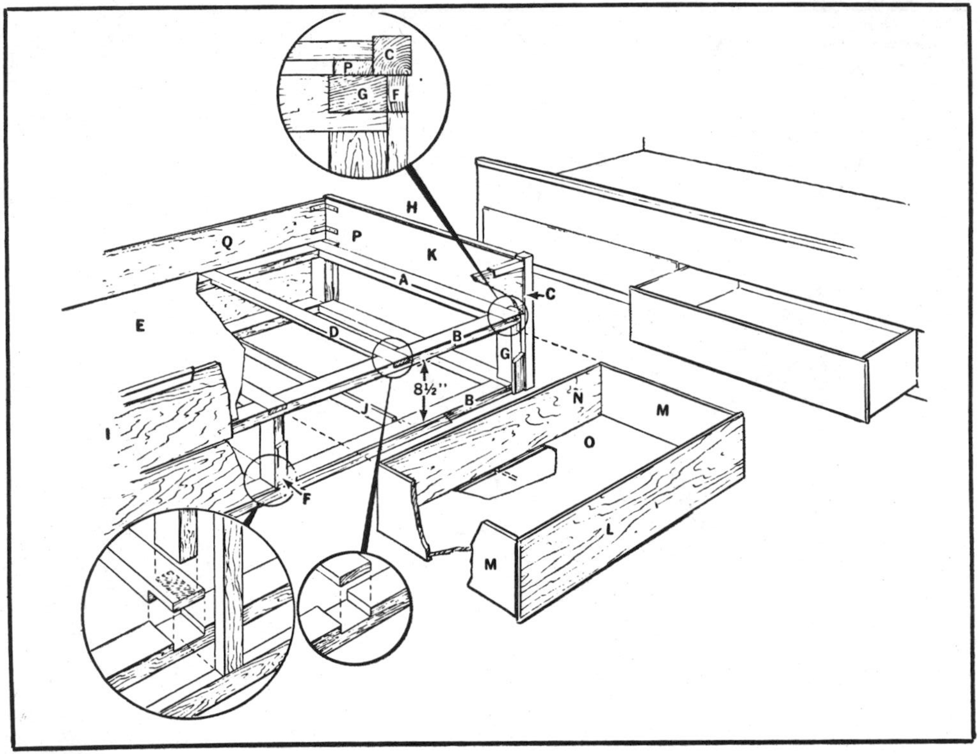

Fig. 8-6. Diagram of the built-in bunk beds.

Table 8-3. Necessary Materials For the Built-in Bunk Beds.

A. 6 pcs., 2 × 3 × 38"	I. 1 pc. ¾ × 10 × 6'2"
B. 4 pcs, 2 × 3 × 6'2"	J. 1 pc. 1 × 2-⅛ × 32 ½"
C. 2 pcs. 2 × 2 × 21"	K. 2 pc. ¾ × 20-½ × 36-⅝"
D. 2 pcs, 1 × 3 × 38"	L. Drawer front, 1 pc. ¼ × 9-⅛ × 35-¼"
E. 1 sheet, ⅛ × 38 × 6' 2"	M. Drawer sides, 2 psc. ½ × 8-⅜ × 28"
F. 3 pcs. 1 × 2 × 8½", 1 pc. 1 × 2 × 5'10"	N. Drawer back, 1 pc. ½ × 8-⅜ × 34"
G. 4 pcs. 2 × 3 × 8½"	O. Drawer bottom, 1 pc. ¼ × 27-¼ × 33"
H. Corner moulding, 1 pc. ¾ × ¾ × 6'2"	P. 2 spacers, 1 × 11-¾"
2 pc. ¾ × ¾ × 36-¼"	Q. 1 pc. ⅜ × 20-½ × 6'3-½"

The front of the shell has two drawer fronts, one of which (the left) is a dummy, and one long piece (I) which forms the upper part. The upper part is nailed and glued along its lower edge to the frame and is attached to the corner posts (C) with angle irons. The ends of this piece should be driven through the corner posts into these glued ends. To make the rest of the front flush with the upper part, 1 × 2 material is nailed to the spaces (F) around and beneath the drawer fronts.

The drawer sides and back are made of ½" plywood and are rabbeted together. The bottom is ¼" plywood and fits into a groove ½" from the bottom of the sides. The front is made of ¾" plywood and is rabbeted all around its inner edges to overlap the front by ⅜". The outer edges of both drawer fronts are slightly rounded. The bottom edge of the back is notched to ride on the drawer guide (J).

HIDEAWAY BED COMBO

Ever try to shoehorn a teenager and a younger child into the same room? You could with this hideaway bed combo and have room to spare (Fig. 8-7). Not only does this project provide both a measure of privacy, but the beds fold up when not in use.

The utility of this project is increased by the large amounts of storage space it provides above and below the beds. The room divider doubles as a hideaway for two full-size beds. The novel way the beds are supported does away with the need for fixed supports.

Joining Pieces

The entire project can be made from pine. As is usual in projects of this type, the fixed portions of it should be built first, with movable portions such as the bed (S, T) and its supports (R)

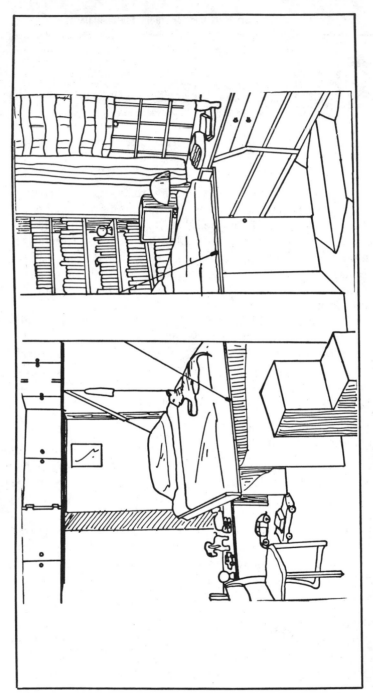

Fig. 8-7. These beds fold up when not in use.

Table 8-4. Materials For the Hideaway Bed Combination.

A. Two pieces, each: 84-⅛ × 2 × 1″
B. Four pieces, each: 8 × 2 × 1″ (not shown)
C. Four pieces, each: 9 × 2 × 1″ (not shown)
D. Two pieces, each: 84-⅛ × 2 × 2
E. Three pieces, each: 84-⅛ × 12 × 1″
F. Two pieces, each: 84-⅛ × 14 × 1″
G. Four pieces, each: 72-½ × 3 × 1″ (one not shown)
H. One piece, 36 × 12 × 1″
I. Eight pieces each: 10 × 2 × 1″ (six not shown)

J. Four pieces, each: 35-9/16 × 12 × 1″
K. One piece, 72-½ × 14 × 1″
L. Twelve pieces, each: 72-½ × 12 × 1″
M. Two pieces, each: 14 × 12 × 1″
N. Two curtain cods, each: 72-½″
O. Twelve doors, each: 18 × 12 × 1″ (eight not shown)
P. One piece, 86-⅛ × 11-⅞ × 1″
PP. One piece, 86-⅛ × 12 × 1″
Q. One piece, each: 86⅛ × 1 × 1″
R. Eight pieces, each: 36 × 18 × 1″
S. Two pieces, each: 72 × 36 × 1″

T. Two pieces, each 71 × 3 × 1″
U. Three pieces, each: 12 × 12 × 1″ (one not shown)
UU. Two pieces, each: 13 × 12 × 1″
V. Three pieces, each 72-½ × 2 × 1″
W. Four angle irons, 2 × 2″ (three not shown)
Y. Two piano or continuous hinges, each: 71″
Z. Eight piano or continuous hinges, each: 35″
AA. Twenty-four hinges, each: 2 × 1″ (eight not shown)
AB. Four eye-bolts (one not shown)
AC. Sixteen door pulls (twelve not shown)
AD. Eight bullet-stop catches (six not shown)

being built last (Fig. 8-8). There are bullet-stop catches (AE) embedded in the edge of piece S that serve as a bed stop.

Most pieces of the project can be joined together using simple butt joints, nails and glue. One of the exceptions to this is the bookcase portion, most of whose shelves (L) are dadoes into the uprights (E), also using nails and glue. The overhead storage cabinets located in the upper portions of the room divider open from either side and use a different type of joint. Both its center and end boards (M) are notched in the middle to receive the cross pieces (L, PP). The center piece (H) of the storage space underneath the beds is notched on either side of its lower end to fit into the space between the two horizontal pieces (G).

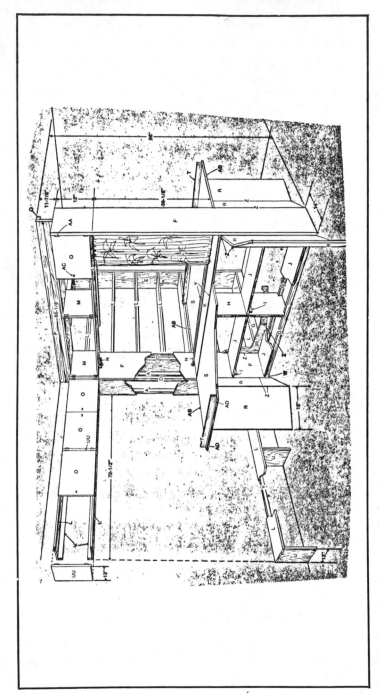

Fig. 8-8. Sketch of the hideaway bed combination.

242

Building The Frame

When starting to build this project, it is recommended that you start by building a frame against the wall using items B and C in Table 8-4 as part of the horizontal framing elements at top and bottom with pieces A and D forming the vertical elements of the frame. Pieces E and F are then used to cover the frame. Before installing the piece (E) that forms one side of the bookcase, it is a good idea to cut dadoes in it to receive the horizontal member (L).

Two of the uprights (F are anchored to the floor using angle irons (W). Additional anchoring is obtained by securing Q to ceiling joists with screws and attaching PP to it.

BUNK BED AND ROLLING STORAGE SHELF

Here's a great project that will take care of the needs of two young boys in one room (Fig. 8-9). This easy-to-make bunk bed has

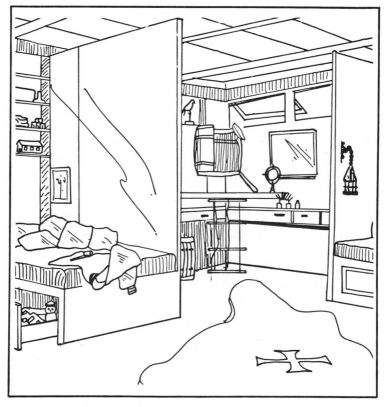

Fig. 8-9. The bunk bed has a storage platform underneath it.

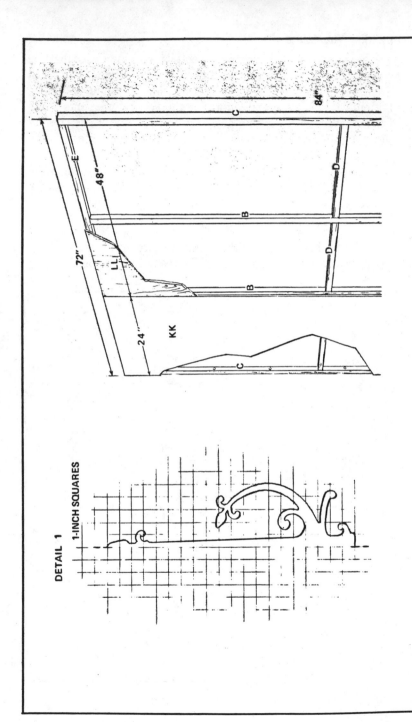

KK

LL

DETAIL 1

1-INCH SQUARES

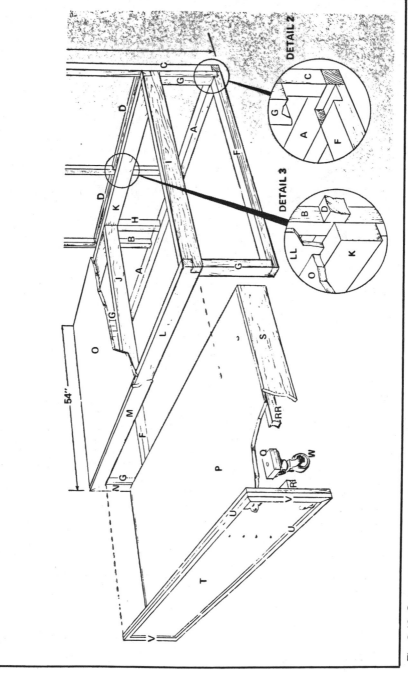

Fig. 8-10. Construction details for the bunk bed and rolling storage shelf.

Table 8-5. Necessary Materials For the Bunk Bed and Rolling Storage Shelf.

A. One piece, 72 × 1½ × 1½"
B. Two pieces, each: 81 × 1½ × 1½"
C. Two pieces, each: 82½ × 1½ × 1½"
  (one not shown)
D. Six pieces, each: 22 × 1½ × 1½"
E. One piece, 69 × 1½ × 1½"
F. Two pieces, each: 54 × 2½ × 1½"
G. Four pieces, each 11¾ × 2½ × 1½"
H. One piece, 11 × 2½ × 1½"
I. Two pieces, each: 54 × 3½ × 1½"
  (one not shown)
J. One piece, 50¼ × 3½ × 1½"
K. One piece, 69 × 3½ × 1½"
KK. One piece, 68 × 24 × ¼"
L. One piece, 72 × 3½ × 1½"
LL. One piece, 68 × 42 × ¼"
M. One piece, 72 × 4 × ¾"
N. Two pieces, each: 16 × 2½ × ¾" (one
  not shown)

O. One piece, 72 × 54 × ½"
OO. One piece, 54 × 16 × ½" (not shown)
P. One piece, 67 × 51½ × ¾"
Q. Four pieces, each: 48½ × 3½ × 1½"
  (three not shown; cut to fit)
R. One piece, each: 67 × 1½ × 1½" (one
  not shown)
RR. Two pieces, each: 50 × 1½ × 1½"
  (one not shown)
S. Two pieces, each: 51½ × 5½ × ¾"
T. One piece, 68½ × 12 × ¾"
U. Two pieces, each: 68½ × 1 × ½"
V. Two pieces, each: 12 × 1 × ½"
W. Four plate swivel casters (1½" dia-
  meter wheel; three not shown)
X. Two pieces, each: 20 × 10 × ⅛
  (shown in Detail 1 only)
Y. One piece, 84 × 72 × ¼"

a platform that pulls out on which you can install a good-sized train track layout that can be hidden quickly and simply just by pushing it underneath the bunk. And if your boys' room already has sufficient space for a train track, you could use the platform as a movable storage shelf or as an additional bed if your family grows larger and you find that you need more space. Table 8-5 give materials.

Room Dividing Partition

In addition to its advantages as a combination bunk bed and rolling storage shelf, the partition behind the bed can also serve as an effective room divider to separate the sleep and play areas from the study areas. The framework of the partition is made up of 2 × 2s and is anchored to the wall on the left side with 4" lag screws driven through piece C. See Fig. 8-10. Left side of the partition is covered with painted plywood (KK) and the remainder (LL) with veneered plywood or woodgrain hardboard. The reverse side of the partition is covered with plywood (Y) that goes all the way to the floor.

Construction Details

As can be seen from Fig. 8-10, this project is relatively easy to build. There are, however, a few construction details that aren't too obvious which should be pointed out.

Piece A should be anchored firmly to the floor with screws. Detail 2 of Fig. 8-10 shows the way that pieces A, F, C, and G are joined together to form a strong corner. As can be seen from Detail

3 of Fig. 8-10, piece D has been deliberately installed a bit higher than piece LL and KK. Piece OO, a ½" plywood sheet (not shown), fits on the exposed end of the bunk. Detail 1 of Fig. 8-10 shows one-half of the pattern that fits on the wall which can be made of ⅛" hardboard.

Note that the blocks (Q) above the casters are cut to fit. The thickness of these blocks depends on the total height of the casters. The combined thickness of the blocks and height of casters should allow ¼" clearance off the floor for the front of the rolling shelf (T).

The little rope ladder and the open barrel are play devices that simulate a ship's ladder or rigging going up to a crow's nest. You may or may not wish to add these to the project.

The finishing of the project is up to your own discretion but, as you can see, the method used in Fig. 8-9 does come off quite nicely.

STUDY CENTER FOR THREE

Tired of picking up after kids? Need more shelves for your growing collection of books? Need additional work space for the scholars that board at your house? Get all of these needs filled by building this colorful addition to your basement recreation room (Fig. 8-11).

Each of the three units has a comfortably-sized desk, a drawer, and a storage pedestal and bookshelves in addition to an individual bulletin board for each of three youngsters.

Construction is simple. Plywood and white pine boards constitute the primary building materials (Table 8-6). Sheet vinyl floor covering provides a serviceable top for the desk area. The counter and the bookshelves are constructed separately and assembled later.

While there is no set way of constructing this unit, it does seem far preferable to build the lower portion first and set the upper, bookcase portion on top of it later, Generally speaking, only three different types of joints are used to secure the individual pieces to one another: simple butt, rabbet and dado. The doors have ½" rabbets around their edges, are mounted using ⅜" offset hinges and use magnetic catches. A scrap piece of neutral-colored vinyl is cut to size for the covering of the desk top area and fastened with contact cement. The top, bookcase portion is toenailed to the desk unit. Two extra pieces at the far left (D, F) are added to provide stability for the left vertical (A) (Fig. 8-12). These do not appear in Fig. 8-11 but are shown in Fig. 8-12 in case the study center you build does not happen to butt against a wall.

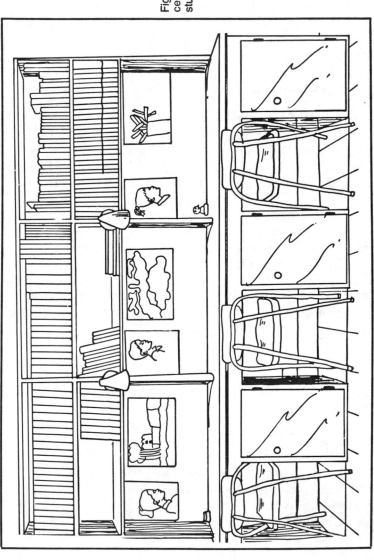

Fig. 8-11. This unique study center has room for three students.

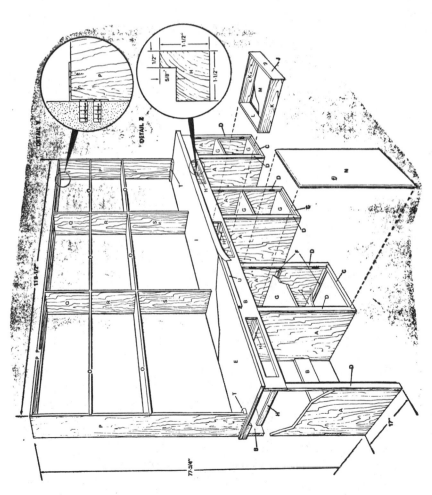

Fig. 8-12. Diagram of the study center.

249

Table 8-6. Materials For the Study Center.

A. Seven pieces, each: 29 × 16 × ½"
B. Three pieces, each: 121½· × 5 × ¾"
C. Three pieces, each: 19'× 1 × ¾"
D. Seven pieces, each: 24 × 1½·× ¾"
E. One piece, plywood: 121½· × 19'× ¾"
F. Twelve pieces, each: 16 × 1 × 1"
  (eleven not shown)
G. Six pieces, each: 19'× 16 × ½"
  (cut to fit)
H. Six pieces, each: 15¼ × 1½·× 1½"
  (two not shown)
I. Vinyl floor covering, 122 × 20"
  (cut to fit)
J. Three pieces, each: 18 × 3 × 1"
  (two not shown)
K. Six pieces, each: 15¼ × 3 × 1"
  (two not shown)
L. Three pieces, each: 15⅝ × 3 " 1"
  (two not shown)
M. Three pieces, ¾" Masonite, each:
  16 × 14½" (two not shown)
N. Three pieces, ¾" plywood, each:
  24 × 16" (two not shown)
O. Six pieces, each: 39¼ × 8 × ¾"
PP. One piece, 119½· × 8 × ¾"
P. Two pieces, each: 48 × 8 × ¾"
Q. Two pieces, each: 11¼ × 8 × ¾"
R. Two pieces, each: 13 × 8 × ¾"
S. Two pieces, each: 22 × 8 × ¾"
T. Two pieces, each: 7× 1½·× 1"
U. One piece, 12½ × 2 × 1"

Epoxy paint was used on the unit to withstand the rough treatment of three children. And you can easily get away with using only two pin-up lamps to provide lighting.

BOYS' BUILT-IN STORAGE/DESK COMBOS

Loaded with counter space, four large drawers, two spacious shelves, and a desk area, each of these twin built-in work surface/ storage combos is a perfect addition for your boys' room (Fig. 8-13). Table 8-7 lists materials.

The construction. mostly of plywood, is not at all difficult; start from the floor and work up, building each of the three basic units: the base (K,L), the shelf/drawer box frame (A, B), and the bridging (M, N) (Fig. 8-14).

The base (K, L) is recessed to allow for toe room and is nailed to the wall and floor. The shelf/drawer frame (A, B) is simply a box

Fig. 8-13. These built-in storage/desk combos have plenty of counter space.

251

Table 8-7. Materials Needed For the Built-In Storage/Desk Combos.

A. 2 pcs, ¾ × 18 × 73	Q. 8 pcs, ¾ × ¾ × 17¼"
B. 3 pcs, ¾ × 18 × 23"	QQ. 8 pcs, ¾ × ¾ × 17¼"
C. 1 pc, ¾ × 19" × 8'	R. 8 pcs, ½ × 11⅛ × 17¼"
D. 1 pc, ¾ × 16½ × 34"	S. 4 pcs, ½ × 6 × 15½"
E. 1 pc, ¾ × 11⅛ × 16½"	T. 4 pcs, 3/16" hardboard,
F. 1 pc, ¾ × 11⅛ × 18"	15⅞ × 17⅝"
G. 1 pc, ¾ × 11½ × 18"	U. 2 pcs, ½ × 4 × 15"
H. 1 pc, ¾ × 18 × 37⅛"	V. 1 pc, ½ × 4 × 14"
I. 4 pcs, ¾ × 11⅛ × 18"	W. 1 pc, 3/16" hardboard,
J. 1 pc, ¾ × 4 × 15"	14½ × 15"
K. 2 pcs, ¾ × 3½ × 73"	X. 4 pcs, ½" aluminum
L. 3 pcs, ¾ × 3¼ × 14½"	angle, 14" long
M 2 pcs, 1½ × 1½" 8'	Y. 2 doors, ¼" hardboard,
N. 4 pcs, 1½ × 1½ × 15"	18 × 23⅜"
O. 2 pcs, ¾ × 1½ × 15"	Z. 1pc, 1/16 × 19½ × 8'
P. 1 pc, ½ × 1½" × 8'	ZZ. 1 pc, 1/16 × 1½" × 8'

affair, without a back, and is set on and nailed to the base (K, L). The partition (B) between the drawer section and the shelf section is one piece with a dado through which shelf (D) is nailed and shelf (H) is inserted and glued. The partition between the two sets of drawers is two pieces (F, G). Shelf (H) is dadoes, nailed to the lower partition (F), and glued to the upper partition (G) which is inserted in the dado. Shelf (D) and partition (E) are recessed 1½" to allow room for the sliding doors (Y).

The four large drawers, of standard drawer construction, have side strips (QQ) (see drawer detail of Fig. 8-14) that ride under the drawer guide (O), and prevent the drawers from tilting down when they are pulled far out. The smaller desk drawer, again of standard drawer construction, has an aluminum L-shaped strip (X) on each side (U) (see drawer runner detail of Fig 8-14) which rides on two other L-shaped strips (X) attached to two of the bridging crossbars (O).

Lastly, the bridging (M, N) is nailed to the top of the frame (A, B) and the wall. The overlapping countertop (C) is set on top of the bridging (M, N), nailed to it—with edging strip (P) added—and covered with sheet (Z) and edging (ZZ) of plastic laminate.

SHOP WORKBENCH

A workbench of the type shown is both sturdy and easy to make (Fig. 8-15). It provides plenty of storage space, can withstand a great deal of hammering on the top, and will last a long time. Table 8-8 gives materials.

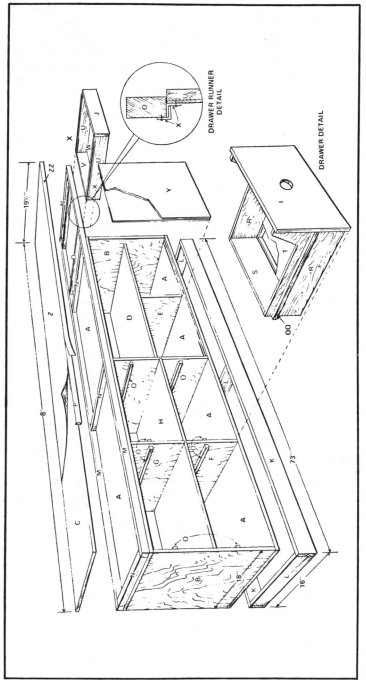

Fig. 8-14. Construction details for the built-in storage/desk combos.

253

Making The Top And Back

The top is made up of 2 × 6s (B) glued edge-to-edge and sanded just enough to make them level with each other (Fig. 8-16). The top is attached to the tops of the double plywood ends and central partition (FF) as well as the tops of the single partitions (F) with glue and 2½" flat head screws driven flush with the surfaces of the 2 × 6s (B). A top wheet (A) of ⅛" tempered hardboard is glued to the upper surface of assembled 2 × 6s.

The back (E) is a solid sheet of ½" plywood glued and screwed to the back edges of all the partitions (F-FF) the ends (FF) and protrudes above the tempered hardboard top sheet (A) by 4" although you can, of course, make this higher if you wish. A board (D) which is fastened to this protruding part of the back with screws and glue acts as a reinforcement here and also helps hold down the back edge of the top (A-B). The bottom is a single piece of ¾" plywood (G) fastened to the bottom edges of the ends and partitions with glue and flathead 1½" screws driven up through the underside of the bottom.

Fig. 8-15. This shop workbench will last a long time.

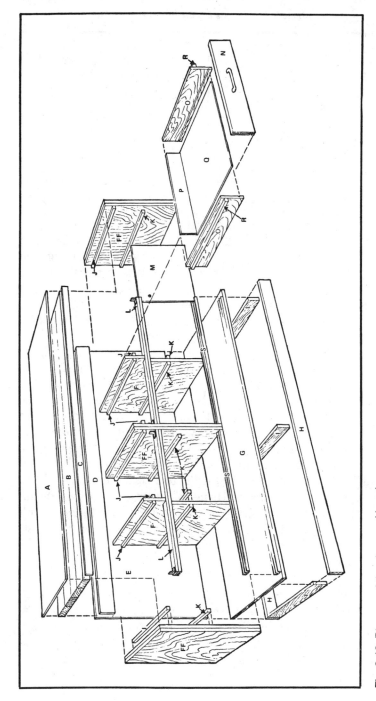

Fig. 8-16. Diagram of the shop workbench.

Table 8-8. Materials For the Shop Workbench.

A. 1 pc, 8' × 22' × ⅛"	I. 3 pcs, 19" × 3½" × ¾"
B. 1 pc, 8' × 22" × 1¾"	J. 8 pcs, 22" × ¾" × ¾"
C. 1 pc, 8' × 1⅞" × ⅛"	K. 8 pcs, 20¼" × ¾" × ¾"
D. 1 pc, 8' × 4" × ½"	L. 2 pcs, 45¾" × ¾" × 1¾"
E. 1 pc, 8' × 31⅞" × ½"	M. 4 pcs, 24" × 20" × ¼"
F. 2 pcs, 26" × 22" × ¾"	N. 1 pc, 22½" × 5" × ¾"
FF. 3 pcs, 26" × 22" 1½"	O. 2 pcs, 17¼" × 5" × ½"
G. 1 pc, 8' × 22½" × ¾"	P. 1 pc, 21½" × 5" × ½"
H. 2 pcs, 8' × 3½" × ¾"	Q. 1 pc, 22" × 17" × ¼"
	R. 8 pcs, 17¼" × ¾" × ¾"

Base, Cleats And Tracks

Note that the base (I-H) is flush with the back and ends of the bottom but is recessed 3" in front for toe room. Fasten the base to the bottom with glue and flathead 1½" screws driven through the bottom into the back, front (H) and central cross piece (I).

The cleats (J) near the top of each end and the partitions (F-FF) are drawer guides which support the cleats (R) on the sides of the drawers. Wax these cleats with paraffin or spray them with silicone lubricant for easy movement. The cleats (K) in the middle of each' partition and ends are meant for shelves, if desired.

Tracks (S) for the sliding doors may be made of wood, plastic or aluminum and are available in many hardware stores and lumber yards. There are four sections of tracks, one pair on each side of the double central partition. The lower tracks are fastened to the bottom with ¾" flathead screws driven flush with the bottom of the track groove. The upper tracks are fastened in the same way to a stringer (L) which in turn is fastened to the ends and doubled middle plywood partition (FF) with steel right angle braces. The two partitions (F) are notched to permit the tracks to pass by them.

The drawers are simply butted together and fastened with finishing nails and glue. Finish with paint, using a primer first, followed by a good quality enamel.

BEDROOM FROM A BARE WALL

The built-in storage theme carries emphasis in this project which is designed to make the most of that potential wall in a girl's bedroom. The vanity-dresser and divided built-in bed with storage space underneath is well within the scope of the average handyman and can easily be finished in a couple of weekends (Fig. 8-17). See Table 8-9 for materials.

Floor Frame

The floor frame is built first by nailing 2 × 4 pieces (E-E-F-F-F-F) to the floor and to the wall studs after the wall-to-floor molding has been removed (Fig. 8-18). Cabinet shelf (C) which is notched to fit around risers (H) is then nailed to the bottom frame, and the risers (note overlap on bottom for kick-board) are toenailed. The upper frame (E-E-G-G-G-G) is nailed to the risers and also the wall studs in order to firmly anchor the bed-cabinet skeleton; then the top (A) and front face (B) are nailed to the completed frame.

Use a saber saw to cut the front face (B) and the cabinet doors (EE) from one sheet of ¾″ plywood. In doing this, allow 4″ for the width of the four front panel legs when you scribe lines onto the panel for the sides and top of the doors. Make the inside corners square by sawing the door tops from center to side in both directions after making a careful plunge cut into the horizontal.

The wall cleat (K) gives rigidity to the divider (D); and although one is not shown in a ceiling cleat gives added support to the divider. The vanity table surface (J) is supported by cleats (M-M-L), one of which is screwed to the divider panel (D), and by panels (S) which also serve as side guides for the drawers.

Dresser Drawers

Panel (Q) covers a dummy space allowed at the left so that folding doors (shown in Fig. 8-17)) won't interfere with opening of drawers. Shallow groove marks create the illusion that drawers extend all the way to the wall. Another dummy panel (O) covers the space between the right hand drawer and the divider, allowing the opened drawer to clear the vertical panel (I) which overlaps the divider to the left. Formica, glued to the top and front of the vanity, adds durability and washability to the surface.

The drawers of the vanity-dresser have ¼″ plywood bottoms that fit into grooves cut into the sides, front and back pieces; these grooved joints, as well as the butt joints holding drawer sides to front and back, are glued. The overlapping bottom on the drawer faces (BB-X) catches the front edge of the horizontal support panel (U) for a flush fit with the side panels.

A double folding door, shelves to the left and right and a mirror behind the vanity add privacy, function and charm to the completed unit. Wallpaper and harmonizing enamel put on the final touches.

Fig. 8-17. You can convert a bare wall into a complete bedroom.

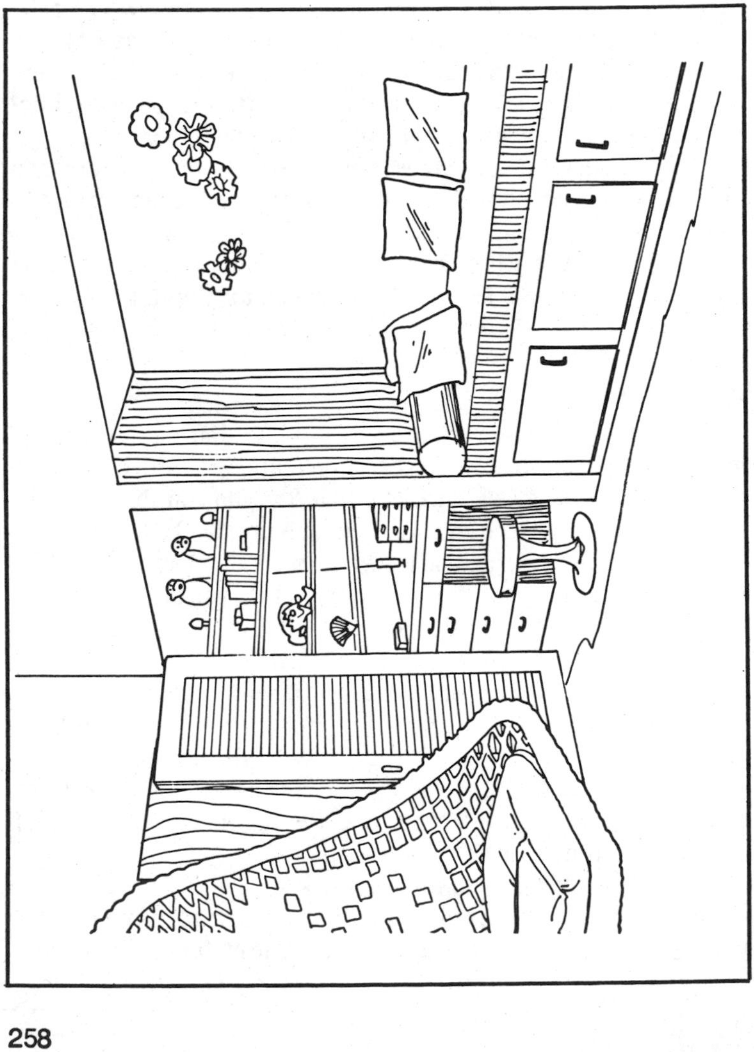

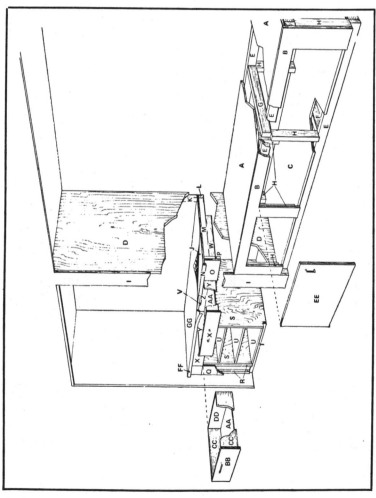

Fig. 8-18. Diagram of the bedroom shown in Fig. 8-17.

Table 8-9. Required Materials For the Project In Fig. 8-17.

A. 1 pc, ¾ × 29¼ × 72″
B. 1 pc, ¾ × 16¼ × 72″
C. 1 pc, ¾ × 29¼ × 72″
D. 1 pc, ¾ × 29¼ × 80¾″
E. 4 pcs, 1½ × 2½ × 72″
F. 4 pcs, 1½ × 2½ × 72″
G. 4 pcs, 1½ × 2½ × 20¼″
H. 8 pcs, 1½ × 2½ × 13″
I. 1 pc, ¾ × 6 × 78¾″
J. 1 pc, ¾ × 26 × 54″
K. 1 pc, 1½ × 1½ × 51¾″
L. 1 pc, 1½ × 1½ × 54″
M. 2 pcs, 1½ × 1½ × 22″
N. 1 pc, ¾ × 1½ × 54″
O. 1 pc, ¾ × 4¾ × 8″
P. 1 pc, 1 × 1 × 4¾″

Q. 1 pc, ¾ × 4 × 25¾″
R. 2 pcs, 1 × 1 × 25¾″
S. 2 pcs, ¾ × 28¼ × 24¼″
T. 1 pc, ¾ × 2½ × 25″
U. 5 pcs, ¾ × 19½ × 22″
V. 2 pcs, ¾ × 2 × 26″
W. 1 pc, ¾ × 1¾ × 26″
X. 2 pcs, ¾ × 4 × 21″
Y. 4 pcs, ⅜ × 3¼ × 20″
Z. 2 pcs, ⅜ × 3¼ × 20¼″
AA. 5 pcs, ¼ × 20½ × 20¼″
BB. 3 pcs, ¾ × 7½ × 21″
CC. 6 pcs, ⅜ × 6¾ × 20″
DD. 6 pcs, ⅜ × 6¾ × 20¼″
EE. 3 pcs, ¾ × 12¼ × 18″
FF. Formica, 1½ × 54″
GG. Formica 26¾ × 54″

BUNK BEDS FOR TWO YOUNGSTERS

These bunk beds for two young fellows are just about the simplest to make that you could possibly find (Fig. 8-19). They are also sturdy and good looking. Table 8-10 lists materials.

These bunks are designed to accommodate standard 6′ mattresses, 36″ wide. The width. The width inside the bed frame (D-C-D-C) is 39″ to allow 1½″ on each side for blankets and bed covers (Fig. 8-20). For the same reason, the inside length is 75″

The vertical support (A) that connects both beds is a 4 × 4 fastened to the outer sides (C) with ¼″ carriage bolts. These bolts should be driven into their holes with a hammer to seat the square part of the shaft under the head. This prevents the bolt from turning when the nut (and washer) is tightened with a wrench. The nut should be countersunk and flush with the inner surface of the sides (C). The same method should be used to fasten the end posts (B-B) to the exposed end (D) of the upper bunk and the two small posts (E-E) to the end of the lower bunk. As an alternative to carriage bolts you can use 3″ No. 12 flat head screws driven through the sides and ends from the *inside* into the posts.

When fastening the bunks to the walls, use ¼″ lag screws, 3″ long driven from the inner faces of the ends and sides into the studs behind the plasterboard. The lag screws have big square heads which makes it easy to turn them with a wrench. Be sure to use a washer under the head of each of each lag screw.

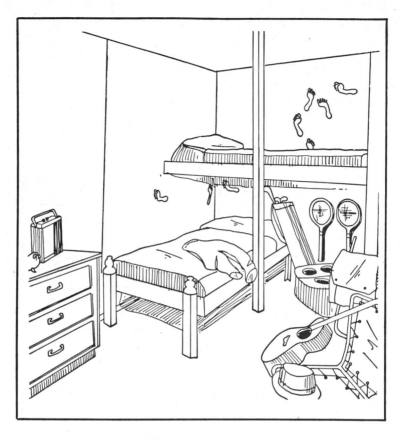

Fig. 8-19. These bunk beds are very handsome.

The plywood bottom of each bunk should be fastened to the sides and ends with glue and 2½″ finishing nails. The underside of the bottom (F) should be about 2″ above the lower eges of the sides and ends of the bunks to permit the lag screws to be driven through

Table 8-10. Materials Needed For the Bunk Beds.

A. 1 pc, 3½· × 3½· × 94½″
B. 2 pcs, 1½· × 3½· × 94½″
C. 4 pcs, ¾ × 5½· × 75″
D. 4 pcs, ¾ × 5½· × 40½″
E. 2 pcs, 3½· × 3½· × 24″
F. 2 pcs, ¾ × 39′× 75″
G. 2 pcs, 1½· × 1½· × 3½″
H. 1 pc, 1½ × 3½ × 3½″

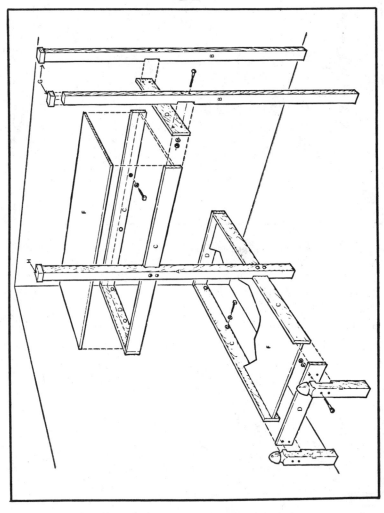

Fig. 8-20. Sketch of the two bunk beds.

them underneath the bunk bottom. The reason for locating the lag screws under the bottom is to avoid bruising Mother's finger on the screw heads when she tucks in the blankets and bed covers under the mattress.

The two smaller posts at the end of the lower bunk (E-E) have rounded ornamental ends turned on a lathe. If you have difficulty duplicating these ends, use any ornamental caps you can find or else simply square the ends of the posts and round their edges with block plane.

Allow about 3' between the top of the upper bunk and the ceiling a similar space between the upper and lower bunks. Finish with an enamel undercoat followed by a good grade of enamel.

YOUTH ROOM

Having two youngsters in one room, even a large one, can be a problem sometimes. They get to the point where each one wants a

Fig. 8-21. The youth room allows privacy for two youngsters.

Table 8-11. Materials Needed For the Youth Room.

LIST OF MATERIALS	
A. 2 pcs, ¾ × 6 × 72"	N. 2 pcs, ¾ × 38¼ × 96"
B. 2 pcs, ¾ × 6 × 37½"	O. 2 pcs, ¾ × 2 × 26"
C. 1 pc, ½ × 37½ × 70½"	P. 2 pcs, ¾ × 2½ × 96"
D. 2 pcs, ¾ × ¾ × 62½"	Q. 1 pc, ¾ × 11 × 24"
E. 2 pcs, ¾ × ¾ × 20½"	R. 1 pc, ¾ × 81 × 24"
F. 4 pcs, 4 × 4" thickness to suit 4 casters 1½" high	S. 12 pcs, ¼ × 1½ × 94½"
	T. 18 pcs, ¼ × 1½ × 24½"
G. 2 pcs, ¾ × 7 × 72"	U. 3 pcs, ¼ × 39 × 94½"
H. 2 pcs, ¾ × 7 × 37½"	V. 4 pcs, 1½ × 1½ × 96"
I. 1 pc, ¾ × 37½ × 70½" (optional)	W. 3 pcs, 1½ × 1½ × 24½"
J. 2 pcs, 1½ × 1½ × 70½"	X. 4 pcs, 1½ × 1½ × 35¼"
K. 2 pcs, 1½ × 1½ × 34½"	Y. 1 pc, ½ × 27½ × 38¼"
L. 1 pc, ¼ × 13 × 72"	Z. 2 pcs, ¾ × ¾ × 35¼"
M. 3 pcs, ¾ × ¾ × 12"	AA. 2 pcs, ¾ × ¾ × 24½"

little privacy and wants his (or her) end of the room to be different (Fig. 8-21).

To secure privacy, the homeonwer hung three light solid screens (U) from tracks on the ceiling (Fig. 8-22). All three are flush with the edge of the closet seen at left when they are pushed all the way back to the wall. For privacy they extend clear across the room, each one overlapping the other. Table 8-11 lists materials.

The built-in bed (G-H) is a box of ¾" plywood without a bottom. Cleats on the inside (J-K) support a box spring. The ¾" bed bottom (I) is optional. The upper bed is bolted to the side of the closet (N) and to the wall under the window. The left end of the bed (H) is bolted to the duplicate closet not seen in Fig. 8-21. Of course, if you don't have space for a second closet, the end of the bed can be fastened to a wall.

The drawer-type bed (A-B) does have a bottom (C) supported on cleats. Four blocks (F) in each corner under the bed bottom have casters under them to allow easy movement of the lower bed.

The closets on both ends of the bed are made of ¾" plywood and have no backs. The closet sidewalls (N) are supported by a framework of 1½ × 1½" cleats (V) at the back nailed to the wall and screwed to the back ends of N. There are similar cleats in the front corners on both sides which, like those at the back sides of the closet, extend from floor to ceiling.

There are similar cleats from front to back (X) which anchor the sidewalls (N) to the floor and ceiling. The door (C) swings on a

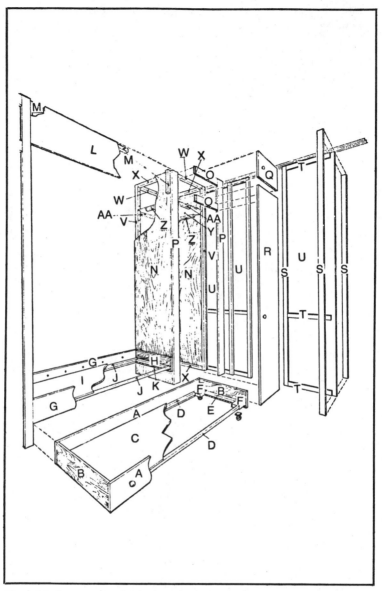

Fig. 8-22. Construction details for the youth room.

continuous hinge. The smaller door (E) has a hinge of the same type.

The valance (L) is made of ¼" plywood and is secured by cleats at both ends and by a third cleat in the middle which is fastened to the ceiling and the valance. A paint finish in keeping with the decor of the room seems to be the best finish for this project.

STUDY CORNER

A corner shelf desk combined with cabinets and a closet as shown on the cover is ideal for the teenage student in your home.

Fig. 8-23. This study corner has a modern look.

Table 8-12. Materials Required For the Study Corner.

A. 2 pcs, ¾ × 24¾ × 65"	K. 1 pc, ¼ × 27¼ × 28"	U. 1 pc, ¾ × ¾ × 25"
B. 2 pcs, ¾ × 24¾ × 31"	L. 2 pcs, 1½ × 1½ × 96"	V. 1 pc, ¾ × 1½ × 26½"
C. 5 pcs, ¾ × 23¾ × 49½"	M. 4 pcs, 1½ × 1½ × 21¾ "	W. 1 pc, 1 × 2 × 27"
D. 1 pc, ¾ × 24 × 44½"	N. 10 pcs, ¾ × ¾ × 21¾"	X. 1 pc, 1 × 2 × 21½·"
E. 1 pc, ¾ × 18 × 55½"	O. 5 pcs, ¾ × ¾ × 46½"	Y. 1 pc, 1 × 2 × 44½·"
F. 2 pcs, ¾ × 14 × 23⅜"	P. 2 pcs, ¾ × 16 × 23¼"	Z. 1 pc, ¾ × ¾ × 21½·"
G. 2 pcs, ¾ × 24 × 96"	Q. 2 pcs, ¾ × 1½ × 18"	AA. 1½·× 120" tape
H. 1 pc, ¾ × 1½ × 44½"	R. 2 pcs, ¾ × 16¼ × 26½"	BB. 2 pcs, 23⅜" piano hinge
I. 2 pcs, ¾ × 16¼ × 27¼"	S. 1 pc, ¾ × 3 × 26½"	CC. 2 pcs, 31" piano hinge
J. 1 pc, ¾ × 1½· × 55½"	T. 2 pcs, ·¾ × ¾ × 16¼ "	DD. 2 pcs, 65" piano hinge

Not only is this arrangement attractive but it also provides ample space for storage and plenty of desk surface. See Table 8-12.

The doors (A-B) are somewhat deceiving in Figs. 8-23 and 8-24. Although they look like two doors, they are actually two pairs with the larger ones (A-A) above and the smaller ones (B-B) below the black paint band. The lower doors extend from the floor to the bottom edge of the paint line and do not have any knobs or pulls because they are equipped with touch latches which allow them to open with light finger pressure.

The sides of the closet (G) are nailed and glued to cleats (M) which, in turn, are nailed to the floor and ceiling beams. Two vertical cleats (L) from floor to ceiling are fastened to the wall studs with nails and provide a nailing surface for the back edges of the sides (G) and keep the whole closet rigid. The five rear cleats (O) support closet shelves (C).

The desk shelf (D) is supported by cleats (X, Y, Z) attached to the side of the closet (G) and the two remaining walls. A ¾ × ¾ strip (H) is screwed under the front edge of the desk shelf to make it 1½" high. The edge is covered with a piece of fir veneer tape.

The same edge treatment is followed for the smaller desk surface (E), using the ¾ × 1½ strip (J) The back edge of the white desk surface (E) is supported by a cleat (W) which is fastened with screws to the wall, and by the cabinet framework.

Both of the desk shelves (D-E) are fastened to the double horizontal strip (Q) with glue and screws driven through the top of D and the bottom of E. The screws through the black desk surface should be countersunk and the holes filled with wood putty.

Note that the sides of the white cabinet (I) are notched at the bottom to provide toe room. The shelves inside this cabinet are fastened with glue and finishing nails driven through the sides (I). Here again, the nail heads are countersunk and filled with wood putty. The finish is high grade enamel applied over a suitable primer.

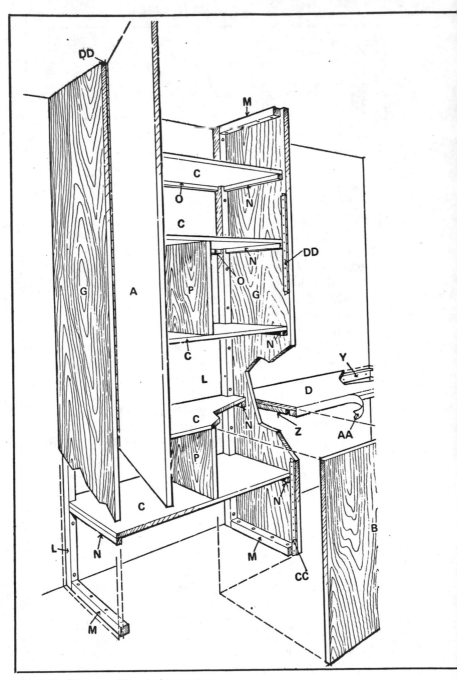

Fig. 8-24. Diagram of the study corner.

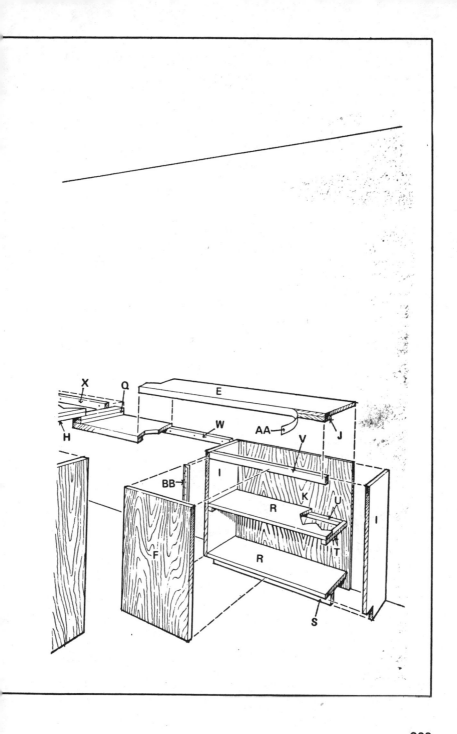

TWIN BUNKS AND CLOSET COMBO

How do you find enough space for playing, sleeping, and storage for two very active youngsters in one room? If this is one of your problems and the room is not as large as you'd want, try this project as a solution (Fig. 8-25). Table 8-13 gives materials.

Building and Fastening the Beds

The bunk beds are simply rectangular boxes of ¾" plywood with corner butt joints that are nailed and glued. Cleats inside these

Fig. 8-25. This neat project provides lots of space for your youngsters to sleep, play and store their possessions.

LIST OF MATERIALS	
A. 4 pcs, ¾ × 9¼ × 73½"	J. 2 pcs, ¾ × 3½ × 46"
B. 4 pcs, ¾ × 9¼ × 39"	K. 1 pc, ¾ × 3½ × 51"
C. 2 pcs, ¾ × 39 × 75"	L. 1 pc, 3½ × 3½ × 51"
D. 1 pc, ¾ × 3½ × 9¼"	M. 2 pcs, ¾ × 6 × 62"
E. 4 pcs, ¾ × ¾ × 72"	N. 5 pcs, ¾ × 6 × 20"
F. 4 pcs, ¾ × ¾ × 39"	O. 2 pcs, bent irons
G. 6 pcs, ¾ × 6 × 28"	P. 3 pcs, 3½ × 3½ × 35¼"
H. 5 pcs, ¾ × 6 × 35¼"	Q. 10 pcs, ¾ × ¾ × 6"
I. 2 pcs, 3½ × 3½ × 74"	R. 1 pc, ¾ × 9½ × 30"

boxes (E-E-F-F) support a plywood sheet on which a foam mattress can rest (Fig. 8-26).

The right side of the upper bunk (A) is screwed to the studs of the wall with ⅜ × 3" lag screws driven through the side just under the cleat (E) that helps support the mattress platform (C). The back end of the upper bunk (B) is screwed to a 4 × 4 (P) which is fastened to the studs of the wall with lag screws and nailed to the two corner 4 × 4 posts (I). Additional support for the upper bunk is provided by two vertical 4 × 4 posts which are notched at the top to permit the sides (A) to rest on them. The little headboard (R) of the upper bunk is separate piece fastened to the wall to keep pillows away from the wall.

The bottom bunk is of the same construction as the upper one but offers no support problems since it rests on the floor. However, its head end (B) is screwed to the two intermediate posts (L).

Making the Door, Ladder and Steps

The door to the clost under the upper bunk is made of six ¾" slats (G), two posts (J), and a diagonal brace (K) nailed together with finishing nails. The longer slats (H) which make up the other side of the closet are nailed to individual cleats (Q) attached to the two posts (L).

The ladder is easy to make, the steps being nailed through the sides of the rails (M) after the ends are glued. A pair of soft iron straps (O) with ends bent over in a hook hold the ladder to the upper bunk.

The steps (N) must all be parallel to the angle at which the bottom ends of the rails (M) have been cut. One way to do this is to lay both rails on the floor, one on top of the other. Then use the

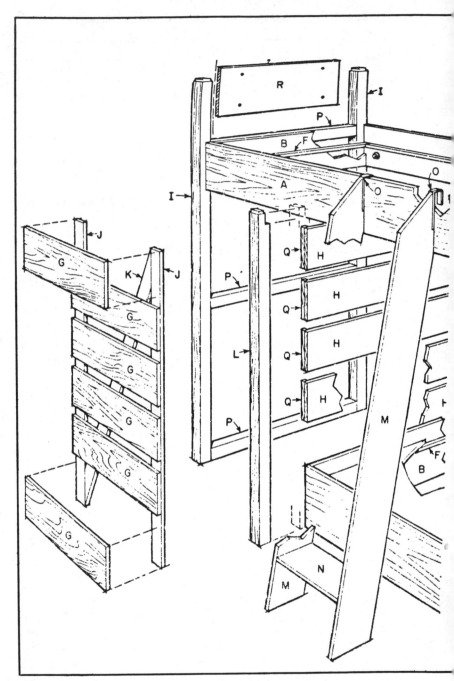

Fig. 8-26. Sketch of the twin bunks and closet combo.

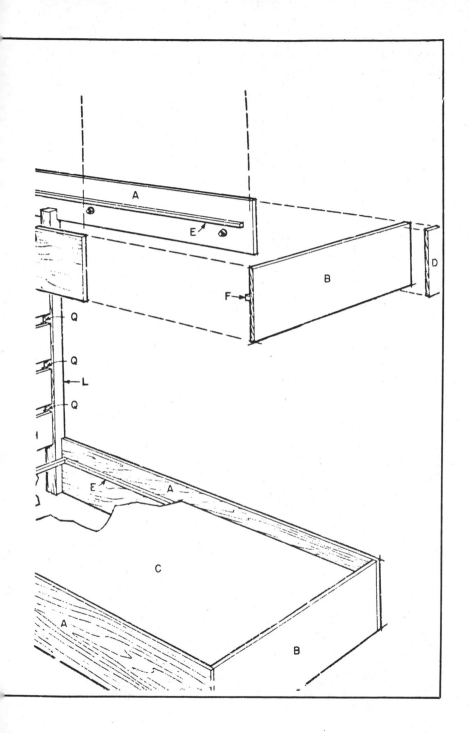

bottom end of the top rail to mark a line along which the ends of the steps are placed when they are nailed. Repeat this process with the unmarked rail. Finish with a primer and good enamel.

CLOSET-BUNK COMBO

The bunk bed-closet combination is a very handy arrangement for the family that has two boys in a bedroom. This particular design will work well also for one boy with room for a guest (Fig. 8-27). The lower bunk can be used either for sleeping or as a couch for sitting. Table 8-14 lists materials.

Upper Bunk and Closet

The upper bunk is supported by the closet and by lag screws driven through the side (A) of the bunk against the wall into the studs (Fig. 8-28). The foot of the bunk (C) is also fastened to the wall in the same manner as A. Two long bolts can be used to fasten the bottom (F) of the bunk to the top of the cabinet (G), although this may not be strictly necessary.

The closet is simply a box made of ¾" plywood with a back (L) of ½" hardboard. Make the floor of ¾" plywood and use finishing nails driven through the front (K), sides (H) and back (L) to fasten it into place. Use both glue and nails for all joints. Nail heads should be countersunk and puttied.

The sliding doors of the closet are made of ½" plywood rabbeted top and bottom to provide an edge which is ¼" thick and rides on rollers of the type used in medicine cabinets for sliding glass mirror doors. If you have trouble obtaining these rollers, use the standard plastic or aluminum tracks with grooves for ¼" material which are available in many hardware stores. You can eliminate rollers and tracks by simply cutting smooth ¼" grooves in K and J and waxing them. Note the arrangement shown in Fig. 8-28 for guiding the doors at the top.

Bottom Bunk and Ladder

The bottom bunk is quite different from the upper one. Basically it is a box with ¾" ends (O) and ½" plywood back. The right front side (covered by the closet) is covered by a solid sheet of plywood. The left side has a deep drawer (V) for storage. Note the 2 × 2 (X) that runs from the lower left front of S to the back which serves not only as a brace for the bunk at this point but also provides a (waxed) rail on which the bottom of the drawer can slide. Of course, the drawer also has side guides.

274

Fig. 8-27. Here's a closet-bunk bed combination where the bunk beds are completely different.

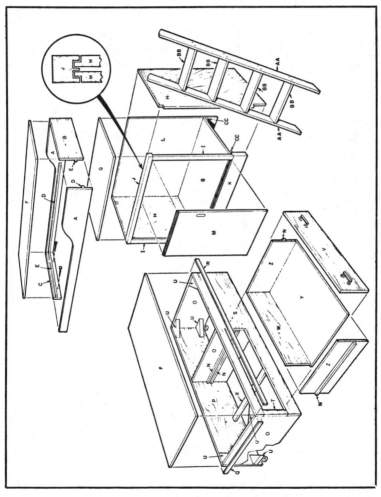

Fig. 8-28. Sketch of the closet-bunk combo.

Table 8-14. Materials Needed For the Closet-Bunk Combo.

LIST OF MATERIALS	
A. 2 pcs, ¾ × 11¼ × 75¾ "	P. 1 pc, ½ × 15¾ × 75"
B. 1 pc, ¾ × 11¼ × 31½"	Q. 1 pc, ¼ × 1¼ × 30"
C. 1 pc, ¾ × 4 × 30"	R. 1 pc, ¼ × 1¼ × 75¼"
D. 2 pcs, ¾ × ¾ × 75"	S. 1 pc, ¾ × 15¾ × 75"
E. 2 pcs, ¾ × ¾ × 28½"	T. 1 pc, ¾ × 1½ × 8"
F. 2 pcs, ¾ × 30 × 75"	U. 8 pcs, 1½" Thick
G. 2 pcs, ¾ × 29½ × 43¼"	Triangles
H. 2 pcs, ¾ × 30¾ × 56"	V. 1 pc, ¾ × 8 × 42"
I. 2 pcs, ¾ × 1½ × 49½"	W. 1 pc, ½ × 7½ × 39½"
J. 1 pc, 1½ × 1½ × 45"	X. 1 pc, ¾ × 2 × 28¾"
K. 1 pc, 1½ × 5 × 45"	Y. 1 pc, ½ × 28¾ × 40½"
L. 1 pc, ½ × 43½ × 56"	Z. 2 pcs, ½ × 7½ × 28¾"
M. 2 pcs, ½ × 21½ × 50"	AA. 2 pcs, ¾ × 3½ × 70"
N. 6 pcs, ¾ × ¾ × 28¾"	BB. 4 pcs, ¾ × 3½ × 20"
O. 3 pcs, ¾ × 15¾ × 28¾"	CC. 2 pcs, ¾ × ¾ × 43½"

Note the triangular braces (U) in each corner to which casters are attached so that the bunk can be pulled out of its recess to be made up when desired.

A paint finish is best for this project. Two coats of primer with light sanding between coats and a finish coat of the desired color should do the job.

BUILT-IN COUCH AND WALL LIGHTS

Here's how a rather ordinary recreation room in a basement can be improved with the addition of a built-in wall seat that provides storage space under it, plus two decorative end tables and a pair of tall "windows" that provide ample light (Fig. 8-29).

Refer to Fig. 8-30 and Table 8-15. The back wall paneling is attached to 2 × 4 studs fastened to the concrete wall of the basement with heavy mastic and masonry anchors. The 63" windows are lighted by two rows of fluorescent tubes, each row having a 3' and a 2' fixture mounted on boards fastened to the concrete wall behind the windows. The window frames are hinged to provide access to the lights. While you may not be able to get the fancy leaded glass in Fig. 8-29, translucent obscure plastic will fill the bill nicely.

The seat and the end tables have a frame work of 2 × 3s held together with nailed and glued butt joints. The front of the seat is covered with the same ¼" paneling as the back wall and is fastened to it with ring groove colored brads. A large piece of ¾" plywood,

Fig. 8-29: Improve your rec room with this couch.

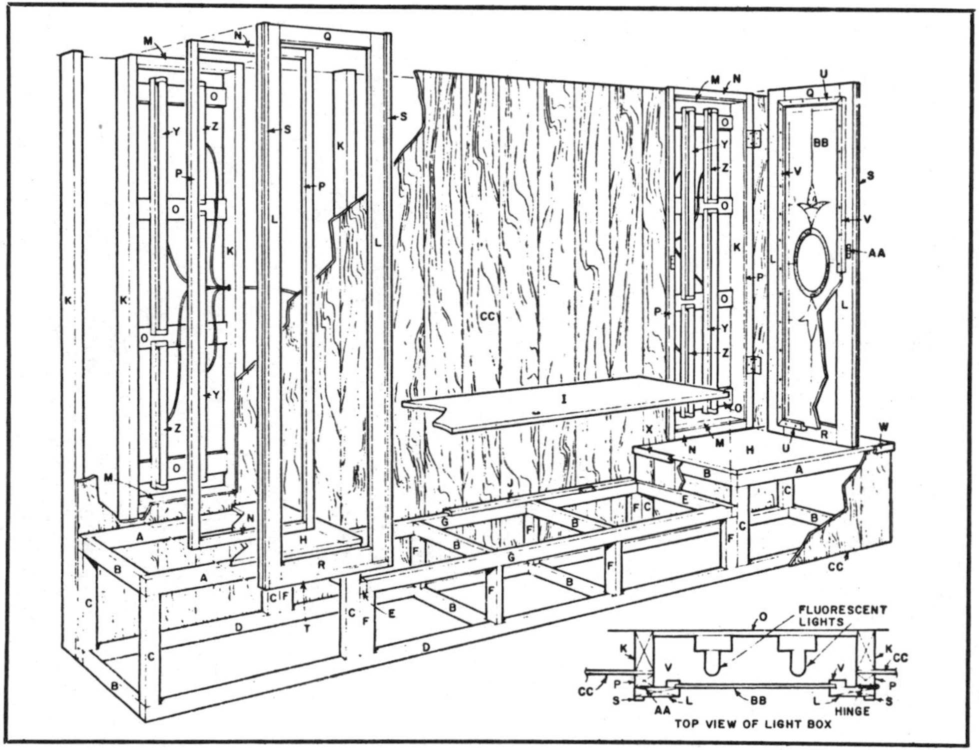

Fig. 8-30. Diagram of the couch and a top view of the light box.

Table 8-15. Materials Needed For the Couch and Wall Lights.

A. 4 pcs, 1½ × 2½ × 36″	Q. 2 pcs, ¾ × 3 × 13″
B.10 pcs, 1½ × 2½ × 21″	R. 2 pcs, ¾ × 3½ × 13″
C.8 pcs, 1½ × 2½ × 13¼″	S. 4 pcs, ¼ × 64¾″
D.2 pcs. 1½ × 2½ × 144″	T. 2 pcs, ¼ × ¾ × 18½″
E. 2 pcs, 1½ × 2½ × 24″	U. 4 pcs, ¾ × 1¼ × 15½″
F. 8 pcs, 1½ × 2½ × 7½″	V. 4 pcs, ¾ × 1¼ × 57¾″
G. 2 pcs, 1½ × 2½ × 69″	W. 2 pcs, ¼ × 1½ × 36½″
H. 2 pcs, ¾ × 24½ × 36¼″	X. 2 pcs, ¼ × 1½ × 24¼″
I. 1 pcs, ¾ × 22 × 70½″	Y. 4 pcs, 36″ Fluorescent
J. 1 pcs, ¾ × 2 × 70½″	Fixture
K. 10 pcs, 1½ × 3½ × 84″	Z. 4 pcs, 24″ Fluorescent
L. 4 pcs, ¾ × 3½ × 64¾″	Fixture
M. 4 ppcs, 1½ × 3½ × 17″	AA. 2 Touch Latch
N. 4 pcs, 1 × 1½ × 17″	BB. 2 pcs, ⅛ × 13½ × 58¾″
O. 8 pcs, ½ × 4½ × 17″	Glass Panel
P 4 pcs, ¾ × 1½ × 64¾″	CC. Wall Panleing

hinged at the back, covers the top of the seat and can be lifted up (after the cushions are removed) to allow storage inside.

The tops of the two end tables are made of ¾″ plywood painted black with narrow 1″ strips around the edges to add a little more depth to the table top. The black paint should be rubbed lightly with very fine steel wool, wet or dry fine sandpaper and water, or pumice and water and then waxed.

Note that the cushions on the seat are about equal in height to the cushion on the armchair. This height is about 17″, which is comfortable for sitting for most people, so plan the height of the seat bearing in mind the thickness of the cushions you expect to use.

MODERNISTIC BUREAU

Here's a project that looks very modernistic and boxy but has a simple, handsome appearance (Fig. 8-31). Although it seems complex, it is actually very easy to put together with butt joints fastened with white glue and 2″ finishing nails. Table 8-16 gives materials.

The top and bottom (C) are single piece of ¾″ plywood cut from one 4′ × 8′ sheet (Fig. 8-32). The end pieces and the two intervening verticals (D are all the same size and are cut from one sheet of plywood. All 11 drawer fronts (A and B) can also be conveniently cut from this same sheet.

The back (E) is also a single sheet of ¾″ plywood and is anchored to the wall behind it with six ¼″ lag screws and washers.

Fig. 8-31. You'll have plenty of space on top of this modern bureau.

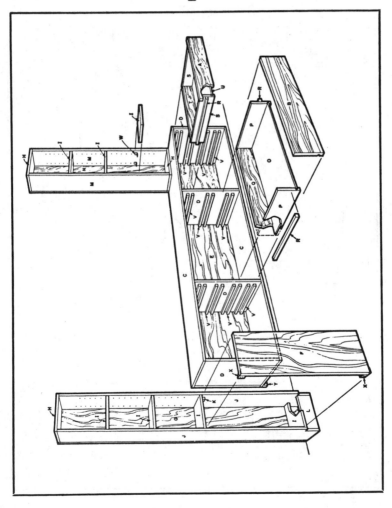

Fig. 8-32. Diagram of the bureau.

Table 8-16. Necessary Materials to Make the Bureau.

LIST OF MATERIALS	
A. 8 pcs, ¾ × 5 × 20"	M. 2 pcs, ¾ × 10 × 62½"
B. 3 pcs, ¾ × 6 11/16 × 30"	N. 1 pc, ¼ × 11½ × 64"
C. 2 pcs, ¾ × 18¾ × 73⅞"	O. 3 pcs, ¼ × 16 × 28"
D. 4 pcs, ¾ × 18 × 20 5/16"	P. 6 pcs, ½ × 5¾ × 16"
E. 1 pc, ¾ × 20 15/16 × 73⅜"	Q. 3 pcs, ½ × 5¾ × 27½"
F. 1 pc, ¾ × 10 × 25½"	R. 22 pcs, ¾ × ¾ × 16"
G. 1 pc, ¼ × 11½ × 78"	S. 16 pcs, ½ × 4¼ × 16"
H. 3 pcs, ¾ × 10 × 11½"	T. 8 pcs, ½ × 4¼ × 17½"
I 7 pcs, ¾ × 10 × 10"	U. 8 pcs, ¼ × 16 × 18"
J. 2 pcs, ¾ × 10 × 77¼"	V. 44 pcs, ¾ × ¾ × 17¼"
K. 2 pcs, ¾ × ¾ × ¾"	W. 20 pcs. "L-Bracket" Shelf Supports
L. 1 pc. ¾ × 5 × 10"	X. 2 pcs, Pivot Hinges
	Y. 1 pc, ¾ × 1½ × 73⅜"

The lag screws are 4" long and are driven into predrilled holes through the plasterboard and studs.

The tall, narrow bookcases are essentially decorative and can be used for books and small ornaments. These bookcases and their shelves are made of ¾" lumber or plywood.. The shelves can be adjustable or fixed. Fixed shelves will make the cases stronger and will require only a ¼" back. The shelves can be fastened with glue and finishing nails driven through the sides and into the edges of the shelves. If you prefer adjustable shelves, make the back ½" thick.

The right hand bookcase is fastened to the top surface of the bureau with glue and 1¼" No. 8 screws driven from below. The top of the case is fastened to the wall behind it with screws and angle braces.

Fastening the left hand case is done in the same way—angle braces at the top to the wall behind and No. 8 screws driven through the left side of the bureau. The door (F) on this book case is optional. The finish in this instance is two coats of white alkyd enamel over a white primer. Of course, the color here depends on your own particular decorative scheme and this applies to the glass drawer knobs, too.

BUILT-IN STORAGE DESK AREA

Here's a project that will brighten a teen-age boy's room and provide him with plenty of space for all his school work and hobbies (Fig. 8-33). The nice thing about it is that you can come up with a professional looking job and you don't need any great carpentry skills. Table 8-17 lists materials.

The desk project is the main job and it's simpler than it looks. Think of it as two topless boxes bridged by the part (E) that forms the top or work surface (Fig. 8-34). Everything is made of ¾"

Fig. 8-33. This project will spruce up a teenage boy's room.

plywood put to gether with butt joints fastened with glue and 2″ finishing nails.

Both boxes stand on hollow squares (D) recessed about 2″ to provide toe space. The left hand "box" has two or three shelves inside and a door hinged on the left. You can simplify the task of making drawers by buying frontless plastic drawers and making the fronts (C) out of plywood. If you can't find such drawers, make them as shown in Fig. 8-34.

The top (E) is a solid piece of ¾″ plywood covered with laminated plastic attached with contact cement. The 1½″ edging around the top is also covered with laminated plastic. Fasten the top to the two boxes with 2″ screws driven from below.

The bookshelves on the wall are the usual metal standards with 6″ boards painted to harmonize with the desk below. Use 3″ screws to fasten the metal standards to the studs behind the plasterboard wall.

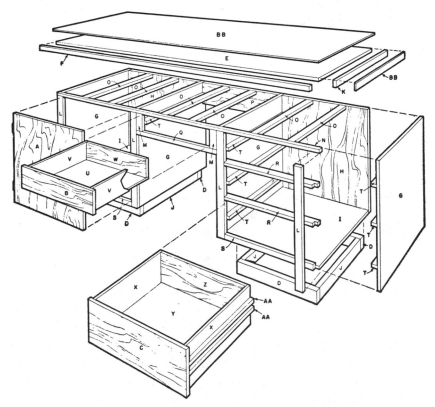

Fig. 8-34. Sketch of the built-in storage desk area.

Table 8-17. Required Materials For the Built-in Storage Desk Area.

A. 1 pc, ¾ × 20 × 22¾"	O. 6 pcs, ¾ × 1½ × 22½."
B. 1 pc, ¾ × 4 × 20"	P. 1 pc, ¾ × 6 × 23"
C. 1 pc, ¾ × 7 × 21½."	Q. 1 pc, ¾ × 1¼ × 23"
D. 4 pcs, 1½ × 3½ × 20"	R. 2 pcs, ¾ × 1½ × 23"
E. 1 pc, ¾ × 24 × 72"	S. 2 pcs, ¾ × 1¼ × 21½."
F. 1 pc, ¾ × 1¼ × 72¾"	T. 8 pcs, ¾ × 1½ × 23¼"
G. 4 pcs, ¾ × 23¼ × 24¾"	U. 1 pc, ½ × 17 × 19"
H. 2 pcs, ¾ × 23 × 24¾"	V. 2 pcs, ½ × 4 × 19"
I. 2 pcs, ¾ × 22½ × 23"	W. 1 pc, ½ × ¾ × 17"
J. 4 pcs, 1½ × 3½ × 20"	X. 6 pcs, ½ × 7 × 19"
K. 1 pc, ¾ × 1¼ × 24"	Y. 3 pcs, ½ × 19 × 19"
L. 4 pcs, ¾ × 1½ × 24"	Z. 3 pcs, ½ × 6½ × 19"
M. 2 pcs, ¾ × 1½ × 4"	AA. 1 6 pcs, ¾ × ¾ × 19"
N. 1 pc, ¾ × ¾ × 24"	BB. Plastic Laminate

Finish with paint, preferably two coats of enamel. The bulletin boards in the corner can be made or bought. If you make them, use mitered corners for best appearance.

BOYS' ROOM BUILT-IN

Here's a charming room idea which clearly uses space to provide sleeping quarters, storage and a study area. Both bunks and study shelf are located in built-in alcoves.

Bunk Beds

The two bunks have 2 × 4 frames attached to walls with ¼" lag screws and washers driven into the wall studs behind the plasterboard. See Table 8-18 for materials.

Both bunks have a front lip (A) which is 5" high to contain the 5" rubber mattress (Fig. 8-36). In keeping with the rest of the room, the lip is masked with the same paneling (S) which covers the walls. The lower bunk platform (F) is supported by the partitions (C) which are notched at the lower front to accommodate the toe board (O) and its paneling cover (U).

The drawers that fit under the lower bunk have casters under them so they can easily be pulled out. All drawer and frame joints are butt type and fastened with nails and glue. The paneling on them is attached with panel cement from cartridges in inexpensive caulking guns and colored nails normally supplied with the paneling.

Study Shelf

The study shelf framing (I-H-I) is made up of 1 × 2s except the front (J) which is a 1 × 3. The framing of the shelf is fastened to studs behind the plasterboard and paneling with nails. Note the

Fig. 8-35. This innovative room idea will be a hit with your kids.

angle irons screwed to the back wall cleat (H) with 3½" No. 10 wood screws.

The crimson color of the shelf may be Formica or any similar laminate attached with panel cement. However, you may find it much easier to use paint from an aerosol can for parts G-J. If you

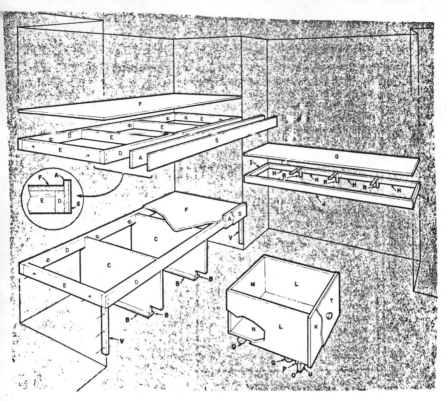

Fig. 8-36. Sketch of the boys' room built-in.

decide to use paint make these two pieces from presanded plywood, good one side and free of patches.

Sand the surfaces with an orbital sander using 100 grit aluminum oxide paper, followed by another sanding with 150 grit

Table 8-18. Materials Needed For the Boys' Room Built-in.

LIST OF MATERIALS	
A. 2 pcs., ¾ × 5 × 76½"	L. 6 pcs., ¾ × 8 × 36"
B. 4 pcs., ¾ × 37" Cove Molding	M. 3 pcs., ¾ × 7¼ × 23"
C. 2 pcs., ¾ × 14½ × 41"	N. 3 pcs., ¾ × 23 × 36"
D. 4 pcs., 1½ × 3½ × 76½"	O. 3 pcs., ¾ × 2½ × 25½"
E. 6 pcs., 1½ × 3½ × 38"	P. 3 pcs., ¾ × ¾ × 24½"
F. 2 pcs., ¾ × 41 × 76½"	Q. 12 Casters (2" wheels)
G. 1 pc., ¾ × 18 × 60"	R. 3 pcs., Angle irons
H. 4 pcs., ¾ × 1½ × 14¼"	S. 2 pcs., ¼ × 5 × 76½" Paneling
I. 2 pcs., ¾ × 1½ × 16½"	T. 3 pcs., ¼ × 8 × 25½" Paneling
J. 1 pc., ¾ × 3 × 60"	U. 3 pcs., ¼ × 2½ × 25½" Paneling
K. 3 pcs., ¾ × 8 × 25½"	V. 2 pcs., ¾ × 1½ × 8"

sandpaper. Remove all dust with a vacuum cleaner and a tack rag (available in hardware, paint, and home center stores).

Prime the raw wood surface with a primer recommended by the manufacturer for the final color you choose. Use finishing nails to attach these two parts to the frame. Countersink them and fill the nail holes with wood putty. Sand the putty smooth when dry, then prime and paint.

Chapter 9
Outdoor Furniture

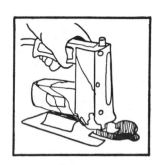

Is there webbing on your outdoor chairs that needs to be replaced? Would you like to substitute redwood slats for worn webbing? Do you need an outdoor table which can double as a patio bench? Are you having problems with rust and missing ornaments on patio furniture? This chapter has remedies for all these problems.

REPLACING WEBBING ON OUTDOOR CHAIRS

Do you have an aluminum lawn or patio chair whose webbing is falling apart and looks so shabby you are thinking of throwing it out? If the aluminum frame is still in good condition, hang on to your old chair and save yourself the cost of a new one because new plastic webbing is readily available in hardware stores and installing it is very easy (Fig. 9-1).

There are two basic types of plastic seating and back material—flat webbing strips about 2½" wide and thin, flexible tubing which is wound around the frame. Let us consider flat webbing first since this is the most common.

Flat Webbing

When removing the old webbing, look carefully at the way the ends are anchored to the frame. Sometimes there is a brass plated grommet (a beveled metal circle) with a flathead sheet metal screw that goes through the grommet and webbing into a hole in the

Fig. 9-1. It's not hard to install some bright new webbing.

frame. The grommet serves the same purpose as a washer which is to increase the gripping power of the screw head.

You won't be able to use the old grommet but you can buy them in most hardware stores along with a special pair of pliers for clamping them to the ends of the webbing. Some chairs simply have zinc plated washers and round head sheet metal screws to anchor the plastic webbing; others have special anchoring devices held by sheet metal screws. When removing the old stripping, be sure to save these special anchors if possible. No matter what method of anchoring is used, the screws should go through at least two thicknesses of webbing (Figs. 9-2 and 9-3). In some chairs the double thickness has been folded over to form four thicknesses. Wherever possible use the manufacturer's method of anchoring and the same number of folds as in the old webbing.

Measure the length of the new webbing from an old piece removed from the chair without cutting. This is especially impor-

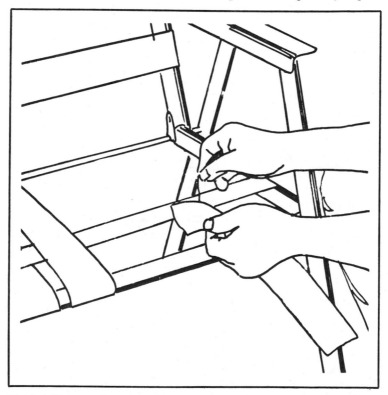

Fig. 9-2. Use an old piece of webbing as a guide for the proper length. Metal stamping with hook is pushed through the double thickness.

Fig. 9-3. Barbed hook is then inserted into the slot in the frame.

tant if your chair is of the folding type since the webbing in these have more slack in them than the rigid kind (Fig. 9-4).

Vinyl Tubing

The second type of material used in outdoor aluminum chairs is a thin, flexible, very tough vinyl tubing. This is anchored with a copper plated steel staple driven through a single fold of the tubing into two holes in the frame. If the staple breaks or gets lost use two ½″ zinc plated screws with small washers (Fig. 9-5). The tubing can usually be found in coils in hardware stores.

Unlike the webbed chair, the type that's covered with tubing has a separate seat and back so you need two different lengths of tubing. Once you have anchored the starting end of the back, you wind the tubing from side to side as tightly as you can until you get down to the bottom where you anchor it just as you did at the start (Fig. 9-6). The same method is used to cover the seat, the only difference being that the length of tubing is shorter.

If you also wish to improve the appearance of the aluminum frame by polishing it, use No. 0000 steel wool followed by a hard

294

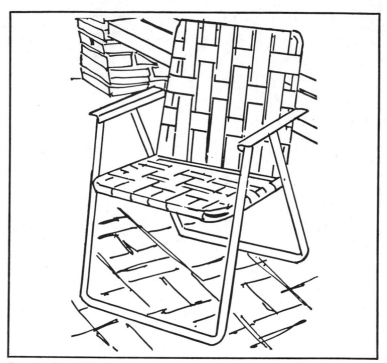

Fig. 9-4. The finished chair, when open, will have the proper tension.

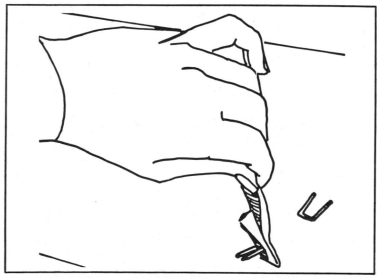

Fig. 9-5. Plastic tubing wound on chairs is fastened with sheet metal screws or heavy staples, which are pushed into holes in the frame.

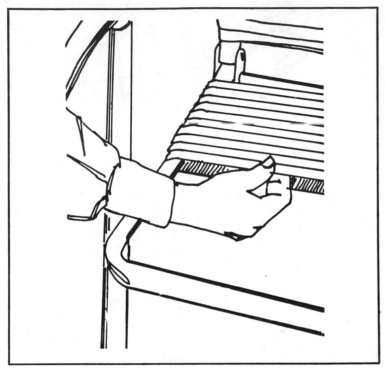

Fig. 9-6. When winding, pull each strand tightly to prevent sagging. Tension flattens the tubing like a ribbon. Do not twist tubing.

paste wax (Fig. 9-7). For a really high polish, put a cloth wheel in the chuck of an electric drill, charge its edge with jewelers' rouge and apply the wheel to the aluminum frame. Of course, any polishing should be done before the tubing or webbing is applied.

REDWOOD CHAIRS FROM ALUMINUM FRAMES

Do you have a folding aluminum lounge chair whose woven plastic webbing has seen better days? In fact, the webbing may be in such sad shape that you are think of struggling with replacement webbing or even throwing the whole chaise away. Well, you don't have to do either. Instead, replace the worn webbing with strong, redwood or pine slats that will give the tired old chair a whole new beautiful appearance without affecting its compact folding (Fig. 9-8 and 9-9).

First strip off all the old webbing and webbing fasteners (Fig. 9-10). Then snug up all rivets by tapping with a hammer against a solid metal back-up block.

Fig. 9-7. To complete the renovation job, polish the aluminum with steel wool and coat the frame with paste wax for a lasting finish.

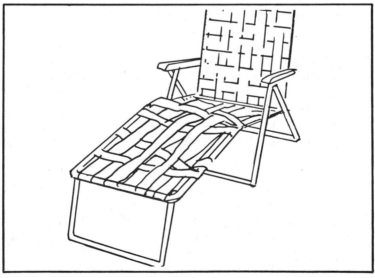

Fig. 9-8. If you have a folding aluminum lounge chair which has broken plastic webbing, don't throw it out or struggle with replacement webbing. that will only break again.

Fig. 9-9. The worn webbing can be replaced with redwood stained slats.

Measuring and Cutting Cross Supports

With the frame in an opened-up position on the floor, measure and mark the locations for the cross supports (Fig. 9-11). There should be six 1 × 2 supports of redwood, or pine stained to look like redwood. Pine is recommended because it does not splinter or split easily and costs less than redwood. The cross supports should be located 8 to 10″ apart. One of the back cross supports should be located 6″ above the point where the backrest boards meet the seat boards, and the other cross support 8″ above this. Mark locations on tubing with a pencil.

For the seat, the front cross support should be centered 6″ from the footrest hinge joint and the rear support 9″ back from this. The two footrest cross supports should be located 6″ and 16″ respectively, forward of the hinge joint. Using the twelve locations you have marked on the tubing, center punch and drill clearance holes for No. 8 screws.

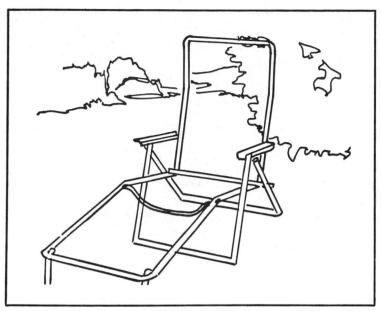

Fig. 9-10. To begin the project, strip off all old webbing and webbing fasteners. Then check and tighten up the joints of the frame.

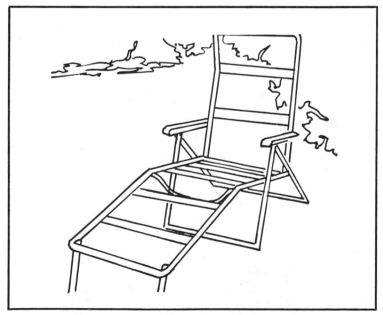

Fig. 9-11. Mark locations on the frame of the lounge chair for six cross supports which should be located about 8 to 10″ apart.

Fig. 9-12. If you have used pine slats and cross supports, finish them with redwood stain at the proper time during the project.

Cut the 1 × 2 cross supports to the proper width. The best way to measure these is to hold the 1 × 2s against the tubing at each pair of holes. Mark off each piece so it reaches the outside of the tubing on each side. Each piece will have to be measured in this way because the frame might be distorted a bit from use.

When all six cross supports have been cut to size, rabbet out a piece at each end to permit them to set inside the tubing ¼". The rabbet should be ¼" deep and 1⅛" long. This will bring all slat sections up to a point ¼" under flush with the front face of the tubing for a better looking finished job.

Sand all six cross supports, rounding off all sharp corners at the ends. Apply a coat of redwood stain and set aside to dry (Fig. 9-12).

Preparing Slats

While the cross supports are drying, prepare the slats for the back, seat and footrest using ½ × 2⅝" lumber (Fig. 9-13). For the back slats, measure from a point 2" below the inside of the top aluminum cross bar to within 1" of the point where back boards and seat boards will meet. This is the length of the back boards.

For the length of the seat slats, measure from a point 1″ in front of where the back boards and seat boards will meet to a point 1½″ back of the footrest hinge joint. For the footrest slats, measure from a point 1½″ in front of the folding joint between seat and footrest to a point 1″ back of the folding end leg.

After you get these measurements, it is a good idea to cut up some scrap lumber to length and check the fit. After cutting the slats, sand them, making sure to round long edges.

Stack six pieces for each section together with the bottom side up. Clamp the stack tightly together with 2 "C" clamps and apply a coat of redwood stain to the ends and sides. Release clamps and lay slats out on bench with the bottom side up and apply stain to bottom side; leave front side unstained until later.

Attach the proper cross support to the proper pair of holes in the frame. Square each cross support with the frame and drill through the holes in the tubing and through the wood. Attach loosely with 2″ No. 8-32 round head machine screws. Put a washer on the screw against the back of the crossbar, then a spring washer and then a hex nut.

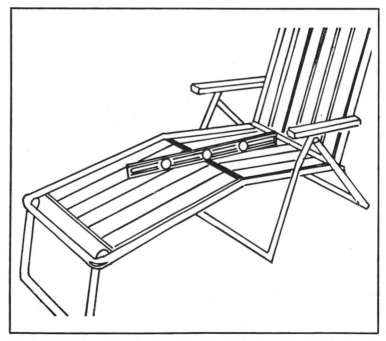

Fig. 9-13. Cut slats for the back, seat and footrest using ½″ × 2⅝″ lumber. A level is used to check the slant of seat and footrest.

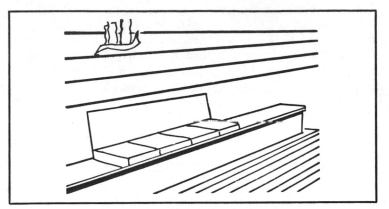

Fig. 9-14. This patio bench converts into a table.

Wipe excess stain off slats and lay them out on the cross supports with the unstained sides up. Mark one slat from each section with the location of the center of each cross support. At the two marked locations on each group of slats, drill clearance holes for screws.

Lay out the slats again in their proper sections and determine the spacing between each slat. To do this, push all the slats to one side and measure gap that is left. Divide this figure by seven and you have the spacing between slats and between outside slats and frame.

With the slats properly located, fasten with No. 8 by 1″ flat head wood screws.

Remove all three completed secretions from frame, sand and apply stain to all unstained surfaces. Use a steel wood soap pad and give all the tubing a good scouring, followed by a thorough rinsing with clear water. Finish off wood parts with clear gloss polyurethane and attach permanently in place. Wood or plastic arm rests can be finished off with a warm brown enamel.

OUTDOOR BENCH THAT CONVERTS TO A TABLE

This ingenious patio bench not only offers storage space under its seat but also converts readily into a handy table for outdoor eating (Figs. 9-14 and 9-15). While this particular bench rests on a wooden deck, it can just as easily be anchored to a concrete slab with masonry anchors.

The table top is 72″ long and 32″ wide. The width is made up of two 16″ sections of tongue-and-groove boards. Table 9-1 lists materials. One section is hinged to the wall of the house and a

Fig. 9-15. Enjoy eating on this handy buffet table that disappears when not in use.

303

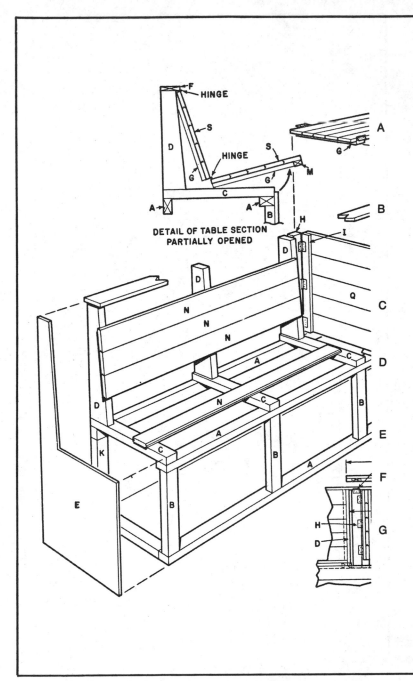

DETAIL OF TABLE SECTION
PARTIALLY OPENED

Fig. 9-16. Construction details for the outdoor bench/table.

304

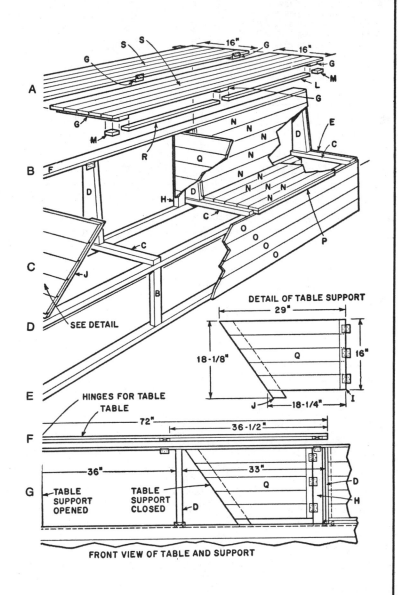

DETAIL OF TABLE SUPPORT

29"

18-1/8"

Q

16"

J

I

18-1/4"

HINGES FOR TABLE
TABLE

72"

36-1/2"

36"

33"

TABLE
SUPPORT
OPENED

TABLE
SUPPORT
CLOSED

Q

D

H

D

FRONT VIEW OF TABLE AND SUPPORT

Table 9-1. Materials for the Outdoor Bench/Table.

A. 3 pcs, 1½· × 2½· × 168″ B. 7 pcs, 1½· × 2½· × 12¼″ C. 7 pcs, 1½· × 2½· × 19¾″ D. 7 pcs, 1½· × 16⅝″ × (See Detail) E. 2 pcs, ½· × 19¾ × 33⅜″ F. 1 pc, ¾ × 3½· × 169″ G. 6 pcs, ¾ × 2½· × 16″ H. 2 pcs, 1½· × 2½· × 18⅛″ I. 2 pcs, ¾ × 1½· × 16″ J. 2 pcs, ¾ × 2½· × (See Detail)	K. 2 pcs, 1½· × 2½· × 10¾″ L. 1 pc, ¾ × 1½· × 1½· × × 32½″ M. 2 pcs, ¾ × 1½· × 1½″ N. 2p pcs, ¾ × 3½· × 48½″ T. & G. O. 4 pcs, ¾ × 3½· × 169″ T. & G. P. 1 pc, ¾ × 1½· × 169″ Q. ¾ × 3½″ × (See Detail) T. & G. R. 1 pc, ¾ × 1½· × 29″ S. 10 pcs, ¾ × 3½· × 72″ T. & G.

second set of hinges (3) in the middle of the table connects both sections. Thus when the table top is not in use and swings down, the section nearest the wall becomes part of the back of the the bench while the outermost section becomes part of the seat.

The table top is supported by two "wings" (Q) also made up of tongue-and-groove boards held together by cleats I and J (Fig. 9-16). The wings are hinged vertically to the housewall and fold back against it. When the table top swings down, it conceals the wings behind it. Note the 2 × 3 cross members (C) that rest on the front wall of the bench and on boards at the back and support the seat section of the table top. The pieces of trim (R-L) at the front edge of the table acts as a stop to prevent the seat from going back too far and also lines up with the trim on both sides of the movable section.

A handy outdoor storage place for cusions and outdoor garden and lawn tools is readily available by simply lifting the hinged seat. Of course, you don't have to make your bench out of 1 × 4 tongue-and-groove boards if you prefer plywood. However if you do use plywood make sure you get the type designed for exterior use which has waterproof glue between the plies. Also be sure to use zinc coated nails to prevent rust streaks and brass screws on the hinges.

The finish is up to you but a good grade of latex exterior paint over a previously applied primer will do the job. Using the same color of paint as is now on the wall behind the bench will help make it an integral part of the house.

Buttons and Ornaments

The glass top of metal furniture tables usually rests on little plastic or rubber buttons. Sooner or later these buttons or pads get squeezed down or dry out and fall off. Don't bother to try to get replacements. You won't have much luck. Instead, get a roll of sponge rubber of the self-sticking type (Fig. 9-19). Apply this to the metal shelf on which the plate glass rests and go all around the four sides. The weight of the glass is enough to keep the rubber in place.

Leaves, flowers and other metal ornaments sometimes get knocked off and this spoils the appearance of the furniture. The ideal way to fix this is to spot weld the broken pieces. However, spot welding is for professionals with special equipment.

Epoxy glue will often do the job but not always. Apply a liberal amount to the bare metal where the break occurred and tape the broken piece firmly in place. After 24 hours if it still holds it will probably hold forever.

If this doesn't work, some solder and a soldering gun probably will (Fig. 9-20). Acid core wire solder is best for this purpose.

Replacing And Tightening Screws

Aluminum furniture with webbed seats and backs is often subject to hard wear. Generally the webbing weakens first because

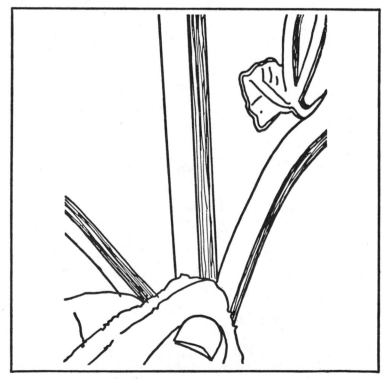

Fig. 9-17. You can fix the finish on your metal porch furniture when it gets rusted or chipped. Start by clearing away loose particles and cleaning the surface with steel wool.

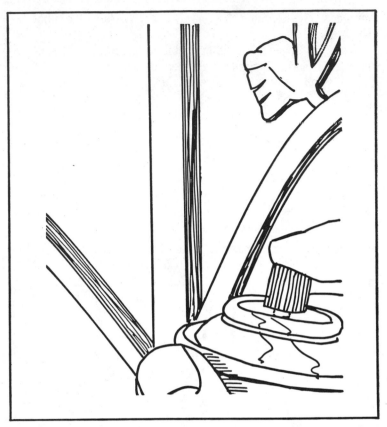

Fig. 9-18. Spray a light coat of primer on the cleaned area. Smooth with fine sandpaper and apply several finish coats until this area matches the rest of the surface.

of exposure to summer sun and soaking rains. Since the webbing is the most vulnerable part of this furniture, it should be inspected first. Look for frayed or torn threads especially where the ends are wrapped around the frame and in the seat area (Fig. 9-21).

Screws that anchor the webbing should be examined and if loose should be tightened (Fig. 9-22). If the screws are too loose to be tightened, replace them with others of the next larger size. Be sure that the replacements are rust-proof, sheet metal screws with threads that go all the way up to the head. Buy aluminum washers along with the screws and webbing.

Usually the directions on the webbing box tell you how long to cut each strip so that you have two or three (preferably three) extra folds at each end. The new screw goes through the washer, the

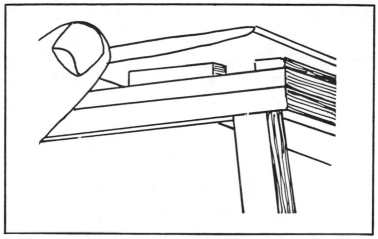

Fig. 9-19. The button pads on which a glass table top rests often flatten within a season. You can replace them with adhesive-back weatherstripping in long or short pieces.

webbing folds, and then into the hole. The washer gives the screw greater gripping power and the extra folds minimize fraying and tearing.

FIXING METAL PATIO FURNITURE

Many homeowners have metal porch furniture and right about now these well used items should be dragged out from the cellar for

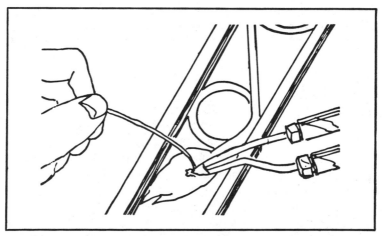

Fig. 9-20. Small ornamental elements can be reattached to metal porch furniture with a soldering gun. However, be sure to have structural parts welded by a professional.

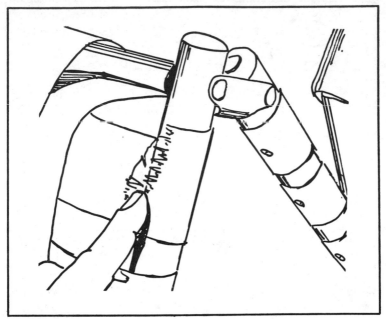

Fig. 9-21. If the webbing frays and begins to separate, replace it. New webbing can be bought in rolls and is available at most hardware stores.

inspection. Usually this inspection is apt to reveal rust spots in the painted steel furniture, missing screws, loose rivets, and worn out webbing on aluminum chairs as well as metal tables with loose tops or wobbly legs.

With only a modest amount of effort all these faults can be corrected and if it's still a little cool in your region of the country, all the work can be done indoors in your garage, shop or basement.

Removing Rust

Most steel or iron furniture shows little wear and lasts forever if its finish is properly maintained. If you find that the entire finish is peeling and showing rust spots, you might as welll remove all of it with paint remover. Then remove the rust, spray on a metal primer from an aerosol can and follow this up with the enamel color of your choice.

What is more likely to happen is that you will find scattered areas of peeling paint and rust spots. Remove all peeling or loose paint and rust with coarse steel wool (Fig. 9-17). Then go over the remaining rust with medium grade emery cloth until all rust is removed. The rust removal will go faster if you use a rotary wire brush in the chuck of an electric drill. Another method of eliminating rust is to use one of the rust inhibitors now available in hardware and paint stores. Some will affect the surrounding paint, others will not.

Once the rust is removed the surrounding paint edges would be sanded with fine sandpaper to a feather edge. Then spray the bare metal with zinc chromate metal primer from an aerosol can, being sure also to cover the nearest feather edged old paint. You may have to spray the bare metal area several times to build up the low spots caused by previous paint removal. The edges of the metal primer should be sanded with 100-grit open coat aluminum oxide paper and all primed areas should be smoothed, working the sandpaper back forth until the primed spots blend smoothly with the old finish (Fig. 9-18).

Apply a matching finish from a spray can, adding two or three light coats. You may have to search in several stores for a color that comes closest to matching the original finish. If the new finish is a little too glossy, use very fine steel wool to bring the gloss down.

Aluminum patio chairs and chaises often have adjustable backs. The hardware that allows for this adjustment is held by retaining screws that may have become loose. If the threads of these screws are stripped or they are too loose to be tightened, replace them with larger sheet metal screws.

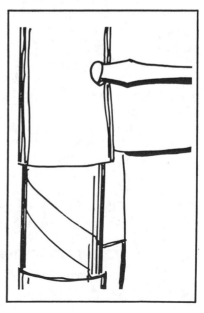

Fig. 9-22. Tighten loose screws. If any are badly worn, replace with screws of slightly larger diameter. Use sheet metal screws with threads up to the head.

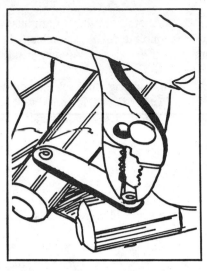

Fig. 9-23. Use a pair of pliers to crimpt the heads of loose rivets such as the one shown. If the rivet cannot be tightened, replace it with a blind rivet which can easily be installed.

Rivet Problems

Your inspection may also reveal some loose rivets. Sometimes crimping the head of a loose rivet with a pair of pliers is enough to tighten it and make it useful again (Fig. 9-23). If this doesn't work, the rivet will have to be replaced.

You will probably find it almost impossible to replace these rivets with the same type used by the manufacturer. There is, however, a type of rivet which is readily available to the homeowner in most hardware stores. This is known as a blind rivet and is sold with a rivet gun which looks like a pair of pliers.

Remove the old rivet with a hammer and punch applied to either end. If you find this difficult use an electric drill to drill out one of the rivet heads, then draw the rivet out with pliers from the opposite end.

Finally, if you don't care to fuss with rivets after removing the old one, use a machine screw with a large enough diameter to make a close fit in the holes in the aluminum frame. Two hex nuts tightened against each other on the end of the screw will hold it in place. To prevent the nuts from loosening put a few drops of clear epoxy glue on the nuts and on the threads of the screw behind them. Be sure to use zinc-coated nuts and screw.

HOW TO RECYCLE PATIO FURNITURE

Some aluminum framed chairs that should be out on the patio or lawn are gathering dust in the garage because of broken web-

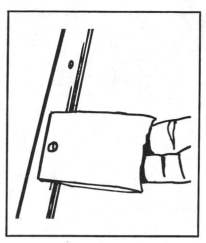

Fig. 9-24. Anchor held by spiral nail is removed by turning webbing.

bing. However, if the frame is still in good shape, you can easily replace the vinyl webbing in as little as two hours. Replacement kits, available in most home center and hardware stores, contain both a large roll of woven vinyl webbing and new aluminum self-threading screws.

The old webbing is usually anchored to the back of the frame with a strip of metal and a screw or spiral nail with slotted head. To start this job, unfasten the old webbing by removing the old screws with a screwdriver (Fig. 9-24). If the chair has spiral nails, you'll find them harder to remove since their slots are usually too shallow for the screwdriver to grip. If you have this problem, cut the old webbing with a pair of scissors all around the frame and remove it. Then give the metal anchoring strips a few turns and the nail will come out.

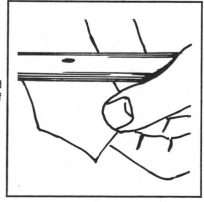

Fig. 9-25. Webbing strip is folded into peak to provide four layers of vinyl.

313

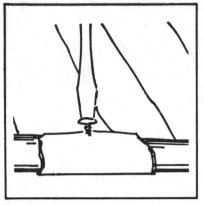

Fig. 9-26. Screw is driven through folded webbing into a hole in the frame.

Install the horizontal webbing first, allowing 1½″ extra at each end of the frame. Fold each end into a triangular peak, as shown in Fig. 9-25, and bend the triangle around to the back of the frame over the holes. Put a screw through the folded webbing and into the hole in the frame. Tighten screw firmly. The four layers in the folded ends of the webbing will provide ample strength to resist tearing.

Once horizontal strips are in place, push the back of the chair down and extend it full length (Figs. 9-27 and 9-28). Fasten one vertical strip to the top of the chair and interweave it through the horizontal webbing (Fig. 9-29) of the frame. Allow about 2½″ beyond the bottom of the frame. Before fastening the bottom ends, cut the remainder of the vertical strips to the same length as the first one.

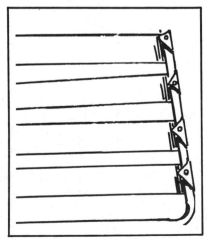

Fig. 9-27. Horizontal strips are installed first, beginning at the top of the chair.

314

Fig. 9-28. Chair with installation of horizontal webbing completed.

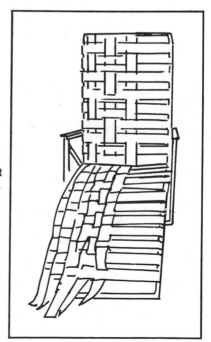

Fig. 9-29. Fasten vertical strips at top and interweave with horizontals.

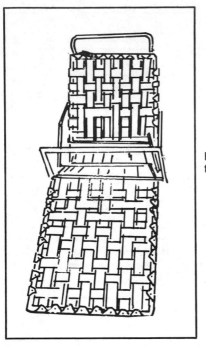

Fig. 9-30. Rear view of webbing fastened in place.

Fig. 9-31. Completed rewebbing job should last several years.

Then raise the back of the chair one notch and fasten the remaining vertical strips to the top of the chair, interweaving them through the horizontals until you come to the end. Pull the loose ends as tightly as possible, then fasten to the bottom of the frame. The reason for raising the back of the chair slightly is that, when fully extended, the frame will keep the lengthwise webbing strips taut and provide more support (Figs. 9-30 and 9-31). The cost of the total project may be no more than about $3.

Chapter 10
Two Alternative
Furniture Materials

If you're tired of seeing and having furniture made from fine woods, you might consider making some pieces out of plywood or plastic. Both materials are relatively easy to work with.

FAST (PLYWOOD) FURNITURE

"Fast furniture" grew out of a need to furnish a house quickly, easily and inexpensively. If a person is a master craftsperson or cabinet maker, building furniture is natural. But what about everyone else?

Do-it-yourself furniture made from fine woods (oak, maple, walnut, mahogany) is rapidly reaching the point where the cost of materials makes the investment of time impractical; that is to say, the total cost is nearly equal to prices charged by stores for similar pieces. Pine, although still relatively inexpensive, is quite soft and splits, checks and warps easily, particularly if used outdoors.

Cross-lapping

We've settled on ¾"-thick plywood as the most viable alternative, used with what we call the "fast furniture" system or the Zegel system. Settling on plywood as the material, we set about creating designs for comfortable furniture which could be cut from flat sheets of plywood. The results offer look and comfort, but require less work and few skills. And since few tools and virtually no hardware are needed, it costs less.

We did not invent the "fast furniture" system of joining wood together. In official carpentry parlance it is called "cross-lap." It also has several slang names, the most common is "bird's mouth."

Since cross-lapping is the method of assembling the furniture, plywood is a good choice. The slots required for cross-lapped joints are prone to break in ordinary wood if the slot is too close to the end. Even with plywood, slots should be no closer than 1⅛" to the end.

Construction Techniques

The "fast furniture" system has been designed to require only a few tools, including saber saw with plywood blades; straightedge (yardstick, meter stick or similar); 8′ folding ruler; four C-clamps, drill (hand or electric) and drill bits. The slot is the opening cut to receive another component; the tab is the section of wood between the slot and the nearest edge parallel to it (Fig. 10-1). The curve is the rounding off of a corner.

The shelving illustrated is just the tip of the iceberg of possibilities for making shelves and room dividers using the "fast furniture" system. The shelves are simple to lay out and make, since all lines and cuts are straight. You can round off the corners if you like, but this is not as important as it would be if the project were an easy chair or other piece where the profile is important.

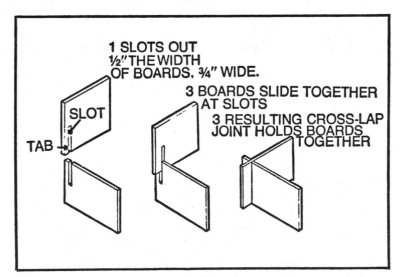

Fig. 10-1. Shown are tabs and slots.

Fig. 10-2. The room divider/shelves is a project that employs the basic cross-lap method.

It is best to make a scale drawing of the piece you are going to do. We like graph paper ruled with eight squares to the inch, because it works well with the two scale sizes we use most often: 1½″ equal 1′, and 3″ equal 1′. It is also a good idea to draw a scale-sized piece of 4 × 8′ plywood: you can cut out the pieces from the graph paper and position them on the scale drawing of the plywood sheet, to be sure you're making the best possible use of the the plywood. For complicated pieces of furniture a scale model, made of cardboard, will allow you to experiment with various shapes and design a piece with pleasing lines.

Lay out the pieces on the plywood to the size indicated in Fig. 10-3. Cut the pieces to the lengths indicated. You can make the pieces as wide as you wish, but a shelf width between 8″ to 12″ is a good choice for bookshelves. Mark the slot locations off with a square. We like to cut the slots 1/32" for a tight fit. In ¾" wood this would be ¾" minus 1/32" or 23/32 slot width. Cut the slots out with your saber saw.

The measurements in Fig. 10-3 are on center, or from the center of one slot to the center of the other. When the slots are cut, slip the shelves into the upright supports. You will have to tap the pieces together using a mallet or hammer. Use a small wood block placed over the piece to protect the edges from the hammer as you tap the two pieces together. If the pieces will not fit into the slots with moderate tapping, sand or rasp the slots slightly larger and rub them with a bar of hand soap. The soap will serve as a lubricant to help slip the pieces into place.

If you like you can use dowels to make a permanent joint (See Fig. 10-3). If you are careful in cutting the slots the shelves will be very sturdy, and dowels won't be needed. You can then disassemble the pieces and pack them flat, making them easy to move.

For a wood finish you can choose either paint or stain. If paint is the choice be sure to use a good primer first. Follow the directions on the paint can for new "wood." Other choices include

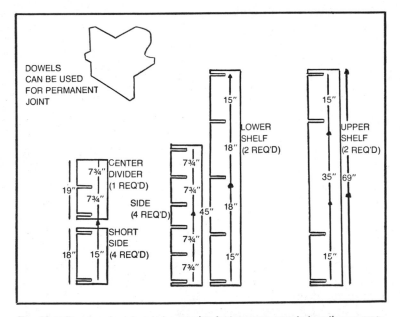

Fig. 10-3. Pegs or dowels can be used to fasten components together permanently. The slot width should be equal to (or slightly smaller than) the thickness of the piece of wood that will slide into it. The length of the slot must be one-half the length of the shorter of the two components.

Fig. 10-4. Chair and desk made with the "fast furniture" system. The desk breaks down for easy moving.

stain, followed by a sealer and varnish; clear varnish or polyurethane for a natural finish; or tung oil, our personal favorite. Tung oil can be applied with a lint free cloth, or your hand. Just rub the tung oil into the wood. You can apply as many coats as you wish. The more coats of tung oil, the more glossy the finish. Figures 10-4 through 10-10 show some "fast furniture."

PLASTIC FURNITURE

If a home handyman finds a lovely-to-look-at but expensive piece of wooden furniture, he'll try to build one just like it, and

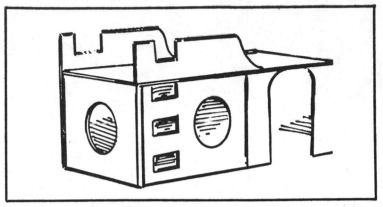

Fig. 10-5. A superbed gives kids a place to sleep with a playhouse down below. Build it for either purpose, or both.

usually he achieves a neat creation. Wood has always been a favorite of do-it-yourselfers. Plastics, however, being relatively new, still frighten a great many people. But working with plastic is in many ways easier than working with wood, once you learn the basic differences.

By the time you've finished this chapter, you'll know these differences. Better still, you'll know how to build $575 luxurious shelves for about $150 (closer to $100 if you shop carefully; closer

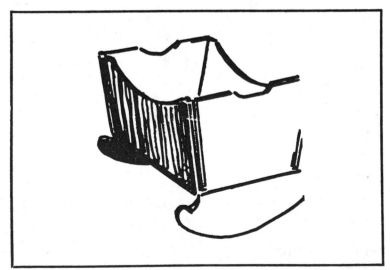

Fig. 10-6. The cradle, besides its obvious use, can be used as a planter or for magazine storage.

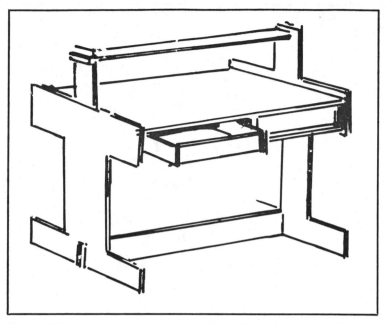

Fig. 10-7. Two-faced desk provides two desks in the space of one. Both sides have drawers.

to $200 if you take the easy way out. You'll be able to build the $100 coffee table for $10 to $15.

Types of Plastic

Furniture shown here is built from a clear acrylic type of plastic sold under brand names such as Plexiglas, Lucite and Acrylite. Acrylic plastic is just as clear and sparkling as glass; yet it is incredibly hard to break. It comes in sheets of various thicknesses. The thicker your plastic, the more luxurious your finished furniture will look.

However, price is a big factor too. Acrylic plastics aren't cheap. So in designing the furniture here we've kept thickness to a minimum.

Acrylic plastics scratch more easily than glass. That's the major problem you'll find in building and enjoying furniture like this. However even glass will scratch if you slide gritty or sharp-edged metal or glass objects over it. With plastic you can do something about the scratches; with glass you can't. If you do happen to get a scratch on some highly visible part of your plastic furniture, you can buff it out.

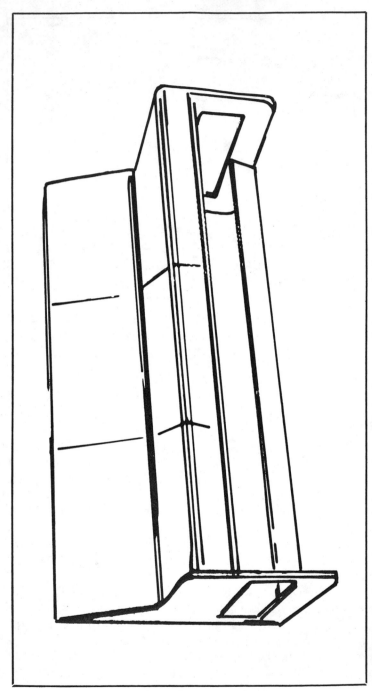

Fig. 10-8. Same end pieces are used for this sofa, easy chair or love seat. Only seats, backs and spreaders change.

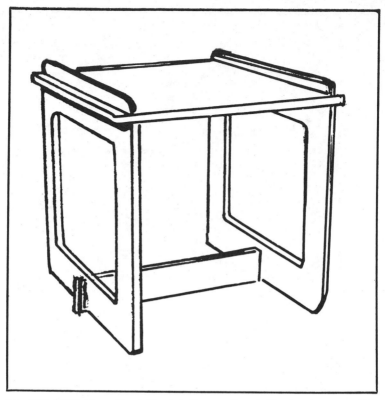

Fig. 10-9. End table, coffee table and ottoman all are built using the same side pieces. Just change the top and spreader length.

Most acrylic plastic you find on the market is sandwiched between lightly glued protective papers. Leave the paper in place while you're working to avoid scratches.

Tools and Methods

You can cut acrylic plastics with any saw that cuts soft metal—hacksaw, coping saw, sabersaw or circular saw (Fig. 10-11). However, when you're building furniture such as the two items shown here, many local plastic suppliers will cut pieces to size if you don't ask for too many different-sized cuts.

Cut with the finest-toothed blade you have available, be sure it's sharp, and use the slowest speed possible. You have to be sure that your blade is cutting through the plastic and not melting its way along. Best approach of all is to buy an acrylic-cutting blade for your saw.

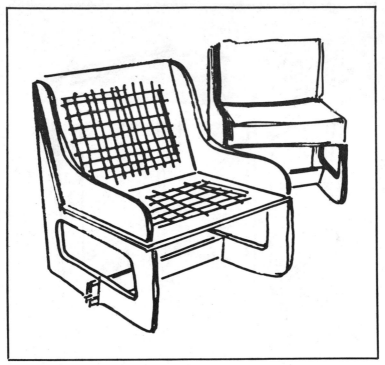

Fig. 10-10. Easy chair uses two cushions, a love seat uses four, and a sofa uses six cushions.

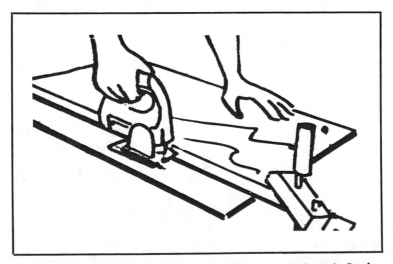

Fig. 10-11. Saber saw with special or sharp metal-cutting blade works fine for cutting acrylic plastics. Other saws capable of cutting soft metal work fine, too.

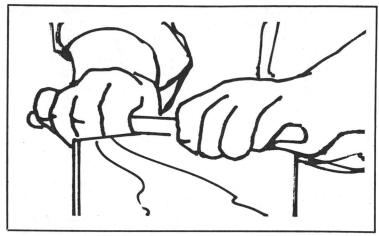

Fig. 10-12. Scrape off the tool marks with a sharp instrument such as the back of a hacksaw blade, a file or a special tool made for scraping plastics.

A drill made for boring into plastic makes the neatest holes. But any drill that works on soft metal will work on acrylics. Again be sure to use a sharp drill and use it slowly.

After sawing or performing similar operations, scrape away tool marks with a file or a sharp edged instrument such as the back of a hacksaw blade or a scraping tool made especially for finishing plastics (Fig. 10-12). Sandpapering somes next (Fig. 10-13). Use "medium" at first, and then work your way down to "superfine." To turn dull looking sawed or drilled edges into the same gleaming, clear surfaces as the rest of your plastic, buff the edges with a powder or paste polish such as jeweler's rouge.

The same store that sells plastic should stock several types of polishes. The easiest way to polish acrylic is to put a buffing tool in your electric drill and let the accessory rub the polish until the edges shine like diamonds (Fig. 10-14).

Whether you polish the insides of drilled holes is up to you. If you like the frosted glass appearance, leave them alone. If you do polish them, they will become as reflective as mirrors, usually concealing whatever hardware you run through the holes.

You can assemble shelves such as these with stainless steel nuts and bolts. Select the length carefully so the bolt just peeks through the nut. Polish the nuts and bolts until they are as shiny as the acrylic plastic.

Alternately, you can glue acrylic plastics together if you don't plan on moving frequently. (If you're occasionally on the move, it's handy to have knock-down shelves.) Unlike glued joints in wood, acrylics that are glued with acrylic cement remain absolutely transparent. Acrylic cement is usually a solvent that dissolves a bit of the two surfaces you want to join. When the solvent evaporates—usually within minutes—you're left with a very tough, chemically welded joint. And like metal welding, it's not easy to unweld an acrylic joint without damaging the plastic surface.

Buy acrylic cement from the company that supplies your plastic. There are many cements available for different plastics, so be sure the solvents in the cement you buy are designed for acrylic. Using a squeeze-bottle with a tiny opening is the most convenient way to apply cement. It also exposes you to fewer fumes than using a small paint brush, the second-best technique. In any case, work with the cement in a well ventilated room since it is quite toxic. And don't smoke, since many cements are also flammable.

Acrylic pieces to be cemented together have to be very, very clean. Use soap and water to insure that grease and dirt are removed. Slightly rough up one or both surfaces with "extra fine" sandpaper. Apply a generous dose of cement to one of the surfaces to be joined. Then quickly, but carefully, push the parts together.

The cement acts very fast so you can't count on sliding one part around until you find the right place. You have to match up the parts in advance. Generally the cement does its work within a few seconds. However, to be safe, don't disturb the cemented joint for several minutes. And before piling books on the shelves, give them several hours of setting time.

There's a jellied cement available for acrylics, but it's hard to find in most localities. It's stronger than the ordinary solvent cements, and it dries much slower. If you have trouble finding the thickened cement locally—or special tools made for acrylics—the Rohm and Haas Company, which makes Plexiglas brand acrylics, sells them by mail at competitive prices.

Shaping Plastic

In working with plastics, you have one unique property on your side—it softens enough at relatively low temperatures that you can bend it easily and smoothly. Using only a single sheet of plastic, you can create diverse shapes without having to glue separate pieces together. The coffee table shown is a fine example. The entire piece of furniture is made from a single sheet of plastic.

Fig. 10-13. Production grade sandpaper, from medium down to superfine, helps turn the edges into a glassy finish.

A strip heater is used to soften acrylic plastics (Fig. 10-15). It is a simple heating element fabricated into a long strip and comes in many lengths, most of them inexpensive. Some come pre-wired; some require five minutes of simple wiring. But all come with instructions showing how to mount the heating strip so it will soften acrylics. Some heaters can only handle acrylics up to ¼″ thick, so be sure the one you buy can cope with the plastics you intend to use.

To bend plastic, accurately mark the site of your bend. Use a magic marker or china marker to draw a straight line where the

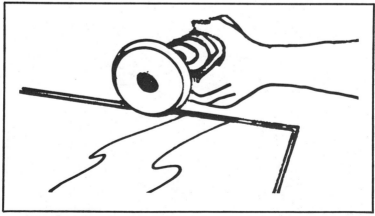

Fig. 10-14. Buffing edges, with drill and polisher or by hand, imparts the same gleaming reflectivity to the edge as to the face of your acrylic furniture.

bend should be. Lay your plastic sheet over the strip heater. Be sure the line you've drawn is on top, and be sure it runs exactly over the center line on your strip heater.

It's advisable to invest a pittance in a piece or two of acrylic scraps so you can make a few practice bends before plunging into the real thing. In general, strip heaters take 10 minutes to soften a ⅛" thickness of acrylic plastic. That means a sheet of ⅜" thick plastic, will require approximately 30 minutes to reach the required softness. You can test for softness by gently lifting one edge of the plastic sheet; if it starts to bend easily over the strip heater, the bend is ready to be made.

Remove the plastic from the strip heater and carefully lay it on a flat surface. Grab one end and—in a smooth, steady, firm motion—bend it to its desired position. Always bend away from the side of the sheet that was resting against the strip heater. Have a guide handy to insure that your bend will come out precisely the way you want it.

For example, if you want a right angle, you can set a box on your workbench, and then bend the plastic against the side of the box. Give the plastic at least 15 minutes to cool, 30 minutes for pieces thicker than ⅜".

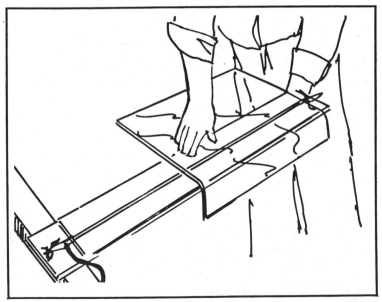

Fig. 10-15. A strip heater softens acrylic plastic until you can easily bend it to your desired shape.

Coffee Table

The table here is known as a waterfall table (Fig. 10-16). You can make it in dozens of sizes—short sides, or long sides, long tops or short tops, narrow or wide, very squared off or very elongated. This model is made from a piece of ½″ thick plastic, 18 × 48″. The best way to determine your dimensions, however, is to go shopping for a bargain-priced piece of plastic longer, shorter, wider, narrower, thicker or thinner. Regardless what size plastic you end

Fig. 10-16. Among the more luxurious furniture on the market today, clear acrylic etagere and waterfall table look expensive, and are expensive, if you don't make them yourself.

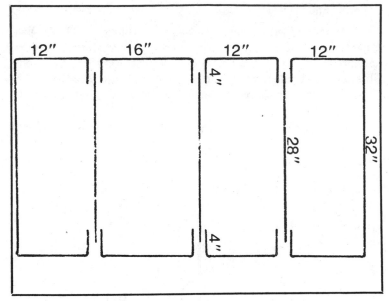

Fig. 10-17. Etagere dimensions.

up with, this is an ideal first project. It looks great, it doesn't involve a large investment in materials, and it's extremely easy to make.

Carefully measure 16″ from each end of your plastic and draw the two bend lines that will form the legs. Lay one line over your strip heater until you can bend it. Let the bend cool and then form the second bend. That's it! Your table is finished. Polish away any scratches you may have put into the table; then call in the neighbors so you can show it off.

Etagere

This project is at the opposite end of the plastics spectrum (Fig. 10-16). It involves much more material than the waterfall table, and it will take more time. But the working methods are identical to the simple table. To make the top and bottom sections, you'll need two pieces of ⅜″ thick Plexiglas 12″ wide and 60″ long. The side supports are ⅜″ thick Plexiglass 12″ wide and 16″ long. Shelves are ½″ thick Plexiglass which are 12″ wide and 28″ long (Fig. 10-17).

For a less-expensive etagere, you can use ¼″ acrylic instead of ⅜″ for the supports, and ⅜″ instead of ½″ for the shelves. With this material, it will look only slightly less elegant, and won't hold quite as much weight. But the overall cost will drop substantially.

Using the sketch as your guide, mark the bend lines. Form the 4" "legs" on the top and bottom sections. Then form the 12" "legs." Stack all of the parts together to be sure they fit well.

You can cement the shelves and supports together for a permanent assembly. Or you can drill two ¼" holes into all of the 4" "legs" and matching holes into the shelves, and buy ¼" carriage bolts 1½" long to assemble the units. Either way, when the etagere is completed, you will have a piece of furniture that you and your friends will truly admire.

Chapter 11
Kit Furniture

Unless you have the experience, building your own furniture can be a massive undertaking. And, at today's prices, buying quality furniture can take a big bite out of your budget. Between building from scratch and buying outright is a wide range of furniture available as kits in styles varying from classic colonial to modern.

INDUSTRY BEGINNINGS

The whole idea is as American as apple pie. It was started on a large scale by the Shakers nearly 150 years ago. They set up central production workshops at a settlement in New Lebanon, New York, where their most experienced carpenters mas-produced simple, sturdy furniture from pattern pieces.

A group of elders supervised the design and construction of the furniture in sections that could be shipped economically to other Shaker settlements. The structures were made mostly of hardwood, but the joints and overall design were purposefully simple so anyone could assemble the pieces correctly.

It has taken some time for kit furniture to become a thriving industry. But the business of packaging kits is growing up fast in today's economy. Reason? You can put together your own furniture at a savings of up to 50 percent without sacrificing either style or quality!

Many of the major suppliers of furniture kits first got into the kit business with the more familiar grandfather clock kits. Furniture kits were a natural sideline.

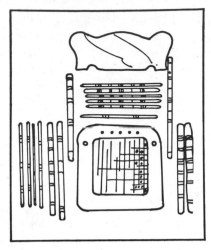

Fig. 11-1. This chair kit from Crown of Fairhope, comes with prebored holes and preinstalled seat.

For example, Emperor Clock Company, largest clock kit manufacturer in the country at Fairhope, Alabama, first offered a Queen Anne Secretary around Christmas, 1974, and found the demand excellent. Shortly, Emperor added their popular Queen Anne Lowboy in 1975, followed by a Butler's Tray Table in the fall of 1976. Today the company's kit offering have multiplied substantially and new items are being added to the kit roster regularly.

Many of the original kit offerings were replicas of classic furniture pieces such as Emperor Clock Company's Queen Anne Secretary. Crown of Fairhope, also of Fairhope, Alabama, offered its first furniture kit just three years ago. Today, Crown of Fairhope offers a total of 50 kits. Their hottest furniture kit is the sculptured cane chair, shown in Figs. 11-1 through 11-3, which is a faithful reproduction of a classic 1890's design.

But kit furniture today no longer is confined to Victorian or Early American styling. Although Emperor recently just introduced kits which reproduced the classic round oak table, the company at the same time introduced a full series of modern walnut sofa and coffee tables. It's easy to see the substantial savings possible by checking kit prices on modern furniture pieces with prices on comparable items in traditional furniture outlets. Nine times out of 10, kit prices will be half or less.

COMPARISON WITH UNPAINTED AND KD FURNITURE

So we're talking the same language, let's distinguish between unpainted (or ready-to-finish) furniture, KD (knock-down) furniture, and furniture kits.

Unpainted furniture is usually preassembled and you save by finishing the already completed piece yourself. KD furniture parts are almost always prefinished, but you must do light assembly work yourself. Generally KD furniture is designed to go together fast with clips and special fasteners. Few, if any, tools are required and in many cases an allen wrench or key needed for assembly is supplied.

Kit furniture, on the other hand, requires both assembly and finishing. Like KD furniture, kit furniture allows substantail savings in packing and shipping. But potential savings are higher with

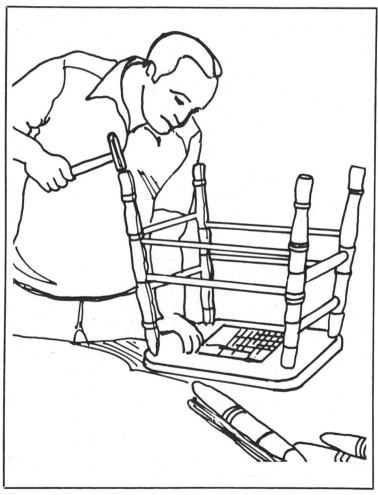

Fig. 11-2. Tools required are a hammer and screwdriver.

kits than with either unpainted or KD furniture, simply because you do more work yourself.

Although kit manufacturers are making substantial progress in designing furniture for fast assembly, kits generally require more effort to build than KD. Time required varies considerably, from one hour for a simple chair design, up to three weekends of spare time for more intricate and larger pieces such as a Queen Anne secretary.

Depending on the quality and complexity of the kit, some fitting or trimming may be necessary. Most kit furniture is cut on machines with permanent settings or jigs to exactly duplicate a prototype which is designed to fit perfectly. But, due to the nature of wood, you may encounter some variations that need a rasp, a plane or just some sanding to correct.

Obviously if major modifications are required, you can and should go back to the manufacturer. Minor discrepancies may not be the factory's fault though, particularly if the kit has been shipped to an area where the climate is radically different from where it was built.

ASSEMBLY AND QUALITY CONSIDERATIONS

It pays to find out as much as possible about the kit you want before ordering. Here are some things to look for that will help you spot high quality and ease of assembly.

- **Hardwood**. These tight-grained woods are more resistant to the effect of climate, will wear better in the long run and are considered to have a more desirable appearance for furniture than softwoods.
- **Kiln Dried Lumber**. This means that the wood has been effectively seasoned in kiln that you can count on only the most minimal shrinking or warping, if any.
- **Finishing Materials Included**. In some cases this may include sandpaper, screws, washers, bolts, glue, stain and of course, a set of well-illustrated instructions. Keep in mind you may need other items such as brushes to apply the finish and clamps to hold the work in place as the glue dries.

If you have experience in woodworking you won't think much of having to sort out pieces A to Z and six different kinds of screws. But to the uninitiated, a complicated kit can seem like a jigsaw puzzle with no solution. Best bet is to methodically lay out each

Fig. 11-3. Assembly takes 30 minutes or less.

piece of wood and hardware on the floor in a kind of exploded version of the finished kit to help you visualize the sequence of assembly.

When assembling, take care not to mar the finish, particularly on pieces that will form the front, top and sides. If light hammering is needed to tightly set a joint, make sure the hammer blows are cushioned. You can do this first of all by hitting a block of wood laid against the full length of the joint and, secondly, by wrapping the block in a soft cloth to further deaden the blow.

APPLYING GLUE

With kit furniture, pay special attention to applying the glue. On prefinished pieces, excess glue can be wiped away easily. But on raw wood, glue quickly penetrates the surface. Even if you wipe it away before it has hardened, some residue will remain in the pores of the wood. When it comes time to apply the stain, the hardened glue residue acts as a barrier to stain penetration, leaving a light, uneven finish.

You can prevent glue problems by keeping a damp cloth handy to wipe away any excess immediately. To be safe you should also give these areas a light sanding with fine paper before applying the stain.

Some manufacturers have made it unnecessary for you to have a wide array of clamps for gluing by making joints that clamp themselves. You'll notice this on the ends of chair legs where they fit into the seat and on the stretchers where they fit into corresponding holes in the leg. The dowel-like ends of these pieces are often compressed by machine. As the moisture in the glue is absorbed, the compressed end swells against the hole to lock the joint together as the glue dries.

The swelling takes place quickly, so it's a good idea to apply the glue to the interior surface of the hole and not the compressed end itself.

Putting together kit furniture will do more than save you money. It's a good way to introduce yourself to woodworking. You don't need a shop and need only the most basic tools to start with. After trying your hand at some small projects, you'll gain the confidence and experience to tackle more complicated pieces.

Chapter 12
Making Furniture
From Scrap Material

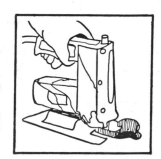

Don't believe people who say it's impossible to make attractive furniture out of scrap lumber. This chapter shows you how it's done.

FURNITURE FOR PENNIES

You don't have to be a Duncan Phyffe to begin duplicating prize colonial furnishings and antiques that your friends and neighbors would happily give their eye teeth for (Figs. 12-1 through 12-3). Reclaimed or scrap lumber, a handful of tools and a lot of imagination are all it takes. Fill your new house almost completely with homemade early Americna pieces. The amazing thing is you can do it for less than $400.

You might think you'd need all sorts of power equipment and finishing apparatus to get started. But when you realize that the early pioneers had made their pieces using crude, hand tools, you may decide to give it a try. A small project at first will give you the confidence to work your way into something a little more challenging.

The prohibitive cost of lumber may be another near setback. But you can salvage the boards from old, discarded furniture, packing crates and wooden skids. Most scrap lumber of this type comes with enough irregularities to qualify for whatever projects you have in mind.

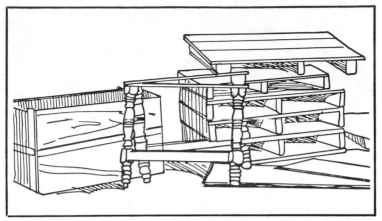

Fig. 12-1. You can make fine furniture from this scrap wood.

Projects Are Easy To Find

Many projects copied from furniture catalogs or photographs. But if you feel more comfortable with step-by-step outlines, the monthly project features such as those found in *Family Handyman* will be a great help. Techniques used in wood joinery are no secret, thanks to the availability of several good books on the subject.

Before starting your project, decide how much lumber you'll need, by composing a list of materials. The materials list should

Fig. 12-2. The benches and rocker were made from scrap wood.

tell length, width, thickness and number of pieces required for the job. This will give you a good guide. Next, start carefully disassembling your accumulation of skids, pallets, packing boxes crates or whatever used pieces you have (Figs. 12-4 through 12-7).

Try to manage your choice of boards so that any undesirable features will remain inconspicuous in your pattern. For painted furniture, you can mix or match different types of wood, but for stained pieces use the same type. This will assure uniformity of grain and color.

If your particular project will be enhanced by nail holes, then leave them open. Otherwise, try your hand at plugging them. Wood plugs are simple enough to make with a portable electric drill. Plug cutters to fit ¼" and larger drills are available in many hardware stores (Fig. 12-8).

If you want the plugs to blend inconspicuously, then use a piece of waste wood identical in type and grain characteristics to

Fig. 12-3. This dry sink was also made out of scrap material.

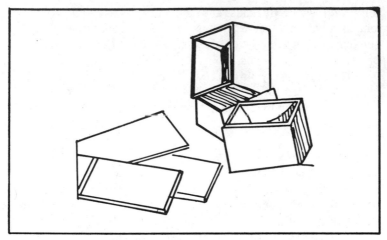

Fig. 12-4. When building from boxes, crates, skids and pallets, emphasis is on matching type of wood ang grain characteristics unless the finished furniture surfaces are going to be painted.

the wood being plugged. Be sure that the grain of the plug runs parallel with the grain of the board.

If you want the plugs to stand out, use a waste piece with a different grain and insert the plug with the grain running perpendicular to the grain of the board. In either case, make sure the plug

Fig. 12-5. Unfinished shelf and hutch.

Fig. 12-6. Side pieces for the hanging shelf were cut from the upper part of the hutch.

Fig. 12-7. The completed hutch.

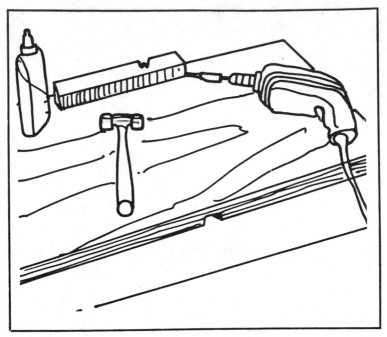

Fig. 12-8. Plug technique is shown here. Plugs are cut from similar wood with matching grain and inserted into carefully drilled holes. Plug cutters as well as screw counterboring bits are available in most hardware stores.

is made from the same type of wood so that the finished surface will sand evenly. Sometimes, a few extra plugs will add to the symmetry of the pattern and to the antique appearance of the piece.

Combination countersinking and counterboring bits are also widely available in hardware stores. Both bits and plug cutters come in various sizes, and a full set of both would be a wise investment for the serious or beginning furniture maker. In many cases, assembly screws cannot be hidden, but they can always be plugged.

If after selecting most of your material you find yourself in need of a few wider boards and do not have access to a jointer/ planer, you can always resort to buying this stock. The bargain bay at your local lumber store can provide an economical answer to this problem.

Cut And Shape First

In reclaiming scrap lumber, you usually cut all pieces to size and preliminarily shape them before sanding, stripping or planning

(Fig. 12-9). This avoids a lot of back-and-forth repetitive work. Weathered or discolored boards can be used with unpainted wood; however slightly more sanding will be required to make them match.

An orbital or disc sander can be used to remove the bulk of the discoloration using a medium grit aluminum oxide production grade (# 120) paper. Use care to achieve a uniform sanding depth. Finishing sanding in line with the grain will remove swirl marks left by the orbital sander. Use a finer grit paper (# 220 or # 320) for this. If you're fortunate enough to own a planer, you can use it to advantage in removing thin layers of surface stain or discoloration.

A saber saw or jigsaw can be used to cut curved or odd-shaped pieces in your project. To make furniture look old, all exposed edges should be rounded to imitate the effects of time. A simple cornering tool, which sells for about two dollars, is excellent for this job (Fig. 12-10). A good grade of non-staining furniture glue should be used on all joints.

Once it is assembled and sanded, your furniture piece is ready for finishing. A good oil stain can be applied and allowed to dry. Burnt umber oil coloring, available from art supply dealers, can be applied with rag and fingertip to shade corners and outside edges.

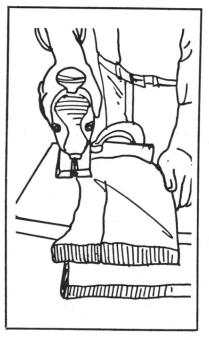

Fig. 12-9. Practically all scrap boards have areas which are split, warped or otherwise unsuitable for the project intended. Aim to get the most usable amount of material from each board by cutting around such areas.

Fig. 12-10. Cornering tool is used here to round the edge of a tabletop. This treatment produces the aged look which is all the more desirable in early American work. Small inexpensive tools of this sort are a valuable aid in furniture projects.

This will further help to simulate the ravages of age (Fig. 12-11). (Let this dry 24 hours before further finishing.)

The *easiest* finish *to apply* to homemade furniture is a finishing wax that is put on over the stained wood. Another good finish, however, is a more durable varnish that stands up well to abuse. Apply a coat of satin finish urethane varnish, rub the dried surface lightly with extra fine grade (# 000) steel wool and finally put on the finishing wax. Buff to a high luster.

A good deal of authenticity can also be achieved with the popular antiquing kits available in most hardware and department stores. The antiqued finish require less sanding and less work generally than the stained and varnished ones.

Any Old Wood Is Usable

Old wood for furniture making can come from almost any source. Often, old broken furniture pieces can be dismantled and cut down. For example, an aging bureau can be made into a blanket chest. The decorative mirror supports found on many bureaus can also be used in several ways. Ripped down the middle they become steeples that can be used to restore or remodel old pendulum shelf clocks, tavern signs and candlestick holders.

A fine set of discarded oak table legs will become the framework of an attractive rope-strung bed or maybe an elegant foot stool. Aged-looking store signs depicting Ye Olde Bootery or what have you can be made with little effort from old discolored boards of any thickness and dimension. Scrap 1 × 4 pine works very nicely to focus attention on a fireplace wall when arranged in a paneled pattern.

Waste Pieces Useful

Sometimes the waste pieces from one project can provide enough material to complete another. For example, pieces from a C-roll hutch can provide you with the material for a hanging shelf. The uses for old wood are limited only by one's imagination.

Furniture making is like any other craft. The more you work at it, the better you become. Using the techniques described, you can make pieces that look as good as any factory-built units and at unbelieveably low prices. You can duplicate a Fort Henry payroll desk. which sells on the market for about $170, using only $4 in scrap lumber.

CRATE CRAFT

In her book "Crate Craft." *Family Handyman* technical editor Lura LaBarge shows how building furniture from scrap lumber

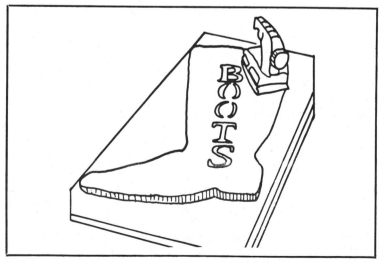

Fig. 12-11. Aged appearance is achieved on this decorative sign by sanding lightly over painted finish. Scrap pine is a good choice for such novelty pieces because designs can be easily cut using a portable jig or saber saw. The attractive grain enhances the finished work. Three-quarter or 1″ stock is most preferred.

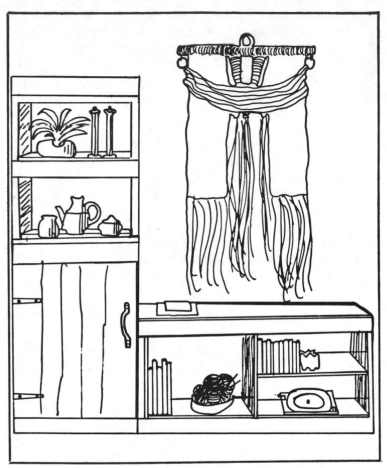

Fig. 12-12. Shown are 4' doored and open shelf modular units.

offers a rewarding way to save money—whether it's furniture to house a sound system, or to furnish a second bedroom, rec room, den or living room.

"Crate Craft" is not about how to stack boxes and call them bookshelves. Rather, it outlines a system you can use to find and process scrap lumber into projects you'll be proud of. The units shown here were built using her system, and are living proof of the possibilities (Figs. 12-12 through 12-14).

Be a Scavenger

In this day and age, it pays to be a scavenger. Every buck you can save on scrounging up scrap lumber is money that can go into some other project. There's a lot of scrap lumber waiting to be utilized. And you'll probably find that the owners are more than happy to have you cart the scrap away.

LaBarge points out that crating materials also offer a uniqueness. Knots, rough texture and grain are inherent to second grade scrap and crate lumber. Don't be alarmed by the poorer grade rating, though. Cared for properly, it'll take all the rough stuff your family can deliver, yet still look good.

Shop around and get a general idea of what your first project will be. Then make a list of the materials you'll need. Common stock sizes such as 2 × 4s, 2 × 6s, 1 × 4s or 1 × 6s, will be the easiest to find. Also look for scrap pieces of plywood and possible 4 × 4s.

Where to Look

Check out building sites and scavenge for wood that normally is junked. Be sure to ask, before picking up any pieces. It's better to be safe than sorry.

Furniture stores or companies that receive shipments of breakable items usually have an abundance of wood-framed cartons. Large musical instruments and equipment are generally shipped in corrugated boxes with wood frames. Several food items are shipped in wood boxes or palletized. You can pick up these

Fig. 12-13. Modular units complement tea-for-two table and chairs which are also easily built from scrap lumber.

Fig. 12-14. More examples of what you can build. They include a coffee table, love seat, armchair, footstool, lamp table and table lamp.

boxes and use them as they are, or dismantle them for use in shelving or small tables and bookcases.

Paper companies and printing companies ship and receive paper on pallets, and that's where your sturdiest wood will come from. Also check out grocery warehouses, petroleum wholesalers and just about any company that ships materials on pallets. Check with lumber yards as a last resort. They may charge for scrap materials. Remember what you're looking for is free.

Get it Ready

Because the material you're looking for will be made into a permanent fixture in your home, you can afford to be choosey.

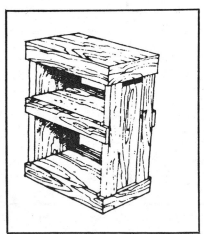

Fig. 12-15. Check your wood supply for boards that will make up the 16″ width. Use stock sizes such as 1 × 4 for this job. Boards should be square and smooth on the sides.

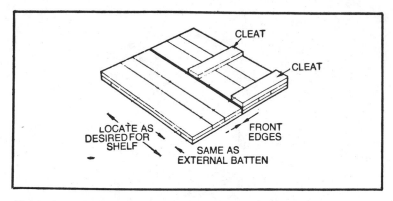

Fig. 12-16. Start by making the planked ends to the exact size (16 × 36″), minus the thickness of what you'll use for the top planks. Lay the two ends with their front edges together, inside up, facing you. Locate the cleats flush with the bottom to align with external battens that'll be added later.

Don't take the first scraps you see unless you're absolutely sure the quality is first rate. Weather damaged or warped materials may be common because scrap is quite often stored outside.

Procedure

Building furniture using the "Crate Craft" concept allows plenty of room for improvising. Modular units are 36″ high, 16″ deep and 24″ wide. But you can tailor-fit them to the space you have available (Figs. 12-15 through 12-29).

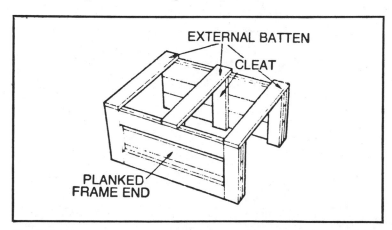

Fig. 12-17. Set the two planked ends on their front edges. Glue and nail three external battens across the back, aligning them with the cleats inside and with the top edge.

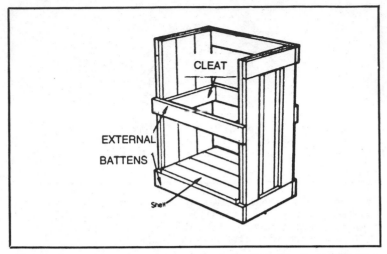

Fig. 12-18. Glue and nail the external batten across the bottom front. Select the boards for the two shelves so that laid out side by side they will come out flush with the external battens front and back. Then cut to fit between the planked frame ends. Glue and nail the bottom shelf, then the center front batten, then the shelf and finally the top batten.

All units consist of two planked frame ends, held parallel and perpendicular by three or four external battens. The tops are all planked. You can make the units wider by using longer boards and a simple center divider.

Toughest part of building is choosing the right wood. Pick wood that has a good grain, isn't too knotty or warped. You'll want

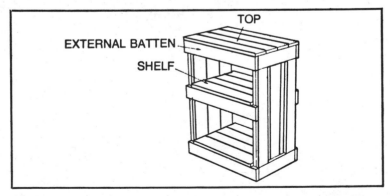

Fig. 12-19. Set the unit upright and glue and nail the top planks, making them flush with the external battens. Note how the external batten and horizontal members make a frame-on-edge in the horizontal plane at the top, bottom and middle. Next step is finishing.

Fig. 12-20. Start this unit exactly the same as the open front module. Locate cleats the thickness of back planking away from each edge. The midshelf can be located anywhere you desire.

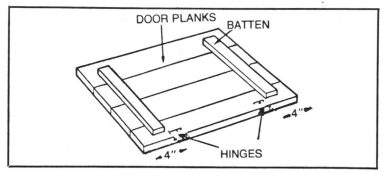

DOOR PLANKS   BATTEN

4"

4"

HINGES

Fig. 12-21. With planked ends on their front edges, glue and nail external battens across the back. Lay the shell on its back and fit in back planks. Then nail the front external battens. Cut these planks the same length as planked frame ends. Glue and nail them in place, then do the bottom and middle shelf. Set the unit upright. Glue and nail the top and top front external battens.

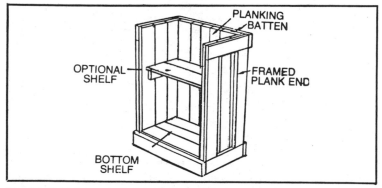

PLANKING
BATTEN

OPTIONAL
SHELF

FRAMED
PLANK END

BOTTOM
SHELF

Fig. 12-22. Make up the battened door to fit between the front external battens with good clearance. The door will be lapped over the planking on the ends, but set in the width of the flat frames.

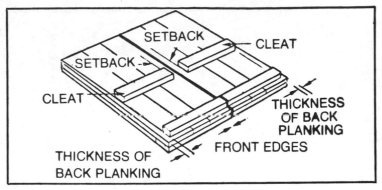

Fig. 12-23. The door is designed for a flush overlay cabinet hinge. Install the hinges about 4" in from the top and bottom of the door. Drill a small pilot hole to prevent splitting. Then attach hinges.

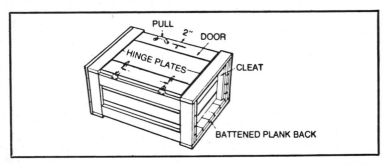

Fig. 12-24. Before attaching the door to the unit, install the door pull. Drill pilot holes and install the pull about 2" from the edge, 6" from the top. Lay the door in position, mark hinges for holes and drill pilot holes. Install screws lightly and try opening and closing the door. If it works, tighten hinges down. The unit is now ready for finishing.

Fig. 12-25. Start by making the planked frame ends using the same dimensions as you did for the open shelf and door modules. Next, construct a planked battened center divider to the same dimensions.

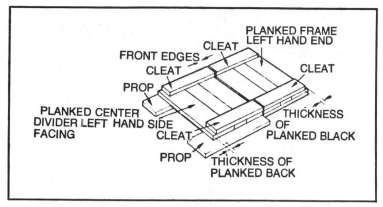

Fig. 12-26. Turn the center over to the right-hand side, facing up, and butt the front edge of the right hand frame to it. Set the battens in from the back edges a distance equal to the thickness of the planked batten back. You can make an optional shelf, which requires a cleat set in from the edges.

to smoothen rough wood enough to make it comfortable to work with. Then follow steps as shown.

Finishing

Once the sawing, fitting, gluing and nailing is done, your job is 75 percent complete. Next, finish the pieces with a suitable paint or stain. Because rough-cut lumber may leave jagged edges, sand it before finishing. Use rough grit paper first, followed by medium and then fine grade paper.

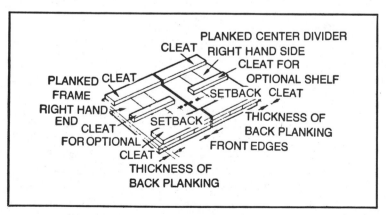

Fig. 12-27. Set the two ends and divider on their front edges and glue and nail external battens in place. Glue and nail by laying the unit on its back. Note that the center divider planking glues directly to the two external battens at the back.

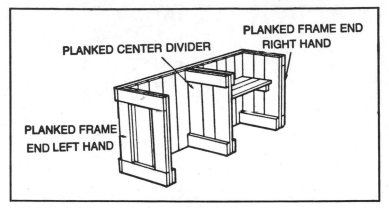

Fig. 12-28. If the unit is to be used with other modules, glue and nail the top batten across the front and glue and nail the top plank.

When choosing a stain or resin, pick a color that highlights the natural flavor of the wood. Penetrating wood resins will bring out natural beauty without adding color. For darker finishes, choose a dye-type stain. For areas that'll receive a great deal of actual wear, consider a liquid plastic or polyurethane finish.

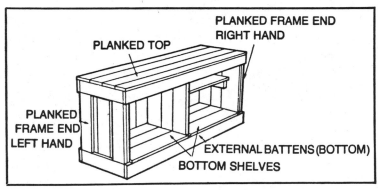

Fig. 12-29. If the unit is to stand alone, glue and nail the bottom front external batten, the two bottom shelves, and the optional shelf before you put on the top.

To match stains when using a mixture of woods, experiment with left over pieces before applying. Always follow the manufacturer's recommendations given on the container.

Chapter 13
Furniture Repairs

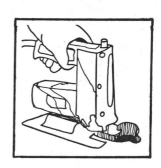

Care to try your luck at fixing furniture? This chapter offers guidelines on stripping furniture finishes, gluing chair rungs, applying laminates and refinishing old pieces.

STRIPPING OLD FURNITURE FINISHES

A refinished piece of second hand or antique furniture is a delight. Coated with three layers of rubbed varnish, the wood glows with its own natural beauty. The item becomes a showpiece deserving appropriate display. Maybe the reward of owning a refinished piece done by one's self explains why yard sales, auctions and flea markets are doing such a land office business. Old but well-built furniture brings high prices because of its appeal when refinished.

However, too often these pieces are obviously being sold for a second time. Someone had started to strip them and never completed the job. It is a hard fact of furniture refinishing that before a surface can be varnished it has to be stripped. And unfortunately stripping is messy, difficult work.

It is impossible to make paint removing neat, but it can be made a lot easier. This process is a bit more complicated than the directions on the back of the can of stripper, but it gets results.

Determining the Job's Nature

The first step is to determine the nature of the job. If the old finish is shellac the best solvent is denatured alcohol used as

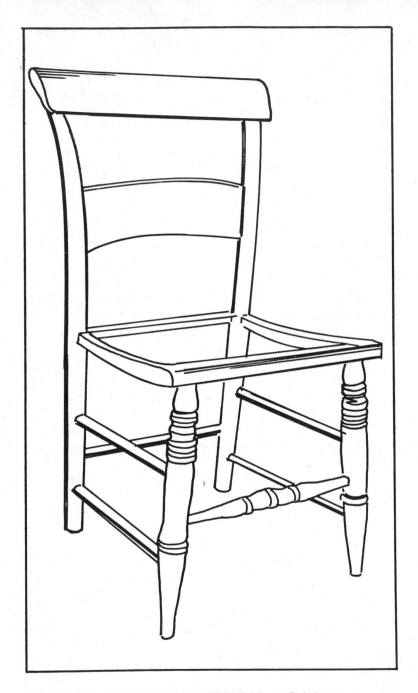

Fig. 13-1. It's not difficult to strip the finish off this small chair.

described for paint strippers. There is a bonus to using alcohol on shellac; it is cheaper. If the piece is covered with paint, of course, stripper will be necessary. A pint should be sufficient for a small table or a chair (Fig. 13-1). Factors to consider are the total surface area and the number of layers of paint covering the wood. Removing three layers of the old finish requires the same amount of stripper as three pieces of furniture covered with only a single coat. As is true of other materials, if the job is a large one, or if there are several pieces to do, it costs less to buy in quantity. Always purchase paint remover by the gallon.

Paste removers are not only more expensive than the liquid kind, but they do not work as well when following this method. To determine, if in doubt, the consistency of the stripper, simply shake the can. Liquids are water thin and sound it. Paste will make a glug-glug noise.

While at the hardware store buy a couple of inexpensive paint brushes, the cheaper the better. They have to be thrown out after each job anyway. Also needed is a bundle of fairly coarse steel wool. Use #1. All the other materials can be found around the house. These include plenty of clean rags, an old tooth brush, a

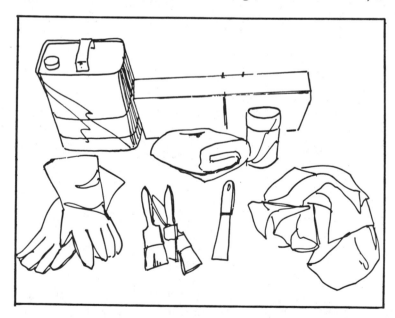

Fig. 13-2. Basic stripping materials neatly assembled include commercial stripper, steel wool, inexpensive paint brushes, putty knife, rags, containers and, of course, rubber gloves.

Fig. 13-3. It's best to do stripping outdoors where fumes will not linger. A drop cloth catches drippings for a neater job. The stripper is brushed on heavily at first.

beer can opener, two clean tin cans and a drop cloth (Fig. 13-2). Stripper can burn sensitive skin, so rubber gloves should be worn by anyone with that problem.

Mending and Gluing

Do any mending or gluing before the paint is stripped. Glue, when spilled on naked wood, seals the surface, even when wiped right away. To top if off, the spot becomes invisible until the surface is varnished. The finish cannot penetrate the sealed area as it does the rest of the wood and the piece ends up with light spots where the glue had been. There is no need to worry about stripper dissolving the bond and causing loose joints. It will not be on the wood long enough to penetrate and what does get into a joint dries rapidly.

It is better to work outdoors (Fig. 13-3). Fumes bother some people, causing headaches. Stripping should be done in the shade to prevent the stripper from evaporating too quickly. The drop cloth will keep the mess from a burning spots on the lawn. Use a sheet of plastic because it is water proof.

Removing Paint

Now to the process. Fill one of the two tin cans half way with stripper. Slop it onto the piece with a paint brush. There is no need to be careful about where it runs, the paint is all coming off anyway. Select a part of the piece, a chair back, an arm, a table top and do it all before moving on. It is best to start high and work down so the discolored stripper does not run onto an area which is already done.

Allow the paint to blister. This means to become ripply and soft. At this point it should be about the consistency of cake frosting. If there are many layers of paint use a scraper to lift each

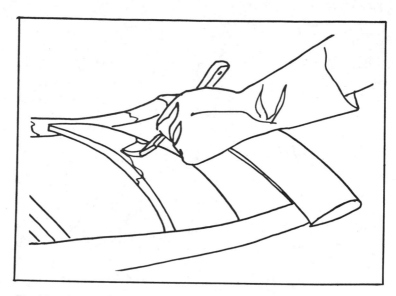

Fig. 13-4. Scraping is done carefully to avoid gouging wood.

of them as they soften. Use a scraper gingerly (Fig. 13-4). On soft wood the blade can leave gouges which will never sand out. Instead of pushing the scraper to remove the softened paint, it is better to simply drag it across the surface. This pulls off the gooey mess

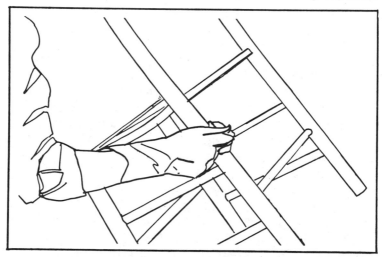

Fig. 13-5. Steel wool is used to remove finish which remains after preliminary scraping. Usse half of a pad at a time, dipping it in the stripper and wiping the area liberally. Discard each piece as it packs up with stripped finish.

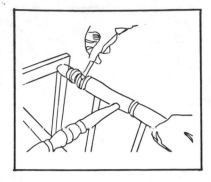

Fig. 13-6. A toothbrush is useful in applying stripper to narrow areas such as turnings and carvings.

without the danger of digging the blade into the wood. Scrape away each successive layer of paint until the surface of the wood is exposed. Of course each coat will have to be softened in turn with another application of remover. Follow this step over the entire piece of furniture, making sure to leave no heavy concentrations of paint.

If there is only one layer of paint on the piece, the work will be much easier. In this case apply the remover as has already been explained. When the single layer has been softened go directly to the next step. Take a pad of steel wool and tear it in half (Fig. 13-5). Steel wool is only good until it packs up, so use it liberally. Dip the pad in the stripper, and without bothering to wring it out, wipe it on the area to be done. Slop the remover all over that surface allowing it to puddle. This will soften the remaining patches of paint which did not come up with the scraper. When they are loose scrub them away with the steel wool. Some will be more stubborn than others, but all will yield with a bit of elbow grease.

If the piece has any turnings, dents, cracks, corners or carving the steel wool will not be able to get at the paint in these areas. This is where the beer can opener and tooth brush come in (Fig. 13-6). Soak the paint well and with the point of the can opener scrape out as much as possible. Next, with the well-soaked toothbrush, scrub away the residue. The bristles of the brush are not as tough as steel wool and the paint may resist longer, but once more it will yield to persistence.

After each part is cleared of all patches of paint wipe the discolored stripper from the surface with a rag (Fig. 13-7). It will streak and make the area look like a poorly washed window. Continue this process of soaking, scrubbing with steel wool and wiping the dissolved paint with a rag until the whole piece is done. This is the most important step and has to be completed properly.

Fig. 13-7. When all paint patches are removed, soak a clean rag with stripper and go the entire piece to wipe off film and remaining traces of old paint.

When this is finished, all that should be left on the piece is the streaky film. Now take the other tin can and fill it half way with fresh stripper. Soak a clean rag in this, again not bothering to wring it out. Simply rub the remover onto the surface and wipe away the traces of old paint. It is the same as washing away dirt with water. As each area is cleaned this final time wipe it dry with a fresh absorbent rag or paper twoels (Fig. 13-8). This is the finishing step and should be done over the entire piece. The wood is now entirely raw. Some pigmentation from the paint may remain in the wood, especially in the end grain. There is nothing which can be done about this other than an awful lot of sanding, but on an antique it indicates authenticity.

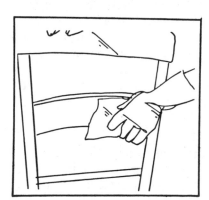

Fig. 13-8. As each area is rubbed a final time with clean stripper, it can be wiped dry with an absorbent rag or paper towel. This step should be done over the entire piece. It will leave the wood entirely raw.

about this other than an awful lot of sanding, but on an antique it indicates authenticity.

One tip. If the piece of furniture to be stripped is missing any parts which have to be replaced, they will have to be made with new wood. This is distinctly lighter in color than the old. When the finish is applied this difference will become glaring. However, the rag used in the last step will contain just enough of the old paint to stain the new part a shade approximating that of the rest of the piece. Simply wet it again with stripper and smear it on the new area (Fig. 13-9). Allow the discolored liquid to dry. This should do the trick. Another technique is to spread some of the thick goo on the light spot while still in the steel wool stage. Let this dry while working on the rest of the piece. When finished simply strip the replacement part the way the rest was done. Avoid the final rinse with clean stripper. That would only remove the stain caused by the smeared paint.

Drying the Piece

The piece is now ready to be dried. If it is put in the sun it will not take long. Sanding is undesirable and should not be necessary unless the item had been badly mistreated. In fact it is surprising just how smooth a stripped piece can be. Plus, the wood has darkened with age. This is the much talked about "patina." The patina is not very deep and sand paper can quickly wear it away. It is the attraction of an old piece and without it there is no difference between aged wood and new furniture. If the patina is sanded off, stripping the antique has been a waste of time. It would have been easier to buy a modern comparable piece at a furniture store.

The dried mess left on hands after stripping old paint or shellac is stubborn. Regular soap will not touch it. The only thing that will is a powdered cleanser, the type used to scour sinks.

This method of stripping will not raise the grain of the wood the way commercial dipping processes will, nor will it loosen joints. So, as soon as the piece is dry (less than an hour in the sun) it is ready to receive the first coat of shellac or varnish. It is possible to start stripping in the morning and have a finish dry enough to handle by night.

EASY FURNITURE FIXING

Americans spend more on furniture, except for food and clothing, than for anything else. It stands to reason, then, that a little care and repair is in order, even if it's only to protect your invest-

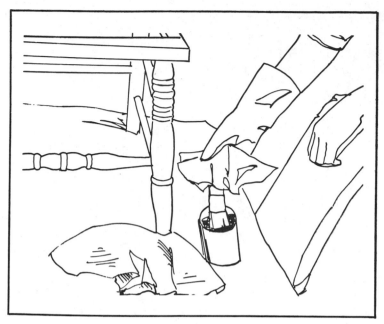

Fig. 13-9. Where new wood is being used to replace any missing parts, the new pieces can be darkened at this time by wiping with one of the used rags. After this the stripped piece is ready for drying, which will take about an hour.

ment. So let's examine what you can do to keep your furniture in shape.

Glues You Can Use

There are many, but chances are you will have at hand and be familiar with three: white glue, household cement (model airplane glue) and epoxy (the kind that comes in two small tubes which you have to mix together). White glue is handy, sure , and it dries colorless, but it will not hold up as a glue for chair legs or where stress is bound to occur. Model airplane glue is a favorite because it dries so fast and is colorless. Better leave it with you model airplane kit. Or use it for the small jobs. Epoxy, however, has no peers. It's hard to get off your fingers, yes, but you can avoid this by applying the material with care. Use small wooden sticks to apply epoxy adhesives.

Epoxy is also available in putty form for filling holes and filling out enlarged holes so legs will fit more tightly.

Plastic resin glue comes in powdered form and is mixed with water. This is a good glue to use in repairing veneers since it is

Fig. 13-10. A padded vise-grip pliers is applied to the epoxied split rung and kept on overnight.

much more water resistant than white glue and not as hard to handle as epoxy. Epoxy does have one major drawback. Its two parts (resin and catlagyst) must be very accurately mixed for best results. The plastic resin can be used with a glue injector (like a hypodermic needle) for injecting glue under raised veneers. Resorcinol is the only truly waterproof glue, and is the only one to use for outdoor furniture. It comes in two parts and must be mixed in precise proportions.

Electrically operated guns, which melt and expel solid sticks of glue, are very handy for those quick, small jobs. A heating lamp, incidentally, will help any glued-up joint to cure faster and better.

Heat, dampness and abuse will cause most kitchen chairs and some living room furniture to need periodic attention. After a winter (even with the fuel shortage) of dry heat, wood legs, rungs and other parts shrink and loosen.

Stools are usually the first to go. Their high legs, thin spindles and casual use often make them loose and shaky. Turn the stool upside down and check the rungs. If one is loose, force some glue in through a drilled 1/16" hole on the underside and clamp it. If several are loose, remove them all, sand the ends clean and reglue the whole thing (Figs. 13-10 and 13-11). Use epoxy, plastic resin or casein, in this case. Casein glue is a powder which must be mixed with water. It has excellent gap-filling properties and is very strong, but you may find it difficult to obtain.

Fig. 13-11. If a rung is loose, clean off the rung end and hole. Apply epoxy with a stick.

Clamping Chair Rungs

Nothing beats a few loops of clothesline or heavy hemp cord for a quick and easy clamp. Loop the rope several times from leg to leg holding the rungs being glued and insert a twist-stick to tighten the knotted rope (Fig. 13-12). Brace the stick to prevent it from coming loose and let stand for 24 hours. Chair clamps can be used if you have them, but contact points must be padded to protect the finish. Use pieces of old rug as pads. Indoor-outdoor carpeting works great. If you have one of the new strap clamps, of course, use it. These tough webbed straps will not mar furniture, and can be

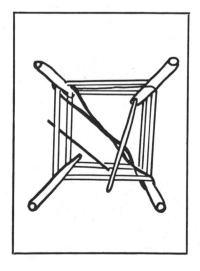

Fig. 13-12. To tighten ropes that hold rungs while drying, twist with a dowel.

Fig. 13-13. Strap clamps have a ratchet gear which can be tightened with a small wrench.

tightened with a small wrench. A ratchet pulls the strap in and holds it (Fig. 13-13).

Broken Chair Rungs

If they are simple dowels, replace them. If the ends are turned, you can still fix them. Most common break is where an end joins the leg (Fig. 13-14). Simple cure is to drill a hole for a medium-sized wood screw, screw it into the snapped off end of the rung in the leg (if it's still firmly glued in; if not, replace it with a short dowel plug) with epoxy on the screw threads, leaving more

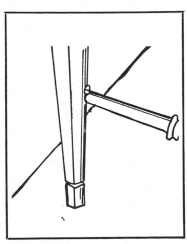

Fig. 13-14. To work on a chair with a rung that's broken at the leg, stand the chair on a padded table.

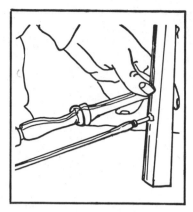

Fig. 13-15. Create a pin to hold the break by inserting a wood screw coated with epoxy into the leg.

than half of the screw sticking out (Fig. 13-15). The other end of the rung will be loose from the original break. Remove the rung, sand or scrape off the old glue on the far end and drill a hole down the center of the leg on the broken end to receive the wood screw pin (Fig. 13-16).

After the glued-in wood screw pin is dry (overnight to be sure), saw off the head of the screw to create a new metal rung pin (Fig. 13-17). Pin shaft should fit tightly into drilled rung. Coat the pin and rung end with epoxy and insert pin into rung hole. Tap into place, matching up the jagged break for a perfect fit. When this is in, insert other end back into its hole with coating of epoxy (Fig. 13-18). Clamp in place for 24 hours.

Other Repairs

Table legs are usually bolted to 45° angle plates at corners. Tighten bolts or lag nuts to take wobble out of table (Fig. 13-19).

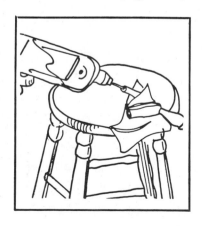

Fig. 13-16. Drill a hole to receive the metal screw pin. Be sure to match the bit to the shaft size.

Fig. 13-17. After epoxy has dried, saw off the screw head and then remove the damaged chair rung.

Table tops are held on with screws which might come loose. These can be tightened, but only if you use the right sized screwdriver. If a screw is loose, remove it, fill the hole with steel wool or with a few toothpicks and glue and replace the screw. Some small benches and chairs have a similar attachment for legs. These can be tightened without any need for glue (Fig. 13-20).

Loose veneer can be glued down by pushing, squirting or forcing glue underneath after cleaning out old glue. Clamp down for 24 hours. Use weights or two 2 × 4s plus large C clamps with a pad just over the area to be glued. One 2 × 4 goes under the table top, one on top.

If glued legs continue to separate, repeat the chore, then add some insurance—some screw eyes, and a couple of turnbuckles with rods—to make a permanent clamp arrangement. These can be

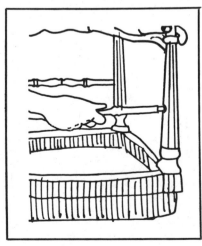

Fig. 13-18. First insert the rung into the sawed off screw. Then insert the other end in the leg hole.

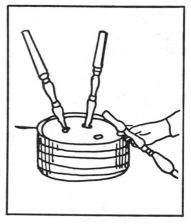

Fig. 13-19. No glue is needed here as the threaded leg bolt screws in the metal plate.

tightened as needed for firm support. Generally used on stools or utility chairs, where heavy use is more important than appearance. As in the use of rope clamps, the rods and turnbuckles would form an X to hold together all four legs.

RENEWING OLD FURNITURE

Decorative laminates let you make an old table—or an entire kitchen—look like new inexpensively, with about the same work it takes to hang wallpaper (Figs. 13-21 and 13-22).

Decorative laminates are particularly suited for kitchen and bath cabinets and counters or other items that require a serviceable surface. Professional grade laminates are heat, stain and scratch resistant; yet they are flexible enough to work with and can be

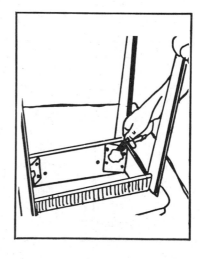

Fig. 13-20. The loose leg needs no glue here. A wrench tightens the square leg screw head.

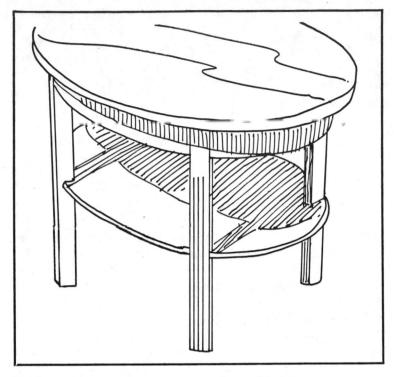

Fig. 13-21. Apply laminate to this piece and make it look like new.

applied over flat or curved surfaces. Laminates come in 30" × 40' rolls, and are available in a variety of woodgrain patterns, marble designs, leather or slate textures. You can apply to surfaces such as wood, hardboard, metal, drywall, or plaster.

Fig. 13-22. A laminated table.

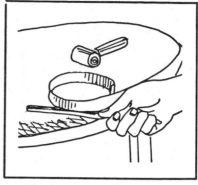

Fig. 13-23. Edge trim is available in rolls to match the surface design, or can be cut from the large laminate sheet. Edges are always applied first. Both table surface and edges are cleaned. Next brush a contact adhesive over the surface and allow it to dry until tacky.

To apply, cut the laminate to the approximate size of the piece to be covered. Leave ¾ to 1″ overlap on all edges. Use edge trim for counter and table edges. Cut trim from larger sections, or buy rolls of matching trim. The trim goes on first (Fig. 13-23).

Either solvent or water base adhesive is brushed on the surface, and allowed to dry a few minutes until tacky. Place a sheet of Kraft paper over the surface leaving only 1″ of adhesive exposed (Fig. 13-24). Align the laminate with the surface and press down pulling the Kraft paper out from between the surface and the laminate.

To insure a tight bond, roll a wooden roller over the surface, radiating out from the point of origin (Fig. 13-25). Then file the edges smooth with a square edge file, using downward strokes. The laminated surface wipes clean with a damp cloth.

Laminates are also effective in decorating doors, even refrigerators, while bar-tops and bookshelves become easy projects for the adventurous do-it-yourselfers, without sanding, painting or

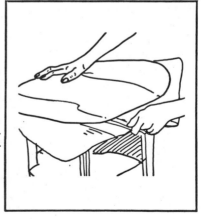

Fig. 13-24. A sheet of Kraft paper is placed over the table surface leaving about 1″ of the adhesive area exposed. The laminate is aligned with the table top and pressed to it as the Kraft paper is withdrawn from between the table surface and laminate.

Fig. 13-25. A wooden roller is used over the laminate surface to insure a tight bond. To finish the application, edges of the laminate are simply filed clean and smooth using downward strokes. New laminate surfaces can be wiped clean with a damp cloth.

varnishing. Decorative laminate such as Conoflex by Conolite are available at most home centers and hardware stores.

REFINISHING OLD FURNITURE

"Thar's gold in them thar hills" was the shout in the early 1800's, but today some handymen are going after old furniture with the same enthusiasm. And the prospectors are almost as thick.

There definitely is money in the refinishing and refurbishing of old furniture. The biggest problem for many folks is in reselling or marketing their finished project. If you like to make a little pocket money and use your hands to recycle something worthwhile, try your hand at "the old furniture business."

Do it one piece at a time until you get the hang of it, and remember old furniture and antiques are not the same thing. A successful antique dealer requires a good knowledge of what really is an antique, what will sell, how to repair it without damaging its resale value, and most of all money.

One of the advantages in dealing in old furniture is that it can be done for almost nothing. Often a $20 bill will handle materials to refinish the project. But it does take time. If you're just starting out, you can also furnish a house with this type of prospecting, and eventually sell off what you desire to replace with newer furniture. However, beware—you'll often end up finding you like the old better than the new.

Finding Old Furniture

Where do you find old furniture? The first step is to look in your neighborhood; almost every area has a second-hand furniture store. Or check with your local furniture store. Often he has to take in used furniture to sell new furniture. The next option is garage or yard sales, which can really be lucrative.

Stay away from the flea markets, although rural farm auctions can often result in a "find." But, like flea markets, these are the places most likely inhabited by the "used furniture" dealers.

What kinds of furniture should you buy? Unless you are a pretty fair upholsterer, stay away from covered or upholstered furniture. Chairs that need only cushions can on the other hand often be done quite easily, or the cushions can be recovered at an

Fig. 13-26. This old chair was picked up reasonably, refinished and sold for a tidy profit.

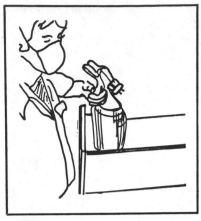

Fig. 13-27. The chair was first stripped and then stained and later sprayed with lacquer.

economical enough price so you can make a bit of profit. Small tables, wooden benches, chests, headboards or bedsets, and all kinds of chairs all make good projects. Stay away from projects with a lot of molding unless they are in exceptionally good shape and none of the molding has to be replaced.

The two pieces shown are examples. The old chair is a Morris chair, one of the first recliners (Fig. 13-26). Because of the number made, and the fact that they were manufactured fairly recently keeps them out of the antique category. However, they can make a great conversation pieces, and refinished properly, they can turn a tidy profit (Figs. 13-27 through 13-29). The chair shown was purchased for $15.

The deacon bench or old church seat was purchased at a farm auction for $10 (Fig. 13-30). It had been sitting on a couple's front porch for many years. After removing four layers of paint as well as

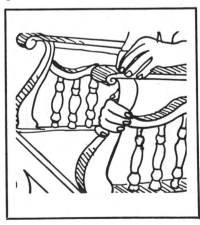

Fig. 13-28. Though the chair had carving, it was easily smoothed with sandpaper and steel wool.

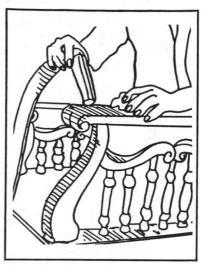

Fig. 13-29. Regardless of finish, all debris is removed between sanding and finish coats.

the old varnish and "red stain," the bench finally revealed its age and past (Fig. 13-31 through 13-33).

It was constructed of white pine boards, 1¼", the back was over 24" wide, one piece bent in place. The seat board bottom was the only surface that hadn't been carefully planed and smoothed down. It had the deep saw texture of an early saw mill and the saw marks were straight across the seat board instead of slightly circular. This dated the bench (or at least the seat board) back to the very early 1800s.

Although modern nails had been used in a place or two to repair the bench, the bench had been fastened together with square, cut nails. The arms and back top resisted easy stripping. Evidently a century of hand polishing and grease and sweat had

Fig. 13-30. This old church bench had many coats of paint and had stood duty on a country porch for several years.

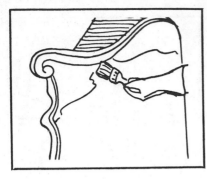

Fig. 13-31. The first step was to brush on pain remover. Then a scraper was used to remove the majority of loosened paint layers.

amalgamated the finishes together and forced them down into the wood.

Marketing Your Products

What about marketing your finished project? It doesn't do any good to refinish a truckload of old furniture if you can't sell it. For the first few few pieces it's a good idea to refinish them, find a good spot for them in your home, and mention to friends and guests that that old chair or table is for sale. Give them a bit of history if you can, and you'll often have a sale.

If you find you like the business you can often take pieces to "antique" stores or used furniture stores and sell them. The best bet is to ask to sell on commission.

Another market is to take your goods to a local flea auction (not a flea market) and sell them there, although you may find this market not very consistent. Some days you might sell everything at a good profit; the next you may practically have to give it away. But at the better auctions you can often ask for a "no sale" if the piece doesn't sell to suit you.

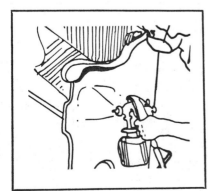

Fig. 13-32. The bench was stained with wiping stain, then given a coat of eggshell lacquer and later rubbed down.

Fig. 13-33. Paint removal revealed a hand-made "primitive" put-together with authentic wrought nails.

Another alternative is to build up a name for yourself in refinishing furniture. You'll soon get requests from friends, and a pretty good business can develop in your garage refinishing and refurbishing furniture for other folks. Like any other small business, or "moonlight" operation, make sure you proceed slowly at first, learn the business, and don't invest a lot of money.

You're in business to make a little money and enjoy a good hobby at the same time.

Glossary

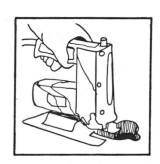

Air-dried lumber. Lumber that has been piled in yards or shed for any length of time. For the United States as a whole, the minimum moisture content of thoroughly air-dried lumber is 12 to 15 percent and the average is somewhat higher. In the South, air-dried lumber may be no lower than 19 percent.

Aliphatic Resin Glue, Wilhold's. A strong all-purpose, all-weather glue. Ideal for porous surfaces.

Alpha Miracle Glue, Vigor Aron. Sets up fast with great strength. Will not work on porous materials.

American beech: This is one of the heavier woods in the United States, rated high in strength and shock resistance. It is used for lumber, distilled products, veneer, railroad ties, pulpwood, barrel making and furniture. It is especially suitable for food containers since it does not import taste or odor. The heartwood is white with a reddish tinge.

American elm. This tree, with moderately heavy wood, grows in most of the United States. It is used principally in the manufacture of furniture and containers. Due to its excellent bending qualities, the wood has been used for barrels and kegs. The heartwood is brown to dark brown.

Anchor. Special hardware designed to fasten together timbers or masonry.

Anchor bolts. A rod-like piece of hardware used to fasten columns, girders and other construction items to masonry.

Ash. Straight, rather coarse grain. Valued for its springiness and bending qualities.

Backband. A simple molding sometimes used around the outer edge of plain rectangular casing as a decorative feature.

Backsaw. Allows accurate cutting of straight lines. Use this tool for finishing work.

Baluster. A type of small column used to support a rail; when several balusters are connected by a rail they are referred to as a *balustrade.*

Batten. A wood strip, usually narrow, used to fasten several pieces of wood together.

Basswood. Basswood is a lightweight hardwood, but weak and moderately stiff. Most basswood is used for boxes and crates, but some goes into doors and general millwork. Heartwood is creamy white to creamy brown.

Black cherry. The wood is stiff and strong, making it difficult to work with hand tools. The majority of black cherry is sawed into lumber to make furniture, woodenware, and interior finishes. The heartwood is light to dark reddish brown.

Black walnut. Black walnut grows in the eastern, central and southern states. It is classified as a heavy wood and is hard, stiff and strong with great durability. It finishes beautifully with a handsome grain pattern. The outstanding use of black walnut is for furniture, but large amounts are used for gunstocks and interior finish. The heartwood is chocolate brown and occasionally has darker, sometimes purplish-streaks.

Beam. A piece of heavy wood used in construction and generally thought of as an item used to support ceilings, roofs or floors. Actually it is a broad term for joists, girders and rafters.

Bearing partition. A partition that supports any vertical load in addition to its own weight.

Bearing wall. A wall that supports any vertical load in addition to its own weight.

Beech, red or white. Tough, close grain. Used for tools. Very good for turning on lathe.

Bevel. A cut made at an angle, or a surface or edge that is prepared at an angle. Also a tool that has a rule and a moveable arm and is used to mark angles.

Blind-nailing. Nailing in such a way that the nailheads are not visible on the face of the work—usually at the tongue of matched boards.

Blue stain. A bluish or grayish discoloration of the sapwood caused by the growth of certain moldlike fungi on the surface and in the interior of a piece, made possible by the same conditions that favor the growth of other fungi.

Board. Wood that is less than 2 inches thick.

Board foot. A unit of measurement for wood. It's the equivalent of a board that's 1 foot square and 1 inch thick.

Bodied linseed oil. Linseed oil that has been thickened in viscosity by suitable processing with heat or chemicals. Bodied oils are obtainable in great range in viscosity from a little greater than that of raw oil to just short of a jellied condition.

Bolster. A short, horizontal timber or steel beam on top of a column to support and decrease the span of beams or girders.

Bottom plate. The lowest part of a stud wall to which the studs are attached.

Brace. An inclined piece of framing lumber applied to wall or floor to stiffen the structure.

Bracket. A support that's used for a shelf or other item. It generally projects from a wall.

Building paper. A thick paper that's used to insulate a building or addition before siding is installed. It's also occasionally placed between double floors.

Build-up. A term referring to an item that has been formed from several smaller ones that have been fastened together.

Butt joint. The junction where the ends of two timbers or other members meet in a square-cut joint.

Carriage bolts. This type of bolt is intended for wood-to-wood use but can also be used for fastening wood-to-metal. Use them in conjunction with a nut and a flat washer. They have round-heads and should not be driven. They are threaded only along a portion of their shafts.

Carriages. An inclusive term for the supports, steps and risers for a flight of stairs.

Casement. A type of window equipped with a sash that opens using hinges.

Casing. The finished wood that's installed around a post or beam. It also refers to the finishing wood and trim around a door or window opening.

Cedar, Western Red. Soft, reddish-brown, straight grained, and available in long lengths.

Chalk line. Used for indicating straight lines and for temporary markings.

Chamfer. A beveled surface made at the corner of a piece of wood.

Checks. Cracks or splits in wood. They are generally caused by seasoning.

Chestnut. Looks and works like oak, but has no figuring when quarter-sawn.

Chisel. Used to make small grooves, notches or cuts. Also useful for trimming and paring. Where space permits, use a plane for smoother results.

Circular saw. Used for making straight cuts in unwieldy materials.

Columbian Pine, Douglas Pine, Oregon Pine, Douglas Fir. One of the harder softwoods, straight-grained, reddish-brown. Raised grain and resin make the wood unsuitable for face work, but it may be used structurally in furniture.

Column. A support for roofs or ceilings that is comprised of a base, shaft and capital.

Common wire nails. A type of nail used in many carpentry projects and for construction and house framing.

Compass saw. Used for making cut-outs or carved cuts.

Construction, frame. A type of construction in which the structural parts are wood or depend upon a wood frame for support.

Conduit, electrical. A pipe, usually metal, in which wire is installed.

Contact Cement, Wilhold's. For adhering large surfaces of almost any material. Sets up almost immediately without clamps. Both surfaces are coated and after a brief wait the two surfaces are brought together very carefully. Hard to change position once cement sets.

Contact Cement, Dura-Safe. Noninflammable and nonexplosive. Works at low temperature. Otherwise, similar to other contact cements.

Coping saw. Designed for making thin accurate cuts and for sawing tight curves.

Corner boards. Diagonal braces at the corners of frame structure to stiffen and strengthen.

Cottonwood. Eastern, swamp, and black cottonwood are moderately light in weight. Most trees are cut into lumber and veneer and then remanufactured into containers and furniture. The heartwood is white to light grayish brown.

Crosscut saw. Used for sawing across the grain of wood.

Cut nails. These are wedged shaped nails with the head on the large end. They are used to nail flooring because of their good holding power and the type of steel used to make them.

Cypress. Grows in swamps. Has a greasy feel and a sour smell. Straight-grained, light brown. Will withstand heat and moisture. Does not take glue very well.

Dado. A rectangular groove across the width of a board or plank. In interior decoration, a special type of wall treatment.

Decay. Disintegration of wood or other substance through the action of fungi.

Decking. A heavy plank floor.

Density. The mass of substance in a unit volume. When expressed in the metric system, it is numerically equal to the specific gravity of the same substance.

Dimension. See **Lumber dimension.**

Direct nailing. To nail perpendicular to the initial surface or to the junction of the pieces joined. Also termed **face nailing.**

Douglas fir. Douglas fir is somewhat more difficult to work with hand tools than soft pine, but it holds fastenings well and can be glued satisfactorily. It is used for lumber, timbers, piling and plywood. The heartwood is orange-red to red.

Dressed and matched (tongued and grooved). Boards or planks machined in such a manner that there is a groove on one edge and a corresponding tongue on the other.

Drill. Used for making small holes such as pilot holes for screws. Attachments are available for electric drills that enable you to make larger holes and to sand. However, better results are usually obtained by using a specific power tool (such as a sander) than by the use of an attachment.

Drip. A projection from a window sill that protects the side of a house or building below it from water.

Elm. Durable, with contused grain that resists splitting. Not of much use in furniture except transitional designs.

End joist. The joist that runs perpendicular to the other joists at a building's perimeter; it is also called a header.

Expansion bolts. These are used in conjunction with an expansion shield to hold materials that cannot accept threaded bolts.

Facia or fascia. A flat board, band, or face, used sometimes by itself but usually in combination with moldings.

Finishing nails. This type of nail has a small head and is made from finer wire than common nails. They are used for interior or exterior finishing work and cabinet making.

Filler (wood). A heavily pigmented preparation used for filling and leveling off the pores in open-pored woods.

Fire-resistive. In the absence of a specific ruling by the authority having jurisdiction, applies to materials for construction not combustible in the temperatures of ordinary fires and that will withstand such fires without serious impairment of their usefulness for at least 1 hour.

Fire-retardant chemical. A chemical or preparation of chemicals used to reduce flammability or to retard spread of flame.

Five Minute Epoxy Glue, Wilhold's. Superlative strength for attaching like or unlike materials together. Fine for adhering very small surfaces and delicate parts. Sets up in five minutes. Two parts are mixed in equal portions.

Flashing. Material used to make the intersecting areas of a roof or other areas on the outside of a building that are exposed to the elements watertight.

Flat paint. An interior paint that contains a high proportion of pigment and dries to a flat or lusterless finish.

Footing. The part of a building that is between the earth and the foundation.

Framing. The wood which forms the rough structure of a building.

Fungi, wood. Microscopic plants that live in damp wood and cause mold, stain, and decay.

Fungicide. A chemical that is poisonous to fungi.

Furring. Strips of wood or metal applied to a wall or other surface to even it and normally to serve as a fastening base for finish material.

Gaboon. Nondurable African wood that looks like mahogany. Used for lightweight plywood.

Gambrel. A symmetrical roof with different slopes on each side.

Gauge. A tool used to make a line parallel to the edge of a board.

Girder. A main horizontal support beam.

Gloss enamel. A finishing material made of varnish and sufficient pigments to provide opacity and color, but little or no pigment of low opacity. Such an enamel forms a hard coating with maximum smoothness of surface and a high degree of gloss.

Gloss (paint or enamel). A paint or enamel that contains a relatively low proportion of pigment and dries to a sheen or luster.

Grain. The direction, size, arrangement, appearance, or quality of the fibers in wood.

Grain, edge (vertical). Edge-grain lumber has been sawed parallel to the pith of the log and approximately at right angles to the growth rings; i.e., the rings form an angle of 45° or more with the surface of the piece.

Grain, flat. Flat-grain lumber has been sawed parallel to the pith of the log and approximately tangent to the growth rings, i.e., the rings form an angle of less than 45° with the surface of the piece.

Grain, quartersawn. Another term for edge grain.

Gusset. A flat wood, plywood, or similar type member used to provide a connection at intersection of wood members. Most commonly used at joints of wood trusses. They are fastened by nails, screws, bolts, or adhesives.

Hacksaw. Used to cut metal.

Hammer (with curved claws. Used for driving nails and for removing nails.

Hammer (with ripping claws). Used for driving nails and for separating pieces of wood that have been fastened together.

Hangar. A vertical support beam.

Header. A joist that is generally short and over an opening or a joist into which ordinary joists are fitted.

Headroom. Unfilled space between the floor and ceiling or between steps and ceiling.

Hemlock. Does not take a fine finish and is more of an external wood than one for furniture.

Hickory. The hickories grow throughout the eastern United States with 40 percent grown in the lower Mississippi Valley region. The wood is very heavy, hard, strong and exceedingly high in shock resistance. The majority of the true hickory goes into the making of tool handles. Other uses include farm implements, athletic goods and lawn furniture. Heartwood is brown to reddish brown.

Hide Glue. Comes in ground form. Also called animal glue. Must be heated in double boiler and used hot. Joints must be put under pressure immediately after glue is applied. This glue works best when the wood is warm so as not to chill glue. This glue is not waterproof.

Hide Glue, liguid. A treated animal glue. Does not have to be applied hot. A fair substitute for animal glue. The big advantage is that no preparation is necessary.

Interceptor trench. A trench filled with stone or gravel which intercepts excess water runoff before it reaches a building.

Jamb. The wood found at the side of an opening—the side post.

Joint. The area where different pieces of wood come together or the various methods of fitting pieces of wood together. Common types of joints: *Butt.* Ends or edges that are squared and adjoining. *Dovetail.* A joint formed by special pins which fit within a corresponding piece. *Drawboard.* A type of mortise-and-tenon joint. It's made with holes that are cut so that the joint actually becomes tighter when pins are inserted. *Fished.* A butt joint strengthened by wood nailed to the sides. *Halved.* A joint that's made from two pieces of wood, each of which has had a section cut away so that they fit together flush. *Lap.* A joint made when two pieces of wood overlap each other. *Mortised.* A joint formed by cutting a hole (the mortise) in one piece of wood and fashioning a section (the tenon) from part of the second piece of wood so that the section fits into the hole. *Miter.* A joint made by butting together two pieces of wood which have been cut at an angle.

Joint cement. A powder that is usually mixed with water and used for joint treatment in gypsum-wallboard finish. Often called "spackle."

Joist. The supporting members of a roof or floor which are 2 inches wide.

Kerf. The term given to a cut made by any saw blade.

Kiln dried lumber. Lumber that has been kiln dried often to a moisture content of 6 to 12 percent.

Knot—natural finish. Softwood lumber, such as framing lumber are dried to a somewhat higher moisture content.

Knot. In lumber, the portion of a branch or limb of a tree that appears on the edge or face of the piece.

Laths. Narrow strips of wood used to support plaster.

Lacquer. A finish for wood made of resins dissolved in ethyl alcohol. When it dries it leaves a tough coating.

Lattice. A framework of crossed wood or metal strips.

Lag screws. Use these when standard wood screws would be too light or too short. They are longer and heavier than ordinary wood screws.

Level. The position of a line or surface when parallel to the surface of still water. Generally thought of as synonomous with "truly horizontal." The term also refers to a tool for determining a horizontal position.

Lumber. Lumber is the product of the sawmill and planing mill not further manufactured other than by sawing, resawing, and passing lengthwise through a standard planing machine, crosscutting to length, and matching.

Lumber, boards. Yard lumber less than 2 inches thick and 2 or more inches wide.

Lumber, dimension. Yard lumber from 2 inches to, but not including, 5 inches thick and 2 or more inches wide. Includes joists, rafters, studs, plank, and small timbers.

Lumber, dressed size. The dimension of lumber after shrinking from green dimension and after machining to size or pattern.

Lumber, matched. Lumber that is dressed and showed on one edge in a grooved pattern and on the other in a tongued pattern.

Lumber, shiplap. Lumber that is edge-dressed to make a close rabbeted or lapped joint.

Lumber, timbers. Yard lumber 5 or more inches in least dimension. Includes beams, stringers, posts, caps, sills, girders, and purlins.

Lumber, yard. Lumber of those grade, sizes, and patterns which are generally intended for ordinary construction, such as framework.

Mahogany. African mahogany comes from the Gold, Ivory, and Nigerian colonies of West Africa. West Indies mahogany comes primarily from British Honduras, Bermuda, and the keys of southern Florida. Torpical American mahogany comes from Mexico, Central America and parts of Peru. It is of moderate density and hardness and has excellent working and finishing characteristics. A high resistance to decay is one of its most important properties. It is used in quality furniture of all styles, and is one of the best woods for boat construction. The heartwood varies from a pale to a deep reddish brown.

Mahogany, African. There are several of these, and not all true mahoganies; but some are suitable for furniture.

Mahogany, Honduras; Baywoods. Lightweight with light brown color. A furniture wood.

Mahogany, Philippine. This wood is grown primarily in the Philippine Islands and is very similar to genuine mahogany in general properties, although it is somewhat coarser in texture. It is a little more difficult to finish, but it is inexpensive, easy to work with and simple to glue. The heartwood varies in color from pale to dark reddish-brown for some varieties while others are light-red to straw-colored.

Mahogany, Spanish and Cuban. Rich brown with close grain. Original furniture mahogany, but there are many more.

Maple. Varies from light yellow to brown.

Moisture content of wood. Weight of the water contained in the wood, usually expressed as a percentage of the weight of the ovendry wood.

Molding. A wood strip having a curved or projecting surface used for decorative purposes.

Mortise. A slot cut into a board, plank, or timber, usually edgewise to receive tenon of another board, plank, or timber to form a joint.

Mullion. The pieces of wood between window frame openings.

Machine bolts. This type of bolt is precision made for use in metal-to-metal applications where close tolerance is important. Heads are square, hexagon, double hexagon, rounded or flat. They are meant to be used in conjunction with a nut that is usually the same shape as the head.

Natural finish. A transparent finish which does not seriously alter the original color or grain of the natural wood. Natural finishes are usually provided by sealers, oils, varnishes, water-repellent preservatives, and other similar materials.

Newel. The main post of the bottom of a staircase or winding staircase.

OC, on center. A measurement of spacing for studs, rafters, joists, and the like from the center of one member to the center of the next.

Oak, English. The oak used for medieval ships and furniture. Brown, open-grained, with prominent figuring when quarter-sawn. Very strong and durable.

Oak, Japanese and Austrian. More mellow and easier to work than English oak. Good furniture woods.

Paint. A combination of pigments with suitable thinner or oils to provide decorative and protective coatings.

Partition. A wall that subdivides spaces within any story of a building.

Pecan. Pecan is primarily a southern wood, but it can be found in most of the eastern United States. It is a heavy wood with an average weight of 48 pounds per cubic foot. It is one of the toughest and strongest American woods in common use. Pecan is used for furniture and can be stained and finished to resemble walnut. The heartwood is reddish-brown in color, often with darker streaks.

Penny. As applied to nails, it originally indicated the price per hundred. The term now serves as a measure of nail length and is abbreviated by the letter *d*.

Pier. Supports, usually concrete, which are separate from the foundation of a building.

Pigment. A powdered solid in suitable degree of subdivision for use in paint or enamel.

Pine, Parana. Brazilian wood, pale straw color, and available in wide boards. Eastern white pine and ponderosa pine are light, with little strength. Sugar pine grows into large trees; it will finish smoothly despite large knots, which may be used as a decorative feature. Western white pine is similar. None of these is very durable if exposed.

Pine, Pitch. Heavy because of considerable resin. Has pronounced grain. Difficult to bring to a good finish.

Pitch. The slope of an item.

Pith. The small, soft core at the original center of a tree around which wood formation takes place.

Plane. Used for edge straightening or shaving wood. Use a long plane for shaving long surfaces. If the job involves cutting along the end of the wood, use a block plane.

Plank. Any wide piece of sawed timber, but generally 1½ to 4 inches thick and at least 6 inches wide.

Plastic Resin Waterproof Glue. Mixes with cold water, and glue sets by chemical action. A fine wood glue, particularly for veneers and joints.

Plasti-Tak. For hanging pictures.

Plate. Loadbearing members spanning between posts which hold either the roof or floor joists.

Plexiglass Cement, Wilhold's. For adhering plexiglass parts together.

Pliers. Used to twist wire, grip objects, remove nails and in conjunction with a wrench to place bolts.

Plough. To cut a lengthwise groove in a board or plank.

Plumb. Exactly perpendicular; vertical.

Ply. A term to denote the number of thicknesses or layers of veneer in plywood, or layers in built-up materials, in any finished piece of such material.

Plywood. A piece of wood made of three or more layers of veneer joined with glue, and usually laid with the grain of adjoining piles at right angles.

Ponderosa pine. This wood is not easily split and has a good resistance to nail withdrawl; it also glues easily. Its principal use is for lumber and veneer. Knotty ponderosa pine has come into wide use as paneling for interiors. The heartwood is yellowish to orange-brown.

Popular, yellow; Canary Wood; American Whitewood. Even, close-grained, yellow wood. Varying quality, but usually easy to work. Similar to basswood and sometimes confused with it.

Pores. Wood cells of comparatively large diameter that have open ends and are set one above the other to form continuous tubes. The openings of the vessels on the surface of a piece of wood are referred to as pores.

Preservative. Any substance that, for a reasonable length of time, will prevent the action of wood-destroying fungi, borders of various kinds, and similar destructive agents when the wood has been properly coated or impregnated with it.

Primer. The first coat of paint in a paint job that consists of two or more coats; also the paint used for such a first coat.

Psf. Pounds per square foot.

Pulley stile. The part of the window frame that contains the pulleys. The edges of the sash slide between them.

Purlin. A secondary roof or floor member spanning between beams, running perpendicular to them.

Putty. A type of cement usually made of whiting and boiled linseed oil, beaten or kneaded to the consistency of dough, and used in sealing glass in sash, filling small holes and crevices in wood, and for similar purposes.

Quarter round. A small molding that has the cross section of a quarter circle.

Rabbet. A rectangular longitudinal groove cut in the corner edge of a board or plank.

Rafter. A beam that forms the main body of a building's roof and that slopes from the roof's ridge to the eaves.

Raw linseed oil. The crude produce processed from flaxseed and usually without much subsequent treatment.

Redwood, Yellow Deal, Red Deal, Red Pine, Scots Pine, Northern Pine. Reddish-brown, straight-grained, some resin. Suitable for internal construction. Redwood grows along the California coast. This is one in a group of woods that has an outstanding decay resistance and a high resistance to termites. It's one of the best lumbers to use on outdoor projects such as outdoor furniture, house siding, etc.

Red Gum, Sweet Gum, Satin Walnut. Soft, even brown color with little sign of grain. Stains well. Twists and warps if not built into other parts.

Red Oak. Red oaks are generally found east of the Great Plains and are similar in properties to the white oak family. Most of the red oak cut in this country is converted into flooring, furniture, millwork, caskets and coffins, boats and woodenware. Preservative-treated red oak is used extensively for crossties and fence posts. The heartwood is grayish brown with a reddish tint.

Resorcinol glue. A glue that is high in both wet and dry strength and resistant to high temperatures. It is used for gluing lumber or assembly joints that must withstand severe service conditions.

Ripsaw. Use this saw to cut wood in the direction of the grain.

Riser. The Vertical board positioned between two stair treads.

Roofing nails. These are round shafted with large heads and diamond points. They are usually 1 inch or 1¼ inch in length but they can be longer. They are used to fasten asphalt shingles.

Sabre saw. Used for cutting irregular or wavy shapes. Can also be used for cutting straight lines.

Sand float finish. Lime mixed with sand, resulting in a textured finish.

Sapwood. The outer zone of wood, next to the bark. In the living tree it contains some living cells (the heartwood contains none). As well as dead and dying cells. In most species, it is lighter colored than the heartwood. In all species, it is lacking in decay resistance.

Sash. The portion of a window's frame that hold the glass.

Scaffold. A platform that helps workmen reach high places and enables them to work on the sides of a building.

Scaffold. These nails have two heads to make it easier to remove them after they have been temporarily positioned.

Scale. A short measure used in drawings and plans instead of actual distances. One-quarter of an inch on a drawing is usually equivalent to 1 foot of actual distance.

Scantling. Lumer that has a cross-section which ranges from 2 by 4 inches to 4 by 4 inches.

Screwdrivers (regular slot). Used for positioning screws with a single slot in the head or for removing such screws.

Screwdrivers (Phillips). Used to position screws that have a + slot in the head or for removing such screws.

Scribing. Fitting woodwork to an irregular surface. In moldings, cutting the end of one piece to fit the molded face of the other at an interior angle to replace a miter joint.

Sealer. A finishing material, either clear or pigmented, that is usually applied directly over uncoated wood for the purpose of sealing the surface.

Seasoning. Removing moisture from green wood in order to improve its serviceability.

Semigloss paint or enamel. A paint or enamel made with a slight insufficiency of nonvolatile vehicle so that its coating, when dry, has some luster but is not very glossy.

Sequoia, California Redwood. Very large trees, so great lengths and widths obtainable. Rather open and porous, reddish-brown, and straight grained. Not very strong.

Shakes. Imperfections in wood caused by high winds or adverse conditions while the tree it came from was still growing. Also a type of siding for a house.

Sheathing. Solid wall covering which is covered with siding.

Sheet metal screws. They have round, oval, flat or fillister heads and are used to fasten metal parts.

Shellac. A transparent coating made by dissolving lac, a resinous secretion of the lac bug (a scale insect that thrives in tropical countries, especially India), in alcohol.

Shortleaf pine. Shortleaf pine has the wideest distribution of the southern pines and ranks with the lightest of the important southern pines. Its principal uses include lumber for interior finishes, ceilings, frames, sashes, sheathings, subflooring, and joists as well as for boxes and crates. Many telephone poles are shortleaf pine. The heartwood ranges from yellow to light brown.

Sitka spruce. Here's another west coast tree which is used for lumber, barrel making and paper pulp. A lot of this wood also goes into boxes and crates. The heartwood is light pinkish yellow to pale brown.

Spray Adhesive 54, Wilhold's. For spraying large areas. A contact-type adhesive; however, pieces may be moved if necessary. Wallpaper and veneer sheets can be mounted with this adhesive.

Spredhesive. A pressure-sensitive, acrylic base adhesive. Takes the place of double face adhesive tape.

Stainless Glue. Excellent for gluing veneers and inlays, as well as other woodworking assemblies.

Siding. The finish wall covering.

Silicone Glue. Used for insulating exposed electrical wires and adhering lamp parts. Remains flexible. Good for filling cavities.

Sobo White Glue. A good all-purpose glue. Similar to other white glues. Dries crystal clear.

Square. A tool used for accurate measurements and for determining right angles.

Splashboard. A horizontal wall member which serves as form around the perimeter of the building for the slab.

Spruce, Sitka, Silver Spruce. A combination of lightness with a strong, straight grain makes this a choice for aircraft construction and yacht spars. Not a furniture choice unless easily obtained.

Spruce, Whitewood, White Deal. Sometimes considered a poorer quality redwood. Near white, with some knots and resin pockets.

Stapler. Used for speed fastening instead of nailing or tacking.

Stove bolts. These have either round or flat slotted heads with threads along the entire shaft. They are used in conjuction with square nuts in metal-to-metal, wood-to-metal or wood-to-wood applications where precision is not a critical factor. Flathead stove bolts should be countersunk. Roundhead types should be tightened until they are flush with the surface.

Stud. One of a series of slender wood or metal vertical structural members placed as supporting elements in walls and partitions. (Plural: studs or studding.)

Subfloor. A wooden floor placed over the floor joists. The finished floor is laid over it.

Sugar maple. The sugar maple grows in a large portion of the U.S. with its highest concentration in the Northeast and the lake states. It is heavy and hard and has a high resistance to shock. Sugar maple ranks high in nail withdrawl resistance and glues easily. It takes stain readily and is capable of high polish. It is used principally for lumber, distilled products, veneer and crossties. Most of the lumber is made into furniture, flooring, woodenware and novelties. It is especially suitable for bowling alleys and dance floors. The heartwood is light reddish brown.

Sugar pine. This is a west coast tree that is very lightweight—averaging about 25 pounds per cubic foot. The wood is used almost entirely for lumber in buildings, boxes and crates, sashes, doors, frames, general millwork and foundry patterns. It is suitable for all phases of house construction. The heartwood is light brown to pale reddish brown.

Sweetgum. Sweetgum grows in the eastern, southern and central states. It is a moderately heavy wood and has a low decay resistance. It is high in ability to resist splitting by nails and screws.

Sycamore. Whitish-yellow, close-grained wood with sometimes a figure or ripple marking visible in the grain. Good for turning on lathe.

Teak. This is a dark brown wood that bleaches to near white in the sun. It may be difficult to work because of its resin. It is very durable even when not treated in any way. Not usual for furniture.

Threshold. A curved or beveled item, generally wood, over which a door swings.

Timber. Wood with a cross-section greater than 4 by 6 inches. Examples are posts, sills and girders.

Toenailing. To drive a nail as a slant with the initial surface in order to permit it to penetrate into a second member.

Tongue-and-groove. Abbreviated "t&g;" a design where the tongue of one member fits into the groove of another member.

Top plate. The wood that supports the ends of rafters.

Tread. That part of a step which is horizontal.

Trim. The finish materials, such as moldings.

Turpentine. A volatile oil used as a thinner in paints and as a solvent in varnishes. Chemically, it is a mixture of terpenes.

Undercoat. A coating applied prior to the finishing or top coats of a paint job. It may be the first of two or the second of three coats. In some usage of the word it may become synonymous with priming coat.

Under layment. A material placed under finish coverings to provide a smooth, even surface for applying the finish.

Valleys. The interior angle formed by the slopes of two intersecting roofing surfaces.

Varnish. A thickened preparation of drying oil or drying oil and resin suitable for spreading on surfaces to form continuous, transparent coatings, or for mixing with pigments to make enamels.

Vehicle. The liquid portion of a finishing material; it consists of the binder (nonvolatile) and volatile thinners.

Veneer. Thin sheets of wood made by rotary cutting or slicing of log.

Wainscoting. Panel work which covers the lower portion of a wall.

Wallpaper Adhesive. One of the best is vinyl wall covering paste, which is a mixture of wheat flour and a special adhesive (Staz-Tite Products).

Wall Sizing. Porous wall surfaces must be sized before wallpaper is applied. One very good size is Wal-Treet, an acrylic base coat (Paint Manufacturers, Inc.). Shellac, flat paint, undercoater, and other materials may also be used.

Walnut, American Black Walnut. A shade of purple mixed with dark brown. Takes a good finish.

Wane. Bark, or lack of wood from any cause, on edge or corner of a piece of wood.

Water-repellent perservative. A liquid designed to penetrate into wood and impart water repellency and a moderate preservative protection.

Western white pine. As the name implies, this tree grows in the western part of the continent. It is moderately light in weight. Practically all these trees are sawed into lumber. The lower grades are used for subflooring as well as wall and roof sheathing. The highgrade wood is used for siding, trim and paneling. The heartwood is cream colored to reddish brown.

White ash. This deciduous tree grows throughout the eastern United States and is a heavy wood with an average weight of 42 pounds per cubic foot. The wood is noted for its excellent bending qualities, its ability to hold fastenings, and its resistance to splitting. It is standard wood for canoe paddles, handles for shovels, hoes, racks, baseball bats, etc. It is good for bent parts on outdoor furniture.

White oak. The white oak family grows mainly in the eastern half of the United States, although some species are found in some of the Northwestern states. The wood is heavy, very hard and must be seasoned carefully to avoid warping. Most white oak is made into lumber for flooring, furniture and general millwork. It is the leading wood for the construction of boats and ships. White oak is grayish brown.

Wood rays. Strips of cells extending radially with a tree and varying in height from a few cells in some species to 4 inches or more in oak. The rays serve primarily to store food and to transport it horizontally in the tree.

Wood screws. Use these instead of nails for extra holding power. They are designed according to the type of head—flat, oval or round. Use the flathead or ovalhead screws with countersinking to hide the screw beneath filler or a covering material. Roundhead screws should not be countersunk. Tighten them until the heads are flush with the surface.

Wrench. Use to assist in turning hardware. Especially useful for tightening or removing nuts and large screws.

Yellow birch. Yellow birch is heavy and hard and is therefore difficult to work with hand tools. It is used principally for lumber, veneer and crossties. Because of its pleasing grain pattern and ability to take a high polish, it is widely used for cabinets and furniture. The heartwood is light reddish-brown.

Yellow-poplar. Yellow-poplar grows in many eastern and southern states. It is moderately light in weight and has an excellent reputation for taking and holding paint. It stains and glues quite satisfactorily. It does not impart taste or odor to foods and therefore is used for food containers. Other uses are lumber, veneer and pulpwood. It is brownish yellow with a greenish tinge.

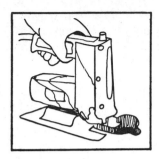

Index